THE POLITICS OF COMMUNITY CRIME PREVENTION

For my parents,
Elmer Schaffner Miller and Anna Lois Longenecker Miller

The Politics of Community Crime Prevention

Implementing Operation Weed and Seed in Seattle

LISA L. MILLER
The Pennsylvania State University, USA

DARTMOUTH

Aldershot • Burlington USA • Singapore • Sydney

Published by
Dartmouth Publishing Company
Ashgate Publishing Limited
Gower House
Croft Road
Aldershot
Hants GU11 3HR
England

Ashgate Publishing Company
131 Main Street
Burlington, VT 05401-5600 USA

Ashgate website: http://www.ashgate.com

British Library Cataloguing in Publication Data
Miller, Lisa L.
    The politics of community crime prevention. - (Law, justice and power)
    1.Crime prevention - United States 2.Community policing -
    United States
    I.Title
    364'.0973

Library of Congress Control Number: 2001086760

ISBN 0 7546 2140 5

Printed and bound by Athenaeum Press, Ltd.,
Gateshead, Tyne & Wear.

Table of Contents

List of Figures and Tables

Preface

This book is an effort to draw attention to the ways that national and local crime prevention policy can be significantly out of step with the priorities of people who are most victimized by street crime. Specifically, it illustrates how implementation of a federal crime policy in an urban minority neighborhood revealed a substantially different set of priorities for urban revitalization than those typically discussed by policymakers. The questions about law enforcement, racial minorities and community crime prevention raised here are much richer and larger than this book can answer. I hope that I have been able to address a small portion of those questions and that the conclusions offered here inspire further research.

I come to this topic by way of a deep and abiding interest in racial justice and a concern for the democratic institutions of government. Crime control and prevention are vital subjects of study since they involve the most restrictive and potentially violent of all government institutions: the police, courts and prisons. As people living and working in high-crime communities are increasingly being asked to participate in the creation and maintenance of public safety in their neighborhoods, the topic of crime prevention becomes even more important because it raises questions about the nature and quality of community involvement. High-crime communities are subject to a wide array of aggressive crime prevention tactics, often with little or no community input. If democracy means anything, it means that citizens at the margins of economic and social life must have the opportunity to participate in the decision-making about policy issues that so directly and profoundly affect their lives.

As a graduate student, my interests in crime and justice were nurtured by Stuart Scheingold's classic work, *The Politics of Law and Order* and by a wide range of law and society scholars whose research in crime and justice have inspired many of the questions I pursue in this book. I became interested in the Weed and Seed program through a colleague and friend, Bill Lyons, whose work on community policing in Seattle was a helpful starting point for my own research. From there, I began my journey to learn the details of the controversy over Weed and Seed and the complex interaction between community groups, law enforcement and government agencies that run the program in Seattle. Throughout my research I was continually impressed by the complex and nuanced perspectives of people living in or near the Weed and Seed target areas and by their persistent desire to redirect policy initiatives to programs and goals that they saw as vital to public safety and community development. I was also, at times, impressed with the capacity of government institutions, including the police, to listen and respond effectively to those perspectives that differed from their own. Perspectives on crime and justice, however, are deeply entrenched in personal attitudes, institutional histories and policy initiatives, making alteration of existing norms an onerous process. This book is an attempt to illustrate how and when existing frameworks might be challenged and altered.

There are many people in my personal and professional lives without whom this book would not have been possible. Stuart Scheingold was a strong supporter of this project from the outset and deserves a great deal of thanks for his intellectual guidance along the way. Michael McCann, Christine DiStefano, Andrea Simpson and Bryan Jones all provided invaluable contributions in their own unique and vital manner and I thank them for their ongoing support of my scholarship. Austin Sarat read the manuscript numerous times and guided me towards a richer theoretical narrative. Regina Lawrence and Judy Aks deserve special mention for their support and friendship. In addition, Mark Donovan, Steve Sandweiss, Sarah Pralle, Bill Lyons, Karin Roberts and Tom Lewis all offered feedback and assistance throughout this project. My new colleagues at Penn State University provided a supportive and friendly environment in which to complete this book. Robin Shepard Engel and Lynette Chow were especially helpful in reading portions or all of the manuscript. The community leaders, police officers, city officials and Justice Department agents who were kind enough to take time from their busy lives to share their stories with me are, of course, the heart of this project and without their cooperation it would never have been completed.

Most importantly, my family has been supportive of this book effort from the beginning and that has been an invaluable resource. My husband Jamie McCrone provided enormous help as he did double-duty childcare on a regular basis. His abiding belief in my ability to finish this project and his intellectual support along the way have been an ongoing source of strength. My children, Fiona, Annie and Jacob patiently accepted the time I needed to spend away from home. And finally, it is my parents, Elmer Schaffner Miller and Anna Lois Longenecker Miller, whose deep sense of justice and fairness inspired the concerns of this research, and to them that I dedicate this book.

List of Abbreviations

CAC   Citizens' Advisory Committee
DHHS   Department of Housing and Human Services
EOWS   Executive Office for Weed and Seed
MAPH   Mothers Against Police Harassment (name changed
            to Mothers for Police Accountability)
SECAC   Southeast Seattle Citizen Advisory Committee
SPD   Seattle Police Department
SSCPC   South Seattle Crime Prevention Council

1 Crime, Punishment and the Politics of Local Community

The advantages of the Weed and Seed program are: the offender is immediately removed from the streets, and the public immediately sees that these law enforcement efforts are effective; the offender is met with swift justice; and those convicted serve longer sentences mandated by federal law and are prevented from committing further criminal acts for years to come.

Weed and Seed Implementation Manual, Department of Justice.

It is my hope that as a result of him [Mayor Norm Rice] reaching out that the Weed and Seed proposal will be changed...so that the fears of what I think is the majority of people in the black community can be dealt with.

Larry Gossett, Director, Central Area Motivation Program.

In 1992 President George Bush announced a new inner-city crime prevention program entitled Operation Weed and Seed, sponsored by the Department of Justice. The program provided funding for federal, state and local law enforcement agencies to weed out criminal elements, specifically violent, gang and drug activity, in a targeted urban community, and seed money to support social services and community revitalization (Roehl 1996).[1] Community policing was the bridge between weeding and seeding: beat officers would perform conventional policing activities while simultaneously getting to know residents and their concerns, utilizing those newly formed relationships to address crime problems.

In cities around the country, including Seattle, Washington, mayors and city council members looked at Weed and Seed as an opportunity to obtain federal funding to address some of their cities' worst crime problems. The mayor of Seattle and the Seattle Police Department (SPD) were interested in addressing crime in a neighborhood known as the Central District, a predominately lower to middle income area with a significant portion of the city's African-American population that had been struggling for years with drug and crime problems. The SPD applied for a Weed and Seed grant for the Central District and was awarded $1.1 million dollars for the first year. Sixteen cities around the country received similar grants, a substantial sum for urban areas in crisis.

1

When news of Weed and Seed hit the streets of Seattle, however, along with San Diego, Los Angeles, Atlanta and other cities that were awarded grants, it quickly became apparent that the Justice Department had underestimated the concerns of urban minorities about implementing a tough law enforcement policy in their communities. Even with its seeding component, some communities quickly saw the program as a threat to young, black males and immigrants. The controversy that surrounded implementation of Weed and Seed focused on three main concerns of minority residents: that city officials and the police regarded their communities as filled with violent criminals; that they would treat all residents as suspicious; and that the seeding component of the program would never materialize.

In some respects, this response of local communities to federal policymaking is not surprising and may even be typical. Scholars of public policy have noted the problems inherent in attempting to graft federally conceived notions of social order onto communities that are far removed, both geographically and often psychologically, from the visions of national policymakers (Wildavsky and Pressman 1973; Derthick 1972; Feeley and Sarat 1980). In addition, the notion of allowing federal law enforcement officials to assist local beat cops in the arrest and prosecution of street gangs and drug dealers seemed destined to cause consternation and alarm in urban minority communities. Relations between black communities and law enforcement throughout American history, while perhaps improving somewhat over recent years, can be characterized by mutual suspicion at their best and downright hostility and violence at their worst (see Skolnick and Fyfe 1993; Kennedy 1997; Tonry 1995).

What is interesting and worthy of note in the Weed and Seed program, however, is that, unlike many federal programs, Weed and Seed deliberately provided for local community involvement through the community-policing component of the strategy and through efforts to empower residents of the targeted areas to preserve their neighborhoods. Indeed, getting communities involved in law enforcement and crime prevention has become an increasingly popular way of framing the government's response to crime. Community policing and community prosecution are popular in both the mainstream press and among law enforcement administrators (see Fleissner 1997 and Lyons 1999). Block watches and citizen patrols have been increasingly popular since the 1970s (Skogan 1988). In addition, programs like Weed and Seed are touted as the latest way of "doing business" which breaks sharply with past practices in which communities, police and social services agencies all operated in separate and discreet realms with little communication and information-sharing (Fleissner 1997; see also Kelling and Coles 1996; for a related discussion see Garland 1996).

Perhaps most importantly, Weed and Seed coupled weeding efforts with seeding monies to help rebuild neighborhoods. Given the popularity of community policing and the calls for more state assistance for social programs from advocates of urban minorities, one might expect such a program to have enjoyed at least a short period of interest and contemplation before being so roundly criticized. Similarly, while some scholars have noted that community policing often serves as a tool for allowing police departments to enter communities more frequently and aggressively, nonetheless, the move towards community policing appears to be a welcome change to existing police practices among those living in crime-ridden communities (see Lyons 1999; Greene and Mastrofski 1988). The fact that Weed and Seed was greeted with immediate mistrust and condemnation by some of the very communities that it was intended to assist is, then, cause for investigation and explanation.

This book is concerned with how federal community crime prevention policy is implemented on the local level and the differences in definitions of crime prevention that emerge during this process. In particular, the research illustrates that residents of a high-crime minority neighborhood can view crime prevention in substantially different terms than policymakers at both the national and local municipal levels. When these views on crime prevention clash, a struggle over problem definitions and policy responses ensues and questions of local community resistance to national crime agendas emerge. This project builds on research illustrating that national policy makers have incentives to exploit the public's fear of crime and support punitive policies, while local leaders have to face more direct electoral pressures and propose more practical solutions (see Beckett 1997; Scheingold 1991).[2] The book illuminates specific local concerns, detailing how those concerns differ from policy ideas of state agents on the federal and local level, and what the prospects are for the transformation of local concerns onto national agendas. Further, this research develops a *community-centered crime prevention model* that is more consistent with the views of community residents in this study than crime prevention models that dominate public policy.

Research on the Weed and Seed experience in Seattle casts doubt on the dominant framework for community-based crime prevention that is prominent in national policymaking and discourse. That framework is largely police-centered and includes a narrow role for community residents, confining them to the role of police informants and promoting symbolic rallies designed to mobilize residents around existing police agendas. The central theme of this book is that, when invited to participate in the direction of crime prevention and control, residents and local community leaders in the Weed and Seed target areas in Seattle worked to shift state resources *away* from the emphasis on punitive law enforcement and mere crime avoidance strategies, and *towards* employment opportunities, and broad economic, educational and social development. In addition, they resisted policing strategies that subjected citizens to increased police authority and those that were unresponsive to community concerns about harassment and abuse. Finally, they advocated for greater control over crime prevention goals and activities.

Politics in National and Local Crime Agendas

Crime control policies frequently emphasize harsh punishment as elected officials both produce and respond to punitive public sentiments (Scheingold 1984; see also Beckett 1997; Marion 1994). That is, elected officials do not simply respond to the punitive will of the electorate; they help create that will by capitalizing on the fear of crime and on the anxieties about social order that lie beneath the surface of crime control debates.[3]

Crime control, in this formulation, is driven by a variety of concerns, not just fear of crime but also concerns about moral decline, family dysfunction and increasing diversity (Tyler and Boeckmann 1997; Scheingold 1984). This is particularly true at the national level where elected officials can deploy powerful symbolic images in an effort to gain support in the electorate without having to be held strictly accountable for resolving local crime problems. The rhetoric of the national government can reassure an anxious electorate by offering solutions to the problem even when those solutions have only marginal effects on the crime rate (Beckett and Sasson 2000; Marion 1994). In a 30-second television advertisement in a Senate campaign, for example, it is difficult to talk about economic development, affordable housing, better schools, and job opportunities. It is far easier to say that criminals are morally bankrupt and that candidate A will lock them up while candidate B will let them go.

Elected officials are reluctant to support policies that make them appear soft on criminals even if those policies may be more fiscally and empirically sound than policies that impose harsh penalties and utilize state resources for increased law enforcement and prisons. One need not look further than the use of Willie Horton in the 1988 presidential campaign, which was designed to make Michael Dukakkis appear dangerously soft on crime, to see how powerful such rhetoric can be.[4] The furlough program that gave Horton a weekend pass had successfully provided opportunities for thousands of felons to return gradually to mainstream society. This was irrelevant in the face of one frightening man who had committed a violent crime as a result of the program.

Public policy scholars have noted that the manner in which social problems are conceptualized and the substantive issues that are discussed in conjunction with those problems help shape the form of public policy (Rochefort and Cobb 1994; see also Baumgartner and Jones 1993). The conception of *individual* fault and wrongdoing is at the heart of American ideas of criminality and leads to particular policy solutions. Thus, gang violence is likely to be discussed in connection with out-of-control, morally corrupt youth and, therefore, the policy solutions put forth by elected officials anxious to quell public concerns are likely to involve giving police more authority to act or trying juveniles in adult court.[5] In contrast, if the issue of gang violence is discussed in connection with poverty, poor education and few job opportunities, than the policy solutions are likely to involve economic development and educational opportunities. On the national level, the "individual wrong-doer" conception is particularly appealing because it lends itself to symbolic politics and to solutions that do not require broad social welfare expenditures.[6] Edelman states succinctly, "The appeal of an emphasis upon the pathologies of criminals and the utility of punishing them lies partly in what it negates: the tracing of crime to pathological social conditions" (Edelman 1988, 28). A clear illustration of this is the dramatic increase in incarceration rates in federal prisons as a result of the federal government's war on drugs. Though the agenda had little connection to actual rates of drug use, it deployed powerful symbolic language and aggressive law enforcement tactics (Beckett 1997; Tonry 1995).

There are a number of reasons to believe, however, that this individualistic conception of criminal culpability and the punitive responses that go with it are much more complicated than a quick overview of national crime policy-making would suggest. For example, the public's punitive attitudes appear to be more latent and contingent than one might think, given broad public support for long prison terms and the death penalty. Katherine Beckett and Theodore Sasson challenge the portrait of the public as simplistically punitive by illustrating that there is considerably stronger support for government spending on social and economic programs to reduce crime than for spending on police and corrections (Beckett and Sasson 1999, 137).   In addition, Scheingold demonstrated that the use of simplistic law and order messages as a campaign strategy seems less likely to be successful on the local level than in national politics (Scheingold 1991). Finally, the presence of powerful coalitions of racial minorities in urban environments may further complicate local crime control politics as minorities are less likely to trust police and more likely to be ambivalent about the role of policing and corrections in their communities (Beckett and Sasson 1999, 140-141). *Thus, while national crime control politics pushes policy agendas towards punishment and law enforcement, local urban politics may present an opportunity for tapping into more nuanced public sentiment that goes beyond simple law enforcement solutions.*

Indeed, at the same time that the national agenda appears receptive to punitive policymaking, community policing, which some would characterize as a less punitive form of policing, has flourished on the local/municipal level. Alternatives to incarceration for non-violent and/or first-time offenders, such as drug courts, are also popular and appear to be proliferating on local agendas. Not only does the local level appear to provide more complex definitions of the problem, attention to the crime issue locally may be less susceptible to manipulation by elected officials and policymakers because they must answer more directly for policy failure. This means that projecting simple, law and order messages at the local level is much less likely to receive a positive response from the electorate than at the national level. Local political climates can transform crime control policies so that they "have a distinctly egalitarian thrust and are intended to curb the state...and [are] derived...to some extent, from an awareness of the structural sources of street crime" (Scheingold 1991, 187).   Furthermore, the internal pressures of local bureaucratic organizations, such as the police and criminal courts, can have an independent effect on crime control practices that are only tangentially related, if at all, to the goals of policymakers (see Walker 1996; Blumberg 1978; Scheingold 1991).

Thus, when local community involvement in crime control is encouraged, the punitive emphasis might be muted and the individual-responsibility rhetoric might give way to more structural explanations and, subsequently, towards different solutions.[7]   Community members, particularly those in urban, black neighborhoods who have been the target of harsh, punitive police policies and/or policies which simply tolerate a level of crime in black neighborhoods, may mobilize around the opportunity to address what some see as crime's root causes – the social, economic and educational breakdown of inner-cities – and in opposition to further empowering law enforcement agencies. Thus, community crime prevention efforts are reformulated to fight crime and reinvigorate neighborhoods beyond a narrow focus on law enforcement and punishment.

Race, Resistance and Marginalization

Racial politics is central to this study both in terms of the impact that the perspectives of racial minorities have on crime control policies and for the effect that those policies have on minority communities.[8] The controversy that surrounded Weed and Seed's original implementation was largely the result of concerns about racial harassment and the differential impact of that policy on minorities. Furthermore, the most vocal proponents of recasting the Weed and Seed strategy in Seattle were black residents of the Central District who saw themselves as representing broader interests in the community. Race is important to almost any discussion of crime control policy and is particularly important here in three specific areas: relations with the police and the criminal justice system, views about the origins of crime, and the impact of criminal justice policy on minorities.

Relations with Police

Scheingold concludes his analysis of local crime control politics by suggesting that blacks were more likely than other groups to criticize police, demand citizen review, be concerned with fairness and advocate for citizen participation in the ways in which their communities were policed (Scheingold 1991). Further, though the black population of the city was small relative to larger urban areas, it was large enough to require those running for local elected office to pay attention to them. Thus, crime control policies that target these populations and promote community involvement open up a struggle over how crime prevention services are delivered.

 Similarly, research from a variety of perspectives indicates that racial minorities are more likely than whites to be suspicious of the police, to have less confidence in the criminal justice system and to express concern about the way governmental services are delivered (Welch et. al.,

1996; Lyons, 1999; Beckett and Sasson 1999; see also Sourcebook of Criminal Justice Statistics 1997). Blacks are also less likely than whites to approve of the deadly use of force by the police (Cullen, et. al. 1996). One need not reach far into American history to understand the suspicion and lack of confidence that African-Americans exhibit with respect to the police and the criminal justice system. Contemporary examples abound.[9] Others have noted that some black Americans are likely to attribute high levels of drug dealing and gang activity in their communities to deliberate efforts on the part of the CIA and other federal agencies to introduce crack cocaine into the black community and allow blacks to engage in a tragic spiral of violence and drug addiction (Sasson 1995).

Randall Kennedy has argued that the stories black Americans share with one another about their encounters with police represent important perspectives on crime control that are too often neglected in policy debates. Kennedy suggests that policing practices that allow law enforcement agents to consider race as one factor in whether to stop motorists, airline passengers or others, contribute to a hostile climate of fear and intimidation. He argues that such practices should be curbed because current strategies "nourish powerful feelings of racial grievance against law enforcement authorities that are prevalent in every strata of black communities" (Kennedy 1991, 151). Similarly, Don Jackson, a former California police officer notes:

> [The] police have long been the nemesis of blacks, irrespective of whether we are complying with the law or not. We have learned that there are cars we are not supposed to drive, streets we are not supposed to walk. We may still be stopped and asked "Where are you going, boy?" whether we're in a Mercedes or a Volkswagen. [The black American] finds that *the most prominent reminder of his second-class citizenship are the police* (Kennedy 1997, 152, emphasis added).

To some degree, community policing is an attempt to address these concerns by encouraging officers to meet residents of the areas they police. Police administrators freely acknowledge that they hope community policing will mitigate some of the long-held anger and hostility towards police that many black Americans harbor. But for Kennedy and other race scholars, the underlying practice of using race as a proxy for dangerousness continues even in the context of community policing and, therefore, hinders any attempt to improve police relations with minority communities and efforts to involve those communities in crime prevention and control.

> The communities most in need of police protection are also those in which many residents view police with the most ambivalence, much of which stems from a recognition that color counts as a mark of suspicion relied upon as a predicate for action - stopping, questioning, patting down, arresting, beating and so forth. This causes people who might otherwise be of assistance to police to avoid them, to decline to cooperate with police investigations, to assume bad faith on the part of police officers, and to teach others that such reactions are prudent lessons of survival on the streets (Kennedy 1997, 153).

Kennedy articulates the oft-repeated frustrations of some black Americans in their day-to-day dealings with law enforcement. These frustrations must be accounted for when considering how communities will receive crime control policies and what kind of input they will provide when invited to participate.

It is also the case, however, that blacks living in high-crime areas are the most victimized by street crime and therefore have a strong interest in effective policing to deal with victimization and the social consequences of crime (see Meares and Kahan 1998 and Lyons 1999 for related discussions). The preceding discussion is not intended to suggest that blacks or any other group living in high-crime areas are uninterested in police presence. On the contrary, because they face greater danger of victimization, law enforcement in those neighborhoods is of vital importance. The tensions between police and minorities, then, suggests that the nature and quality of policing is especially important to urban high-crime area residents.

Origins of Crime

Blacks may be less likely to accept the individual moral failing perspective on criminal behavior, thus making much crime control and public discourse on crime subject to criticism. Blacks are less likely than whites to accept the individualistic explanations for poverty and more likely to believe that inequality is the result of structural economic features and to racial, ethnic and gender discrimination (Gurin et. al., 1989, 246). To the extent that national policy formation begins primarily from the assumption that criminals are morally weak and in need of harsh deterrents from criminal behavior, the perspectives of black Americans may serve to mitigate those individualistic conceptions and introduce alternative explanations for criminal behavior that direct attention towards the actions of state agents. Blacks are also more likely to support an activist government and redistributive social and economic policies than the white electorate (Gurin et. al., 1989, 245) and to think that training and education are the most important purposes in the sentencing of criminals (see Sourcebook of Criminal Justice Statistics 1996). This suggests that black Americans are less wedded to the individualistic conceptions of criminality that resonate so effectively on the national level and that lead to policy initiatives that promote aggressive police tactics and long prison terms.

Impact of Crime Policy on Minorities

Increasing rates of incarceration have generally meant high levels of imprisonment for racial minorities, particularly black Americans. Black incarceration rates are substantially higher than those for white Americans (Sourcebook of Criminal Justice Statistics 1997; see also Tonry 1995). A 1998 article in the Seattle Times noted that 13% of all black men in the United States are disenfranchised because of imprisonment, probation, parole or a criminal record.[10] Thus, the impact of punitive policies is likely to be felt most acutely by blacks.

The literature discussed above indicates that the way in which crime control and crime prevention are defined has a powerful impact on the ability of black Americans to participate fully in democratic polity and not feel that they are marginalized because of their race or economic status. Further, the perspectives of some black communities on crime and its origins are likely to redirect discussion away from punishment and law enforcement and towards structural explanations and solutions. Understanding the involvement of local, black communities in crime control implementation is important because it helps illuminate competing definitions of crime prevention. Furthermore, the impact of social control practices is particularly important for those citizens who are on the receiving end of those practices.

Research Methodology and Case Study Explanation

The key goal of this book is to present a framework for understanding community involvement in crime prevention activities. This involves understanding two important aspects of community crime prevention: first, the crime prevention goals of high-crime area residents in comparison to the crime control goals of federal initiatives, and second, the impact of community residents' perspectives on policy implementation when residents are involved in that process.

The study consists of an analysis of Operation Weed and Seed in Seattle. The case study provides an opportunity to gain in-depth understanding of the perspectives and goals of inner-city community leaders, local officials responsible for crime prevention activities, and the framing of policy goals by federal agencies. Seattle's Weed and Seed site provides the opportunity for a multitude of observations since each Weed and Seed site involves multiple layers of decision-making (federal, state/local, community leaders and community residents in different neighborhoods).[11] Thus, the case study approach in this analysis is a limited but nonetheless useful tool for understanding the perspectives on crime prevention and their impact on policy. Seattle presents a particularly strong candidate for such analysis for several reasons.

First, Seattle was among the original 16 cities that received Weed and Seed money from the Justice Department and generated one of the more protracted controversies about the program. Its status as an original site that generated opposition provides the opportunity to examine the Weed and Seed program in its original Justice Department form, the nature of the local controversy, the views of those who got involved in the program, and the effect, if any, on both national and local program goals.

Second, Seattle has two distinct target areas that implemented Weed and Seed between 1993 and 1997. The first target area, the Central District is a rapidly changing area in close proximity to downtown Seattle. The area was once a thriving, middle-class black neighborhood but shifting demographics, neglect by city officials and local banks in the 1970s, and an influx of crack cocaine and California gangs in the 1980s contributed to declining economic and social conditions that made the area less attractive. More recently, however, in an extraordinarily expensive housing market, the Central Area is becoming a more attractive neighborhood for homebuyers. The second target area is a narrow stretch of the Rainier Valley, a long-time working-class and lower to middle income neighborhood that has diversified substantially in recent years so that its population is approximately one-third white, one-third black and one-third Asian-American. In addition, a third area known as the

International District was added to the first target area in 1995. These three neighborhoods provide an opportunity for some comparison in order to better explore neighborhood dynamics and residents' perspectives.

Third, Seattle had a number of other Justice Department programs operating at the time, which made the Justice Department anxious to see the program work in Seattle. Seattle has been a grant recipient for innovative Justice Department programs for some time, including Comprehensive Communities Programs, and the Youth Handgun Violence Initiative. Thus, the Justice Department was poised to respond to the controversy in Seattle; this provides an opportunity for the views of the target area residents to be heard and potentially incorporated into programmatic goals.

Fourth, the history of citizen initiative in Seattle is strong (see Banfield 1965; Vega 1997; Gordon, et. al., 1998). Citizen mobilization around quality of life issues is not uncommon and the Mayor-city council system provides many opportunities for citizen-initiated concerns to reach the agenda. In addition, the Seattle Police Department has been positioning itself to be in the vanguard of the community policing 'movement' for some time and has, since the late 1980s, been advocating the kind of coordination, cooperation and community involvement that Weed and Seed promotes. Thus if the perspectives of citizens is likely to enter into policy implementation anywhere, Seattle is a good candidate for such activity.

Finally, racial tensions in Seattle are muted, relative to other urban areas that had Weed and Seed programs. The African-American population in the city constitutes about 11% of the population. While that population tends to be concentrated in two areas of the city (not coincidentally, the two Weed and Seed target areas), those areas are also fairly integrated. The Rainier Valley, in particular, is integrated in the sense that whites, blacks and Asians all share numerous neighborhoods in relatively close proximity (A. Gordon 1998). Furthermore, while Seattle has had its share of urban race riots, the relations between blacks and the city government (including the police) are somewhat less contentious than other major urban areas. Thus, if African-American residents of the target areas in Seattle take a position on the role of law enforcement and crime prevention in their communities that is less punitive (less law enforcement-focused) than the one posited by federal crime policy, it is not likely that these views stem from unusually high levels of hostility between blacks and the police in Seattle. In fact, we might expect people living in high crime areas in other parts of the country to be even more wary of aggressive policing and punitive policies.

The data are derived from three primary sources: 1) *intensive interviews*[12] with key Justice Department officials, participants in the Coalition to Oppose Weed and Seed, members of the Citizen Advisory Committees that oversee the program in Seattle, and members of the local political establishment, social service organizations and police department; 2) *observations* of Citizen Advisory Committee and other Weed and Seed programmatic meetings in Seattle; and 3) extensive *analysis of federal and local documents* relating to Weed and Seed and archival materials on the two target areas in Seattle.

Crime Control, Communities and the State

I begin my analysis by developing a framework for understanding community involvement in crime prevention. Three models of community-based crime prevention illustrate this framework: opportunity-reduction, order maintenance and community-centered.[13] The first two models are largely police-centered, top-down models that are aimed primarily at making communities less attractive targets of opportunity. These models tend to dominate public discourse and policymaking. Opportunity reduction focuses on making crimes harder to commit by reducing the number of opportunities criminals have for victimizing persons and property. Order maintenance emphasizes the creation and maintenance of order and stability in high-crime areas by providing police with discretion to deal with low-level disorder (such as vagrancy, loitering, panhandling, vandalism and the like) on the principle that disorder both attracts and breeds criminal behavior. The third model is a community-centered model that provides community residents with the opportunity to define program goals, set priorities and curb police authority. The research in this study illustrates the prominence of the first two models in national discourse and their prevalence in the Justice Department's original Weed and Seed plan. It provides evidence to suggest that while the third model is the least prominent, it is also the one that is more likely to resonate with residents in inner city, minority neighborhoods.

The growth of urban crime control as a governmental priority raises questions about the relationship between the state, crime control policy and minority communities. While the community involvement theme proliferates and raises expectations of strong neighborhoods and decreasing crime rates, it also presents vexing questions about problem definitions, state authority and legal norms. I raise several themes in this book that complicate the dominant models of community crime prevention that are presented as viable solutions to the nation's crime problems. First, a number of governmental and community priorities clash and compete for dominance throughout the Weed and Seed story in Seattle, raising questions about the value of community involvement when it is primarily aimed at serving existing state goals. Weed and Seed inadvertently raised the possibility for community residents to generate crime control policies that were more complex and broad-based than the police-centered, punitive approaches that dominated Weed and Seed at its inception. The community-centered model of crime prevention presented here represents a substantially different way of framing the problems of crime and urban development than the ones promoted by lawmakers, police administrators and even local city officials, undermining the claims of order maintenance and crime avoidance advocates. Second, the Weed and Seed experience in Seattle provides an example of how local community involvement can filter back to national policymaking by providing feedback that modestly reconfigures national policymaking.

However, while Weed and Seed had the *potential* to offer meaningful community involvement in crime prevention because of its local implementation, the program's goals and guidelines perpetuated the punitive, top-down model of community crime prevention that dominates public discourse and policymaking. In addition, community residents are in a relatively (and notoriously) weak position vis-à-vis state agencies and have difficulty translating their perspectives into goals and practice in the absence of external forces in their favor (such as strong political mobilization against the program). This may be particularly true for minority communities. Douglas Massey and Nancy Denton note that blacks in the inner cities are at a distinct disadvantage politically because of residential segregation, which gives them few, if any, political allies in their neighborhood. "Under the best of circumstances, segregation undermines the ability of blacks to advance their interests because it provides ethnic whites with no immediate self-interest in their welfare" (Massey and Denton 1996, p. 145). In Seattle, both Weed and Seed target areas are less residentially segregated than some inner-cities neighborhoods, thus providing a greater opportunity for effective political mobilization. Nonetheless, both areas also have a long history of neglect by city officials and residents can hardly be said to wield substantial power in local politics. While the community involvement theme in Weed and Seed presented an *opportunity* for local communities to inject their goals into policy implementation, the political *realities* of community resources presented challenges to the meaningful realization of those goals. Thus, the stage was set for a struggle between state agents and community members over problem definition, program goals and implementation strategies.

Finally, Weed and Seed, like many urban crime programs, might be seen as an illustration of what Jonathon Simon refers to as governing through crime control, which has particularly troubling implications for inner cities.[14] Simon suggests that the United States is experiencing "not a crisis of crime, but a crisis of governance that leads to prioritizing crime and punishment as the preferred context for governance" (Simon 1997, 173). Others have argued similarly that governments in the U.S. and other Western democracies are experiencing a crisis of authority, illustrated by declining trust in government, low levels of participation among voters and an inability of the state to convincingly make claims to solving major social problems such as crime (Garland 1996; Scheingold 1998). As a result, crime control becomes the primary means of governance because it provides the state with the opportunity to flex its muscle, to exercise authority by aggressively attacking a major social problem.[15] Thus, the inner cities, notorious for hardened criminals, drug wars and gang activity, become central locations for crime control strategies that emphasize government authority. As suggested earlier, this is particularly possible on the national level, though local politics complicates matters significantly.

The governing through crime strategy creates policy opportunities for law enforcement responses to violent crime, gangs and drug activity because authoritarian tactics can be implemented that do not require policy efforts to empower economically disadvantaged groups - a strategy that is politically unpopular, even in good economic times. These strategies mesh particularly well with community-based approaches because they deflect attention away from state responsibility for broader economic issues. Furthermore, they ostensibly promote police-community relations, allowing police greater access to an array of local activities that have not always been the purview of the police (working in schools, for example, or with drug treatment centers). Opportunity reduction and order maintenance strategies are particularly consistent with a governing through crime control approach because they emphasize the value of law enforcement for solving neighborhood crime and disorder problems and they provide opportunities for aggressive policing tactics.

To the extent that the inner cities experience governing through crime control, the struggle between police-centered and more community-centered approaches to crime prevention becomes increasingly important. The community-centered model of crime prevention runs counter to the governing through crime control framework for policymaking and its prevalence (or lack thereof) is crucial for understanding and evaluating the long-term development and revitalization of urban communities.

...Community policing, as long as it remains basically committed to crime as the central justification for order maintenance, runs the risk of reinforcing the imperative of our societies to govern through crime. Indeed, the NYPD [New York Police Department] strategy exemplifies this danger by explicitly justifying the arrest and removal of "squeegee men" out-of-door marijuana smokers and alcohol drinkers, and other public order violators as measures against violent crime (Simon 1997, 180).

As I shall illustrate in the coming chapters, Weed and Seed committed resources to community development only because of the crime problems in the areas, thus using crime control as the justification for all programs, including economic development, recreation opportunities and beautification projects. This approach has several troubling aspects. First, as Stanley Cohen notes, it becomes difficult to sustain these programs in the long-term because they are frequently scrutinized for failure (i.e., no change in crime rates) and therefore easy to eliminate when they do not show clear and unambiguous success. Second, my research in Seattle illustrates that members of the target area are far more interested in community development for its own sake, with crime prevention as one component of that development, not its central focus. While the strategies used in Weed and Seed across the country have been altered as the program evolved and engaged more community members, the original program goals remain and seeding strategies – development, social services, education – are still intimately linked to weeding, justified solely for their crime prevention function. Thus, crime control becomes a kind of leverage for the deployment of resources to address other urban problems.

Finally, that so many Weed and Seed target areas are in largely minority neighborhoods further challenges the value of the governing through crime control framework. If crime control is a primary example of government authority and control, few arenas offer richer opportunities to illustrate that authority than the communities of the hardened inner cities. These neighborhoods tend to be politically weak, rife with criminal activity, and struggle with social pathologies such as drug addiction, teen pregnancy and violence. National elected officials can be seen promoting strong government and exhibiting moral authority with few meaningful repercussions from the electorate.

Outline of the Book

In order to set the context and understand national crime control agenda setting and the role of communities in those agendas, *Chapter Two* begins with a brief discussion of federal crime control policymaking. This chapter also presents in greater detail the three models of community involvement in crime prevention: opportunity-reduction, order maintenance, and community-centered. The chapter concludes by noting that most of the policymaking and public discourse on community involvement in crime prevention emphasizes the first two models. In this chapter I suggest that the third model is the one most likely to fit with the perspectives of residents of high-crime communities.

   Chapter Three introduces Operation Weed and Seed by providing analysis of key federal and local documents and interview data to present a snapshot of the way the policy was first presented to grant seekers and subsequently, to community residents in the areas targeted for funding. The central theme is that the program emphasized coordination between federal, state and local law enforcement, aggressive policing strategies and tactics associated with an order maintenance model, and 'crime avoidance' strategies consistent with an opportunity-reduction model. The community-centered model was almost entirely absent from the original program goals. This chapter also notes the broad array of social problems that are purportedly addressed through Weed and Seed and its crime control emphasis. The chapter concludes with an overview of the controversies that erupted in target areas around the country when Weed and Seed funding was first announced.

   Chapter Four explores the Seattle case in-depth, first providing some historical context of the target area, then detailing the controversy about the program and illustrating how the concerns raised by community leaders in the target area reveal a more nuanced, community-centered perspective on crime prevention and the community role. This chapter uses intensive interview data, analysis of documents associated with the city's grant proposal, and the community response and implementation activities to detail the impact that the controversy and community demands had on the overall program goals and implementation. This chapter suggests that local residents resisted the opportunity-reduction and order-maintenance models of community crime prevention primarily because they were *police-focused* and that the *development-focused* perspective offered a broader range of possibilities for public safety and community development without empowering police agencies.

   Chapter Five discusses the development and implementation of Weed and Seed in Seattle's newer target area in the South End. The primary purpose of this chapter is to illustrate the growing sense of control that community residents articulated, the strong, community-centered model of crime prevention that they advocated, and the conditions under which that model might take precedence over others. This chapter also revisits Weed and Seed as it is conceptualized in the latter 1990s, noting the stronger emphasis on community involvement and the shift towards target areas that have pre-existing community groups with relations with police. The chapter concludes by raising questions about the long-term prospects for meaningful community control over Weed and Seed.

   Chapter Six discusses the community-centered crime prevention model in more detail, drawing out the distinctions between federal and local crime prevention professionals and the local community leaders and residents. This chapter also compares the Seattle original target area to numerous other Weed and Seed target areas in the country on several key variables to place Seattle's Weed and Seed story in context and illustrate the potential relevance of the community-centered crime prevention model for other urban areas.

   Chapter Seven concludes by summarizing the findings, challenging popular crime prevention strategies such as order maintenance and zero tolerance policing and noting the vital importance of listening to the perspectives of urban racial minorities and all residents of crime-ridden areas. It also revisits that governing through crime control theme and offers a brief discussion of the future of community crime prevention in the context of punitive national rhetoric and the trends towards greater control.

Notes

[1]   See Also Weed and Seed Implementation Manual 1992.
[2]   References to 'local' politics refer to city governments. The politicization of crime at the state level is not discussed here and is an important area for future research. Certainly some punitive crime policies have proliferated at the state level (Three Strikes You're Out and juvenile court waivers, for example), suggesting that the

incentives are high for state officials to support punitive law and order frameworks.

[3] See Scheingold (1984) for an eloquent discussion of how crime issues represent society's basic fears about right and wrong.

[4] Willie Horton was given a furlough from the Massachusetts prison where he was serving a life sentence. While on Furlough, he broke into a couple's home, raped the woman and held her husband captive by knifepoint.

[5] For a detailed account of how political aspirations can have an impact on punitive policy, see Butterfield (1995), which explores the case of Willie Boskett, whose many cases in juvenile court finally led the New York State legislature to pass the first law in the country allowing a juvenile to be tried as an adult. The number of juvenile cases waived to adult court grew 25% between 1988 and 1997 (Stahl, et. al. 1999).

[6] Of course, criminal justice expenditures at the national level have risen dramatically over the past 25 years (see Sourcebook of Criminal Justice Statistics, 1996; see also Beckett and Sasson 1999). Clearly, policy makers are willing to spend money to address the problem. The point of contention is the type of expenditures that can be justified; spending public money on prisons and law enforcement is easier than spending it on job programs and economic development.

[7] A note about community: I use the terms "community" and "neighborhood" interchangeably here with the recognition that a community is a rich term with connotations beyond simple geographic boundaries. This project does not address the substantial difficulty of identifying the cultural or psychological boundaries of the inner-cities and does not assume that the high-crime areas discussed in this book constitute discreet communities with common interests. The term is used here to refer primarily to geographic areas, specifically inner-city high-crime areas that have a high percentage of racial minorities and are typically the target of state-sponsored crime control efforts. However, the assumption underlying the thesis of this book is that the high-concentration of minorities in these areas can result in a substantial portion of residents having views of crime and criminal justice that differ – in small or significant ways – from national discourse and from law enforcement views (see chapter two for further discussion of this claim). Furthermore, those views tend to be the ones left out of conceptions of community as they are articulated by policy-makers.

[8] A note about race: In this book I am referring almost exclusively to black-white relations. In Seattle's second Weed and Seed site in the Rainier Valley, which is the subject of chapter five, there is a substantial Southeast Asian immigrant population as well. However, the primary groups involved in the program's implementation have been whites and blacks. Chapter five briefly discusses how the presence of an immigrant population may affect the thesis presented here.

[9] Rodney King is the well-known example and Amadou Diallo (an unarmed African immigrant shot by the New York police in February of 1999) is one of the most shocking but other, less sensational examples exist, including a recent brutal beating of a Latino suspect in New York, the on-going discussions about "driving while black" and the scholarly discussions concerning police misconduct towards black Americans (see Kennedy 1997).

[10] Seattle Times, October 23, 1998.

11   King, Keohane and Verba (1994) note that "what may appear to be a single-case study, or a study of only a few cases, may indeed contain many potential observations, at different levels of analysis, that are relevant to the theory being evaluated" (p. 208). This is true for the case here as it involves multiple levels of government, two distinct target areas, and numerous respondents in the target areas.

12   In order to ensure confidentiality, I have used pseudonyms for all respondents except several high profile professionals whose titles would immediately reveal their identity.

13   These models were established from a combination of literature reviews and policy exploration. While terminology varies, the fundamental principles appear to be generally recognized in community crime prevention literature as the primary approaches to crime control. Beckett and Sasson (1999), for example, describe three approaches and refer to them as opportunity-reduction, order maintenance and social problems.

14   Simon uses the phrase "governing through crime." However, this implies that the government itself is governing through its own criminal behavior, which is not at all what Simon means. Therefore, I use the phrase "governing through crime control" because it is a less confusing description of his claims.

15   Simon suggests that this is a particularly interesting development given that the development of modern societies is generally associated with a decrease in the overt use of state coercive force and a greater reliance on civil, tort and regulatory law. That the criminal justice system has expanded so dramatically in the United States over the past 30 years, raises questions about the relationship between modern, mature democratic societies and the growing use of the criminal justice system as social control mechanism.

2 Federal Crime Control and Community Crime Prevention

> The most interesting aspect of this topic [community crime prevention] is that the very definition of what crime prevention is hinges on the political outlook of the beholder.
>
> Wesley Skogan 1988, 72.

> Frequently, the way a problem is defined suggests the directions needed to address it. There is a set of prescriptions available, for example, to the problems of crime if one defines it as the product of poverty, unemployment, poor education or other social and economic ills. There is a qualitatively different set of directions available if the problem of crime is defined as a genetic problem or a race problem.
>
> Atlanta Police Chief George Napper,
> *Ebony Magazine*, August 1979.

Research on federal crime control strategies reveals that the primary emphasis is on punishment and that symbolic politics is routine (Marion 1994; Scheingold 1991). This chapter introduces the idea that most federal crime initiatives tend to be primarily about punishing criminals and those that involve community members tend to focus on a narrow, opportunity-reduction version of crime prevention (i.e., keeping criminals from being able to commit crimes in the first place). From the perspective of the communities themselves, however, crime prevention may take on a distinct meaning that is often overlooked in national discourse and policymaking.

Research on community involvement in crime prevention has tended to fall into two categories: how and when communities organize (see Skogan 1988; Rosenbaum 1986) and how effective community crime prevention programs have been (see Cirel, Evans, McGillis,Whitcomb 1977; Lindsay and McGillis 1986). The aim of this chapter is to understand community involvement in crime prevention by examining competing conceptions of crime prevention and to begin theorizing about the conditions under which more nuanced versions are able to win out.

The chapter has several aims. First, it illustrates the punitive and symbolic nature of crime control at the federal level and the rise of community involvement in crime prevention. This discussion notes that federal strategies emphasize crime policies that focus on controlling the ability of criminals to commit crime, rather than preventing people from committing crimes in the first place. It further suggests that despite President Johnson's Commission on Law Enforcement and the Administration of Justice, which advocated for broad social programs to address the social conditions that might give rise to crime (such as unemployment and poverty), federal crime control initiatives tended to focus more on punishment and incarceration than broad preventive strategies. And while community involvement has been advocated at the national level – beginning most prominently with the Commission's charge that law enforcement cannot address crime effectively without the help of citizens – that involvement has largely been restricted to assisting police and making citizens, homes and neighborhoods less attractive 'targets of opportunity' for criminals.

The second section of the chapter presents three models for understanding different conceptions of crime prevention and the role of citizens in addressing local crime problems: opportunity-reduction, order-maintenance and community-centered models. The chapter concludes by illustrating that the first two models are most prominent in public discourse on community crime control.

Federal Crime Control

Until Congress passed the Omnibus Crime Control and Safe Streets Act in 1968, the federal government played only a minimal role in crime fighting activities. Generally, state and local governments were seen as responsible for conceiving, funding and implementing policies that addressed crime problems (Feeley and Sarat 1980). "Active participation of the federal government in the field of criminal justice was confined mostly to direct enforcement of a limited number of major crime statutes and collection of the Uniform Crime Reports" (Krislov and White 1977).

The turmoil of the 1960s, however, created a sense that crime problems were more than local governments could handle and attention turned to the federal government for assistance. The punitive, law and order nature of that assistance has its origins in the increased attention to inner-city violence that stemmed from urban unrest and the civil rights movement. Katherine Beckett argues that national crime control efforts were part of the strategy conservatives used in an attempt to move southern Democrats into the Republican Party. This strategy used law and order messages, in part, as a way of responding to the violence and uprising of the civil rights movement and included racially charged "code words" aimed at exploiting fear of racial integration. As the New Deal coalition of Democrats began to fall apart over the race issue, Republicans actively pursued a strategy of appealing to white southerners who were particularly distressed with the civil rights movement and the demands that blacks were making for equal treatment (Beckett 1997). Of course, it is not just conservatives that had incentives to exploit the punitive law and order message. The symbolism of harsh punishments for lawbreakers serves a variety of functions for policymakers across the political spectrum by providing convenient symbols of good and bad that help solidify solidarity around particular candidates and concerns. It has also held increasing appeal to liberals seeking national elected office; President Clinton pressed for increasing the number of police officers on the streets and capital punishment for specific kinds of drug crimes.

While the thrust of federal crime control legislation has been largely punitive, it has also produced a significant amount of symbolic politics that reinforces both the individualistic conceptions of crime and criminality as well as the punitive response to crime. Nancy Marion, in her comprehensive study of federal crime control initiatives, argues that despite the heavy emphasis on crime beginning in the late 1960s, most federal crime control legislation is largely symbolic (Marion 1994).[1] In her 30-year overview of federal crime control policy-making, Marion notes that most policies were a means to an end for the politicians who supported them, rather than representative of any broad strategy for combating crime. Symbolic politics offers a way to frame crime problems and solutions that offer simple answers to complex questions (Edelman 1964, 1971; see also Cobb and Elder 1983; Rochefort and Cobb 1994). For policymakers, then, the range of possible solutions is restricted primarily to policies that send a clear message of right and wrong and place the blame for criminal action squarely on the shoulders of the criminal.

Symbolic politics need not be without material consequences, however, and the fact that the law and order message is geared largely towards punitive solutions has had an impact on incarceration rates over dramatic rise in incarceration rates for federal prisoners between 1980 and 1992, but declining or steady crime rates using National Crime Victimization Survey data from the same period (combined personal and household victimization). Black victimization rates did increase starting in the early 1990s but incarceration rates were on a dramatic upsurge long before then.[3]

Figure 2.1   Number of Victimizations and Prisoners, 1980-1992

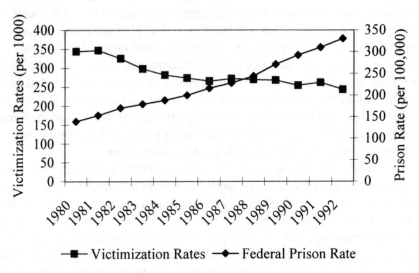

—■— Victimization Rates   —◆— Federal Prison Rate

Source: Sourcebook of Criminal Justice Statistics 1999.

In 1994, Congress passed the Violent Crime Control and Law Enforcement Act which increased federal funding for law enforcement personnel, increased the number of federal offenses punishable by death, lengthened sentences for a variety of offenses and introduced sentencing enhancements for certain types of federal crimes, further solidifying the federal government's central role in addressing crime and promoting punitive, law-enforcement based solutions.[4]

Since national policymaking takes place in the context of national public discourse about social problems, it is also worth noting that the public discourse on rehabilitation of criminals has been on the decline since the late 1970s. A review of articles in the Reader's Guide to Periodical Literature indicates that rehabilitation, as a viable response to criminal behavior, is far less prominent in the public discourse today than it was 30 years ago (Table 2.1). During the 30-year period between 1968 and 1997, there were 94 articles on the rehabilitation of prisoners; two-thirds of these articles appeared during the ten-year period from 1968-1977 and there is a clear downward trend from there.[5]

Others have also observed the abandonment of a rehabilitative model of criminal justice by the late 1970s (see Krislov 1997; Bayer 1981).[6] Even liberals began to express skepticism of the rehabilitative model and became increasingly concerned that the discretion associated with reform-oriented strategies resulted in unfair outcomes for racial minorities (see Beckett 1997).

Table 2.1 Articles on Rehabilitation, 1968-1992

Years	Articles
1968-1972	32
1973-1977	31
1978-1982	10
1982-1987	8
1988-1992	5

Source: Readers' Guide to Periodical Literature: 1968-1992.

What are the implications of these federal crime control efforts and national discourses for community involvement in crime prevention? To a large degree, federal crime control efforts that attempt to involve communities do so in the shadow of punitive solutions and in the context of rhetoric that emphasizes moral failing and individual responsibility for crime. This creates a narrow policy arena in which to craft community involvement.   As we shall see, several models of community crime prevention emerge in the 1970s and 1980s that are consistent with national discourse and policymaking but clash with the richer, community-focused model that is more likely to represent community views.

Communities and Crime Prevention

Historically, responses to deviance were dealt with informally and through collective organizing of local residents to mete out appropriate sanctions to offenders. Early colonial communities, for example, often dealt with those who transgressed social norms in harsh and sometimes brutal ways (Friedman 1993). Adulterers, thieves and others who violated community norms were often required to spend an evening in the local stockade. Floggings for public drunkenness were not uncommon and sex between unmarried persons might land one or both parties in the gallows. Communities inflicted a form of shame on those whose actions were seen as deviant and most of the early criminal justice activity took place around a "morality play" in which criminal activity was regarded as a moral weakness. Because the lack of a transportation infrastructure and the necessity of keeping family ties for childrearing limited mobility, communities were able to be moderately successful in maintaining social order through informal (though often brutal) sanctions.

In the late 17th and early 18th centuries, however, the growing sense of the state and broader national community necessitated more formal social control mechanisms for two reasons. First, the state needed to claim a monopoly on the legitimate use of violence and thus, what had previously been seen as private wrongs began to be seen as public harms - a professional force began to develop in order to formulate, enforce and adjudicate the law. Second, the growing nation had more borders that needed policing (see Dubow, McCabe and Kaplan, 1979). Border disputes were common, circuit court judges needed protection, and fugitives needed to be brought to justice.

In the early part of the 19th century, citizens shared responsibility for crime control through night watches, and private prosecution of crimes. But this also became difficult as the country grew and the need for more of these activities increased. Night watch positions and prosecution of crimes became occupations that were privately reimbursed. "The notion of order as the responsibility of every citizen gave way to growing feelings that direct involvement was an inconvenience that could be avoided by paying others to do the job" (Dubow, McCabe and Kaplan 1979, 68). The increase in public policing paralleled the decrease in citizen involvement and coincided with large-scale forces such as urbanization and industrialization that seemed to necessitate more formal and centralized social control efforts.

By the turn of the 20th century, community involvement in crime prevention was limited and crime prevention activities focused heavily on mobilizing state resources to alter offenders and/or their environments in order to keep criminality from emerging (Lewis and Salem 1981; see also Simon 1993). The Progressive era ushered in visions of the capable state that could successfully integrate new immigrants and those who had been negatively affected by the dual vices of urbanization and industrialization. Furthermore, the penitentiary, initiated by the Quakers as a way of forcing criminal offenders to reflect on their actions, was decisively anti-community as it regarded the communities from which offenders sprang as part of the amoral force which had lead them to vice in the first place (Friedman 1993). Offenders were better off being whisked away by the strong hand of a benevolent state that could bring about a substantial change in orientation and attitude through hard work and solitary reflection. As the century progressed, the rise of the scientific treatment model accompanied the notion of hard work and solitariness as appropriate responses to crime, each of which largely discounted the role of communities in preventing and responding to crime.

In the 1960s, however, rising crime rates and urban riots created a sense that treatment programs and rehabilitative ideals were unlikely to be successful (Lewis and Salem 1981; see also Simon 1993 and Beckett and Sasson 2000). Furthermore, the national government began to take a central role in addressing crime. President Lyndon Johnson's Special Message to Congress in 1965 focused heavily on crime and marked the beginning of an era in which "public expectations for national government action would be encouraged by political leaders" (Marion 1994). President Johnson's crime commission – the Commission on Law Enforcement and the Administration of Justice – recommended major federal support for local law enforcement to expand and become technologically sophisticated. The subsequent Law Enforcement Assistance Administration (LEAA) created block grant funding which provided blocks of funding for a variety of purposes to be determined by the state authorities. This represented a major shift in the history of federal/state relations because it broke with the tradition of direct, categorical grants that were earmarked for specific programs (Marion 1994).

President Johnson's Commission also recommended community involvement and the LEAA funded numerous community crime prevention programs. "Criminal justice professionals readily and repeatedly admit that, in the absence of citizen assistance, neither more manpower nor improved technology, nor additional money will enable law enforcement to shoulder the monumental burden of combating crime in America" (Cirel, et al. 1974, 3). However, while the President's crime commission report called for an active and involved citizenry, most of the money was directed towards *reacting* to crime, rather than dealing with its origins and much of the community involvement funding appears to have been directed at crime awareness and avoidance strategies. Thus, the community involvement was largely confined to *controlling* criminal behavior by making crimes harder to commit, rather than *preventing* criminality in the first place.

This is in part because of the decline in the rehabilitative and treatment ideals noted earlier. Community crime prevention theory emerged as a viable alternative for addressing increasing fear and high rates of crime (Skogan 1988). In addition to the urban riots and general feeling of lawlessness generated by the 1960s, municipal and federal budget constraints made acquiring more police a near impossibility. Encouraging the "off-budget" approaches that were based on local voluntary organizations was a viable alternative to both budgetary problems as well as to the growing sentiment that the criminal justice system could not single-handedly resolve the crime problem. Wes Skogan notes, "The community approach to crime prevention emphasizes collaboration between the criminal justice system and community organizations. It assumes that the police and other elements of the criminal justice system cannot effectively deal with crime and fear on their own" (Skogan 1988, 40). Community crime prevention strategies were also aimed at addressing some of the racial tensions that exploded in urban violence in the 1960s and 70s. To the extent that community involvement was encouraged, it was intended to help police perform more effectively. As such, "community crime prevention meant essentially citizen support for official law enforcement practice" (DuBow and Emmons 1981).

The community approach may have also been attractive because it seemingly deflected attention away from root causes by emphasizing volunteerism and personal responsibility (Skogan 1988). This is consistent with the discussion above that notes the salience of political strategies emphasizing personal failing as an explanation for crime. Thus, the original conception of community crime prevention resonated with an idea of crime that emphasized individual responsibility both for commiting crime as well as avoiding it.

Contemporary Crime Prevention: Local Community Response

Several assumptions about communities and crime have made the local implementation of   federal crime control programs problematic and created a context in which the communities targeted by the policies might resist the conception of crime control and prevention at the center of those policies. First, some policy makers assumed, as did French philosopher Emile Durkheim, that deviant behavior served the function of drawing communities together in a common purpose to drive out the offender, thereby strengthening the community in the process. But research indicates that crime frequently serves to *undermine* the capacity of communities to organize, rather than support that capacity (Skogan 1988; Lewis and Salem 1981). Second, fear of crime in this view was seen as a reflection of objective threats and harms, rather than socially constructed categories. In fact, different communities have different conceptions of crime and its effects (see Sampson, et. al. 1998). Some people view car prowls as the main problems while others view unruly youth as the greatest threat. More importantly, in some cases, police harassment and potential abuse may be viewed as just as deviant and threatening as the actions of street criminals. Finally, when communities do respond to crime and fear, it is not at all clear what those responses will be. Some organizations will want to focus on home security and burglary prevention while others will want to address broader community development concerns such as health care, unemployment, poverty and the like (Podolfskey 1985; McPherson and Silloway 1981; DuBow and Emmons 1981). National policymakers, then, step into a quagmire of questions when they expand policymaking to include input by the communities that are most plagued by crime.

The literature on community crime prevention programs refers to several common strategies that are distilled here into two categories: *opportunity-reduction* and *order restoration/maintenance*. A third category, which I term *community-centered*, is referenced in this early work on community crime prevention but is given comparatively little attention. This model is suggested here to be the potential missing link in understanding community response to federal crime prevention strategies.[7]

Opportunity-reduction and order-restoration/maintenance do not capture the full range of possibilities for community involvement in crime control. The strategies they offer truncate possibilities for community crime prevention and risk losing (or never gaining) the support of local communities. When heterogeneous urban communities are invited into the policy development process, the possibility exists for shifting *away from* the narrow focus on reducing opportunities for criminals and the limited conception of restoring a sense of order *towards* limited police activity and building strong communities that are economically, socially and physically vibrant and offer meaningful opportunities for residents.

Opportunity-Reduction Model

When crime rates rose in the late 1960s and concerns about urban unrest emerged, crime prevention strategies that attempted to address crime at its root causes fell into disrepute (Lewis and Salem 1981, 406). The community crime prevention approach that began gaining popularity shifted the focus of attention away from the environment of criminals and potential criminals and towards potential *victims* and their environments (Lewis and Salem 1981, 406).[8] This approach is the "opportunity-reduction model" and is characteristic of the majority of federal community crime prevention efforts of the past 30 years.

   The opportunity-reduction model is based on the notion that fear of crime is the result of direct or indirect victimization and that communities can and will come together in response to victimization. Further, it assumes that encouraging community residents to assist police through information sharing and neighborhood watches can reduce fear of crime and crime itself. The emphasis is on volunteerism and individual responsibility. It regards community awareness about crime and the ability to resist criminal efforts as the cornerstone of crime prevention. The primary focus is target hardening: making crimes harder to commit by focusing on potential targets such as homes, cars and offices and making those areas harder to penetrate. These strategies include home safety checks, property identification, installing more effective locks, and instituting block watch programs that will encourage residents to look out for one another's property.

   The idea of making crime harder to commit became prominent in the 1960s and 1970s with the emergence of notions of defensible space and Crime Prevention Through Environmental Design (CPTED). These activities focused on a criminology of place, rather than an offender-based criminology (Taylor 1998, 14). In this way of thinking, instead of focusing on how offenders might be altered to integrate them into mainstream life, crime prevention efforts emphasize reorganizing public space and analyzing the features of a neighborhood (such as number and location of high schools, bars, public housing). The primary goal is to explain *"why* criminals commit crimes *where* they commit them" (Kennedy 1990, 240).

A 1979 LEAA publication called "The Community's Stake in Crime Prevention: A citizen's action guide" explicitly noted that law enforcement especially welcomes a role for citizens in making crime harder to commit:

> While citizen involvement in all forms of crime reduction and prevention is to be encouraged, citizen input in reducing the opportunity for criminal acts appears to be the strategy most welcomed by law enforcement..."opportunity reduction" gives notice to the would-be offender that a criminal act may be more trouble than its worth.[9]

Two examples of opportunity-reduction models are environmental design changes and personal safety programs. The former approach emphasizes reconfiguring roads, intersections and other physical characteristics of a neighborhood so that areas that are currently attractive to criminals become less so. CPTED are common in police departments around the country in an attempt to rearrange the physical landscape to make criminal activity less likely. Programs geared towards personal safety are most commonly targeted towards women (rape prevention) and the elderly (avoiding muggings and theft) and emphasize finding ways to avoid assault.

Community groups that advocate these approaches are likely to be what Skogan terms, "preservationist groups" that have a stake in maintaining the current neighborhood composition and to warding off newcomers that appear to threaten the status quo (Skogan 1988, 59). Beckett and Sasson note that block watch groups, for example, are more popular in white, middle-class neighborhoods partly because residents of those neighborhoods "are likely to believe that crime is caused by "outsiders" rather than by members of their own community" (Beckett and Sasson 2000, 152). Two early examples of the opportunity-reduction model that tapped into existing 'preservationist groups' are the Hartford community crime prevention study and Seattle burglary prevention program.

The Hartford study had four major hypotheses:
1) The crime rate in a residential neighborhood is a product of the linkage between offender motivation and the opportunities provided by the residents, users, and environmental features of that neighborhood;

2) The crime rate for a specific offense can be reduced by lessening the opportunities for that crime to occur;
3) Opportunities can be reduced by:
    a. altering the physical aspects of buildings and streets to increase surveillance capabilities and lessen target/victim vulnerability, to increase the neighborhood's attractiveness to residents, and to decrease its fear-producing features;
    b. increasing citizen concerns about and involvement in crime prevention and the neighborhood in general and;
    c. utilizing the police to support the above,
4) Opportunity-reducing activities will lead not only to a reduction in the crime rate but also to a reduction in fear of crime. The reduced crime and fear will mutually reinforce each other, leading to still further reductions in both (Fowler, et. al, 1979, 2).

The primary emphasis here is clearly on reducing crime through reducing the opportunities for offenders to commit crime and involving the community primarily through greater awareness of potential criminal activity. Further, the assumption that reducing fear of crime itself is an important task is made clear in the fourth hypothesis.

A similar emphasis is found in Seattle's burglary reduction program in the 1970s. The local Law and Justice Planning Office found that citizens feared burglary more than most other crimes. The Office developed a prevention program that would focus on key areas in the city in order to affect a significant reduction in burglary rates. The Office received a grant from the LEAA to "hire staff of civilians to organize target communities and implement surveillance and target hardening strategies" (Lindsay and McGillis 1986, 48). The staff worked closely with the police and contacted local civic groups and church organizations to offer three free services: a property identification system, home security checks and neighborhood block watch organizations.

Both programs enjoyed modest success in suppressing the rates of property crimes for a short period, though follow-up research indicated that crime rates crept back to earlier rates or fell back in line with the city's rates within a year or two. Indeed, broader research on opportunity reduction strategies indicates that there is no clear effect on crime rates (Beckett and Sasson 2000, 153).

Order Restoration/Maintenance Model

Order restoration and maintenance as a strategy for community crime prevention has enjoyed some popularity in academic circles through its origin in the Chicago school of sociology and critiques of the belief that the fear of crime stems solely from direct or indirect victimization (Greenberg, Rohe, Williams 1985). The Chicago school argued that urban crises were the result of industrialization, the breakdowns in family structure and informal social control of neighborhoods. Fear, argued these scholars, was as much about the breakdown of social order in the form of loitering teens, public drunkenness and vandalism, as it was about crime itself. This approach challenges the opportunity reduction model by noting the "weakening of traditional community controls that result from increased size, density, and heterogeneity of modern urban society" (Greenberg, Rohe and Williams 1985, 1-2; see also Lewis and Salem 1981). As a result, these communities would not automatically organize around crime issues because there were too many other fears and concerns. The response to crime, according to these scholars, should be strengthening collective local institutions that can respond to these problems.

Some programs were funded in the 1970s with this strategy in mind but James Q. Wilson and George Kelling's 1988 reprisal of an earlier article in the *Atlantic Monthly* brought order maintenance national attention in the form of community policing. Wilson and Kelling suggested that community policing might be able to assist in the restoration of traditional community strength by tapping into the existing strengths of a community and using the police as central figures in helping citizens empower themselves and their neighborhoods by responding to problems of disorder.

Wilson and Kelling claim that disorder itself can be criminogenic. Neighborhoods could decay into disorder and crime when seemingly small problems, such as broken windows on buildings, are allowed to proliferate. Such disrepair leads to the perception that no one cares about the neighborhood and, as a result, encourages more broken windows, abandoned cars and other unpleasantries. This eventually causes people to avoid those streets, giving them over to hoodlums. Crime flourishes. For Wilson and Kelling, the disorderliness of broken windows, public drunkenness and loitering are themselves criminogenic conditions which need to be addressed if the urban decay that is bred through crime is to be resolved (Wilson and Kelling, 1982). If these underlying causes of urban decline are to be addressed, Wilson and Kelling argued, we must empower the police to deal with the day-to-day disorders of urban living.

In a subsequent volume, Kelling and Catherine Coles note, "in its broadest sense, disorder is incivility, boorish and threatening behavior that disturbs life, especially urban life" (Kelling and Coles 1996, 14). They extend this discussion and argue for a community crime prevention strategy that empowers communities by creating relationships between communities and police such that the police are permitted to control the day-to-day disorders that threaten civility and solidarity in urban areas. They note that

> The police are uniquely positioned to assist in order restoration and maintenance through their historical role as problem solvers in the community: in fact, citizen demands for order have been met in many cities with new police strategies emphasizing order maintenance and crime prevention, as well as citizen involvement in crime control efforts in concern with police (Kelling and Coles 1996, 7).

Police departments around the country increasingly embrace the order maintenance approach to crime control advocated by Wilson and Kelling. Police administrators, anxious to respond to concerns about misconduct and to develop policing strategies that generate better police-community relations, generally support community policing practices that involve some type of order maintenance (Fleissner 1997; see also Lyons 1999).

Wilson and Kelling's claim that disorder is criminogenic is a compelling one in some respects. Disorder creates more opportunities for crime and signals that a neighborhood's residents will not take exception if people engage in criminal activity. This is certainly plausible, particularly when we remember that a sizeable portion of street crime is impulsive and opportunistic – an open window, an unlocked car both present an opportunity for a quick heist that may not have been planned when the individual offender began walking down the street. On the other hand, it is harder to believe that otherwise law-abiding citizens are wantonly engaging in criminal activity as a result of broken windows and abandoned cars. In order for the criminogenic argument to be persuasive, we must believe that disorder actually induces people who would not be likely to commit crime to engage in criminal activity. This is a more difficult argument to make. Rather, the order maintenance argument seems primarily rooted in the notion that disorder creates a climate that *attracts* criminals because criminal behavior can more easily blend in with that background and police presence may be less common.

Thus, while this approach moves beyond making individual potential targets of crime harder to harm or acquire, it is still focused on making crime harder to commit by hardening *communities* to criminal activity. The emphasis is on reducing fear so that citizens are present on streets, aware of one another and actively guarding the community from criminals who wander around the area. It is not primarily focused on making communities unlikely to generate criminals in the first place. Like opportunity-reduction, it is oriented towards *controlling* crime, rather than genuinely *preventing* crime.

The Limitations of Opportunity Reduction and Order Maintenance

It is worth noting here that neither of the strategies discussed above emerged from the communities most affected by crime. The opportunity reduction model is a federally inspired, locally implemented model and the order restoration approach was generated primarily by academics who observed slow decay of community life in urban areas. In addition to the policy discussions above, an examination of articles on citizen involvement in crime prevention in the *Reader's Guide to Periodical Literature* illustrates that national discourse on the issue has also focused largely on these two models with very few articles raising the issue of how communities of high-crime might implement crime prevention programs in terms of broader community development and empowerment. The themes are listed in Table 2.2.

Table 2.2 Citizen Involvement in Crime Prevention

Category	Number of Articles
Opportunity reduction	32
Order maintenance	52
Community-centered	4
Other	16
Total	104

Source: Readers' Guide to Periodical Literature: 1970-1997.[10]

Clearly, community-centered approaches to crime prevention are not in the forefront of popular discourse. It appears that order maintenance is the most dominant theme, with articles about citizens taking to the streets to create a presence that would deter criminal activity in their neighborhoods.

But there is some evidence to suggest that urban communities that are dealing with significant street crime problems, particularly those with heterogeneous racial populations, are not as responsive to these types of programs as one might expect, given the day-to-day problems they face with crime. Indeed, researchers trying to understand how communities respond to crime have argued that "the underlying victimization perspective and legalistic conceptualization of the crime problem and crime prevention policy at the federal level serves to limit the range of alternatives that would be considered in local programs" (McPherson and Silloway 1981, 34; see also DuBow and Emmons 1981). McPherson and Silloway go on to note that:

> Politics enters into planning only at the point of implementation when the program or plan must be sold to the citizens in the community; they must be persuaded or forced into accepting the program activities and participating according to plan...the difficulty is that the problem addressed by a program may not be the ones that community members would freely choose (McPherson and Silloway 1981, 35).

Beckett and Sasson also argue that the "social problems approach," which considers the relationships of crime to a variety of social ills including the social, economic and physical environment, is most popular in racially heterogeneous and working class neighborhoods (Beckett and Sasson 2000, 153). Aaron Podolefsky has illustrated this point by noting how an organization representing a poor, multi-cultural area of San Francisco rejected participation in a city-wide crime prevention program because it took a narrow approach to the crime problem rather than addressing what residents saw as real causes of crime: unemployment, poverty and poor education (Podolfesky 1981). And Skogan notes that a group representing blacks in Chicago dropped out of Urban Crime Prevention Program – part of an LEAA sponsored program -- because it was not comfortable with the limited goals that the program had. "Participation," Skogan notes, "...meant the assertion of black interests" (Skogan 1988, 65).

Skogan refers to these groups as insurgents. Contrary to the preservationist groups, which are likely to advocate opportunity reduction strategies, insurgents attack narrowly defined programs advanced by crime prevention specialists as diversionary, preferring instead to focus on funding for social and economic issues. These groups tend to advocate for minority interests and the interests of those in the lower socio-economic strata. Furthermore, and perhaps most importantly, these groups are at pains not to legitimize the role of police because of long histories of abuse and mistreatment at the hands of law enforcement (Skogan 1988, 57-8). Scheingold's study of local politicization of crime noted similarly that blacks were among the earliest advocates of citizen involvement in crime control and prevention and that this advocacy emphasized giving the community a role in disciplinary hearings involving police abuse or mistreatment of citizens (Scheingold 1991, 65). Indeed, public opinion polling data tells us that blacks and whites sometimes have differing views on how crime should be addressed and how criminals should be treated.[11] In general, blacks are less trusting of the police than whites and in some localities these differences are dramatic. In Detroit, for example, blacks "voiced considerably greater distrust of police than did whites. In 1992, three times as many whites as blacks (61% to 19%) said that the police provide enough protection in their neighborhood" (Welch, Combs, Sigelman and Bledsoe 1996, 217).

Table 2.3 illustrates that blacks as a group are less likely than whites to think that the police are doing a good job, more likely to believe that education and training should be a goal of imprisonment and more likely to think that the government should spend tax money on programs to reduce drug addiction and gun violence. Furthermore, the National Black Election Study (NBES) suggests that blacks are more likely to support an activist government and redistributive social and economic policies than the white electorate (Gurin, Hatchet and Jackson 1989, 245). The NBES also showed that blacks and whites supported funding for crime prevention equally but that over twice as many blacks as whites wanted the government to "make every possible effort to improve the social and economic position of blacks and other minority groups…and many more blacks than whites wanted spending on community and social welfare programs increased" (Gurin, Hatchett and Jackson 1989, 245). Given the heavy emphasis on law enforcement that crime prevention programs tend to have, it is not surprising that blacks' preferences for increased spending in this area are not any higher than those of whites. As a result of these other differences in perspectives, blacks and whites as a whole are likely to have distinct and sometimes conflicting viewpoints on what government programs to address crime and revitalize communities ought to look like.

Table 2.3   Black and White Views on Police, Sentencing and How to Spend Tax Dollars

	Good police performance[1]	Training and education in sentencing[2]	Importance of reducing illegal drugs[3]	Importance of reducing gun violence[4]
Black	9	29	76	60
White	31	17	54	32

1 Police doing good or very good job
2 Most important sentencing purpose
3 Extremely important that tax dollars be spent on reducing illegal drugs
4 Extremely important that tax dollars be spend on reducing gun violence

Source: Sourcebook of Criminal Justice Statistics, 1996.

Thus, a gulf exists, Skogan argues, between the federal government's understanding of the crime problem and the ways in which grass roots community groups think about crime and its solutions (Skogan 1988, 66).   However, because many of the early community crime prevention efforts were spearheaded by federal initiatives, it is difficult for groups advocating scrutiny of the status quo to have their input taken seriously in the context of crime prevention.   While groups that are mobilized to focus on education, homelessness, poverty or unemployment may be regarded as outside the scope of crime prevention by federal and state policymakers, many local groups consider them connected. Thus, in examining the role of communities in crime prevention and the response to federal crime initiatives, attention must be paid to how these groups conceive of the crime problem and what solutions they put forth. Because much of the activity around crime prevention and control has taken place in the context of urban, minority areas, the manner in which these communities define the realm of crime control and prevention is important for understanding their reaction to state-conceived programs and the subsequent success of those programs. Podolfesky suggests that "racial minorities are more likely to see the causes" of crime than whites (Podolfesky 1985, 34). As noted earlier, blacks are more likely than whites to see poverty and unemployment as the result of structural factors, such as economic deprivation and discrimination, thus indicating that they may be less likely to buy into the individualistic conceptions of crime that permeate the public discourse.

It is worth noting here that the governing through crime control strategy mentioned in chapter one is likely to run into resistance at the community level because it justifies community development strictly in crime prevention terms, rather than broader economic development. Furthermore, it does so in a narrow, law enforcement-focused manner. When economic and social programs for high-crime areas are promoted primarily as crime prevention programs with police and other law enforcement agencies at their center, there is the likelihood that local communities will resist those policies because their ends are too narrow (crime displacement rather than broader development) and their means are unattractive (aggressive police tactics).

Community-centered Crime Prevention: An Emerging Model

The first two approaches discussed here – opportunity reduction and order restoration – are largely police-centered because they focus crime prevention activities around the police and/or other law enforcement agencies. Furthermore, they draw on the language of legal control and enforcement, and they place police agencies at the center of implementation, thus pitting communities most ambivalent about policing in a struggle for control with law enforcement. In addition, they focus on public safety concerns as the centerpiece of community revitalization and renewal, regarding social and economic development as, at best, a means towards public safety ends, rather than as ends in themselves. Skogan, Scheingold, Beckett and Sasson, and Podolfesky's research all suggest that neither the opportunity-reduction, nor the order maintenance model are likely to be readily embraced by residents in crime-ridden communities.

The work of Paul Lavrakas (1995) provides a baseline for developing a third model of community crime prevention that is more likely to be palatable to residents in urban crime-ridden areas. Lavrakas suggests that most community crime prevention programs have been only moderately successful, if at all, because they have not marshaled "potent enough anti-crime programs given the magnitude of the crime problems faced" (Lavrakas 1995, 112). Lavrakas notes that many of the community crime prevention programs initiated in the years after the LEAA were focused on "secondary crime prevention programs" – reducing opportunities for victimization (see opportunity reduction discussion above). While these programs have their merits, Lavrakas sees them as insufficient for addressing serious crime problems. Primary crime prevention programs, according to Lavrakas, must deal with crime's root causes. Community crime prevention programs that focus narrowly on victimization will miss the mark.

Lavrakas argues that a genuine community crime prevention approach incorporates the following ideas:

1) That the police, by themselves, are incapable of preventing crime;
2) That traditional policing is inadequate for our present needs but new community-oriented policing holds much promise;
3) That citizens must play a central and organized role in preventing crime;
4) That many, if not all, social service agencies (public health, mental health, housing, education, employment, etc.) and other social institutions (the family, churches, the media, etc.) must play important roles in any comprehensive crime prevention program;
5) And that, ultimately, all crime prevention should be viewed as "community-based" (Lavrakas 1995, 113).

The third model of community crime prevention – *community-centered crime prevention* – builds upon this model and presents a potentially more coherent picture of what urban areas plagued by crime are likely to advocate when they are involved in crime prevention activities. The community-centered model does not preclude the first two models – that is, it does not regard them as irrelevant or unimportant. Rather, it sees them as operating as part of a larger strategy which gives community members control over both policing activities as well as broad community development activities.

There are three primary characteristics of community-centered crime prevention. First, at its core, community-centered crime prevention is concerned with *creating a vibrant living environment* in which citizens have an array of viable opportunities for employment, housing, health care, recreation and social activity. This includes using law enforcement activities to address specific crime problems but does not regard those activities as the most central component of crime prevention. This comports with Lavrakas' notion that many other institutions other than the police must be involved in crime prevention and community development.

Second, it acknowledges the importance of police activity but is *wary of existing police practices* that might undermine community solidarity, rather than strengthen it. Thus, it is attentive to concerns of racial minorities and immigrant populations that may be particularly vulnerable to law enforcement activities. It is fearful of strategies that provide police with additional power or that do not provide communities with the ability to have some control over policing strategies. This is consistent with Skogan and others' work which notes the concerns that African-Americans have about police in their neighborhoods.

Finally, it *promotes direct community involvement and some measure of control over the programs to be implemented in the community.* It does not see police or other law enforcement agencies as the central controlling figure in crime control strategies, but rather, as one component of many. It is more likely to advocate community control over, or serious community input into, strategies for addressing crime and revitalizing communities. Lavrakas suggests that police play a "pivotal role in working to mobilize the voluntary potential of the citizenry to engage in crime prevention strategies within their jurisdiction. However, the police should not be given a disproportionately important (i.e., powerful) role in devising the comprehensive crime prevention program that the municipality will implement" (Lavrakas 1995, 115).

Both the opportunity-reduction and the order-maintenance models have potential limitations for crime-ridden communities because they emphasize making criminal activity harder to commit, rather than seriously reducing the activity itself. The opportunity-reduction model, for example, not only focuses almost exclusively on target hardening. It assumes that the primary concern of citizens involves property loss and personal safety from crime, rather than personal safety from police and future opportunities for young people.

This is not to suggest that opportunity reduction and order maintenance are unconcerned with building broader community life. But the community-centered perspective differs from the other models in two important respects. First, the opportunity reduction model assumes that protecting property and persons can reduce crime, and order maintenance assumes that fear needs to be reduced in order to generate strong community ties. The primary emphasis of the community-centered model, however, is not on altering the community environment solely for the purpose of reducing fear or crime but working on community problems for the sake of community. Public safety problems may rank in the forefront of residents' minds, but for many they are perceived as directly connected to economic and social debilitation. Parks and recreation areas, childcare and health care, affordable housing, job opportunities and youth activities may be emphasized not for the sole purpose of reducing crime but because of their necessity for vital, livable communities. Further, criminal behavior by citizens must be addressed but not in a way that promotes allows law enforcement activity that is not subject to inquiry and scrutiny by those subject to greater police presence. Again, this contradicts the governing through crime control mode to which national policymaking seems beholden.

Second, the order-maintenance model assumes that fear of crime and disorder is worthy of police response without questioning whether that fear is justified. It does not, however, assume that fear of the police is equally deserving of attention. Rather, as we shall see in chapter four, fear of police is frequently dismissed as the result of misunderstanding or misinformation. Thus, in communities where tensions with the police are high or even moderate, the order-maintenance model fails to address one of the most important fears in the community (see Lyons 1999).

Given that different groups have different priorities for crime prevention, it appears that neither crime nor fear of crime are objective categories but rather, reflections of ongoing struggles to make sense out of and feel safe in one's social environment. The order-maintenance model is intolerant of fear of crime and disorder, such as unruly youth on a street corner or public inebriation. It does not, however, display an equally zealous intolerance for fear of police presence and the harassment or abuse that presence might bring. Thus, communities that have a history of tension with law enforcement and are not anxious to further empower police in their communities may resist the order-maintenance model.

Table 2.4 illustrates the key tenets of each of the three models of crime prevention. By focusing on the central neighborhood problem, the role of the police, and the extent of community control, we can see the striking differences between the two dominant models in crime prevention discourse and policymaking and the community-centered model.

Table 2.4 Three Models of Community Crime Prevention

	Central Problem	Role of the Police	Community Control
Opportunity Reduction	Multiple crime opportunities	Teach citizens to avoid crime	Identify major crimes, target harden
Order Maintenance	Disorder and unruly behavior	Greater police discretion to respond to fear and disorder	Identify disorderly behavior and work with police to curb that behavior
Community-centered	Low economic and social development, extensive police power	Work with communities to identify community-supported responses to particular problems	Identify crimes, fear of crime and fear of police abuse of power, some community control over policing.

Of course, different community organizations are likely to have different perspectives and goals for their community and for the programs that are brought into that community. Which community groups are most influential and most likely to insinuate themselves into the decision-making process? Skogan's discussion of insurgent groups suggests that they are likely to be left out of the process in part because they will be overlooked by government agencies seeking cooperative organizations and in part because the groups themselves might refuse to participate in the program. Lyons observed that groups that already have police-friendly agendas – such as advocating for greater police presence in their neighborhood or working with police on block watches and neighborhood patrols – are most likely to be embraced by police department outreach and community policing efforts (Lyons 1999). Groups that are highly critical of police tactics or groups that want police to play only a minimal role in their community, are far less likely to receive and sustain the attention of police departments.

Taken together, both Skogan and Lyons' work are significant for this study because they indicate that groups that are critical of the status quo are less likely to participate or be invited to participate in the implementation of crime prevention programs. Because law enforcement is such a central component of Weed and Seed, we might expect community groups that have a favorable disposition to existing police strategies to have more influence than those that do not. And since seeding is only half of the program (and not the half that was originally emphasized, as we shall see in the next chapter), we might expect to see some groups oppose the program altogether on the grounds that it diverts attention away from other, more important issues such as employment, housing, education and economic development. Whether and how these groups are able to influence implementation will be addressed in subsequent chapters.

For our purposes, we will refer to groups that are willing to work with police and focus primarily (though not exclusively) on crime as *police-focused* groups. Organizations that are critical of police and more interested in community development issues will be called *development-focused* groups. The literature discussed above leads us to a hypothesis that police-focused groups would be more likely to promote opportunity-reduction and order maintenance and be willing to work with police on crime prevention programs. Development-focused groups emphasize non-crime issues in the neighborhood, are less interested in working with police (indeed, they may be downright hostile towards police) and are more likely to promote the community-centered crime prevention model. Community organizations with a crime-focus are, according to Skogan and Lyons, more likely than development-centered ones to attract the attention of agents of the state that are implementing a crime prevention program.

Summary

We have seen that the dominant theme of federal policymaking has been punitive; it limits the range of possibilities for community involvement in crime prevention. We have further seen that much of the community crime prevention designed for local implementation has emphasized opportunity-reduction and that the order-maintenance model appears to be popular in public discourse and among police administrators.

The community-centered crime prevention model, in comparison to order-maintenance and opportunity-reduction, forms the central framework of this book. The subsequent chapters explore this framework and illustrate how the residents of the Weed and Seed target areas in Seattle took a community-centered perspective, resisting national policy-making. Further, the intrusion of a community-centered model onto the crime prevention agenda provided an opportunity to modestly transform narrowly conceived national crime policy into broader strategies that incorporate some aspects of the community-centered model.

Notes

[1] Noting that these policies are symbolic is not to suggest that they have no consequences but rather, that they have consequences that are often unrelated to stated goals. Indeed, it is not difficult to see the direct, material consequences of high incarceration rates from the war on drugs which, many have argued, has had a marginal effect, if any, on the actual drug trade (see Zimring and Hawking 1992).

[2] I recognize that Edelman tended to use the phrase 'symbolic politics' to refer to politics that result in inaction or action with no consequence. However, I think the phrase can be used more broadly in the context of criminal justice policy because the punitive rhetoric in which politicians engage has a direct impact on the kinds of policies that are implemented. Those policies, while often not achieving stated goals, do indeed have consequences, as the following section illustrates.

[3] It would be difficult to make the case that lawmakers enacted punitive criminal justice policy in response to the victimization of blacks (especially poor blacks who are most likely to be victimized by crime). In *The Politics of Law and Order*, Scheingold argues persuasively that politicians tend to deploy punitive crime rhetoric to appeal to voters writ large, not necessarily to address crime victimization rates of those on the lower end of the socio-economic ladder.

[4] There is, of course, a great deal more to this act than the law enforcement strategies mentioned here. But the provisions of the program that emphasize more preventive types of strategies – such as education and job training activities for incarcerated young offenders – deeply intertwine social services with law enforcement or justify general neighborhood revitalization strategies (like parks and recreation) in narrow crime control terms.

[5] While the 12 years of Republican presidents from 1980-1992 clearly emphasized punitiveness and focused on individual responsibility with respect to crime control, other research indicates that even liberals have lost faith in rehabilitation as a viable strategy for addressing crime. As early as 1981, Ronald Bayer argued that liberal journals at one time exhibited a strong commitment to viewing crime as a reflection of socio-economic factors..."now those who have changed their positions say that the weight of the scientific evidence makes it impossible to sustain faith in the rehabilitative idea" (Bayer 1979, 176).

6
Daniel Krislov argues that the consensus of a rehabilitative ideal was largely illusory; it combined welfare liberals who had genuine fears about putting people in the hands of a criminal justice system, with crime control advocates whose only interest in rehabilitation was as a means to reduce crime. When rehabilitation appeared to be failing, the crime control advocates quickly jumped ship for, from their viewpoint, more promising terrain, namely the punitive approach. They then allied themselves with what Krislov terms legal moralists, those who see a breaking the law as a moral, as well as a legal, transgression and see punishment as not only necessary but required. This is an interesting perspective and one that goes a long way towards explaining the appeal of punitive policy.

7
One of the most interesting discussions of something akin to a community-centered model of crime prevention is presented by Wesley Skogan who describes insurgent groups involved in community crime prevention as those that have a stake in upsetting the current distribution of property and status and as likely to have much broader notions of what constitutes crime prevention than those presented at the federal level (Skogan 1988, see especially p. 42-3 and p. 50-1). Paul Lavrakas has also articulated a community crime prevention model that notes some of the problems of contemporary strategies (see Lavrakas 1995). Beckett and Sasson (2000) and Rosenbaum and Lurigio (1986) recognize what they term the 'social problem approach' to crime prevention that takes a much more structural view than traditional approaches. However, while these scholars recognize these different viewpoints, to my knowledge, a systematic analysis of how well community residents' views mesh with these models and whether these viewpoints have had an impact on crime prevention strategies put forth by federal agencies has not been systematically explored. Furthermore, none of these approaches includes a critique of police activity and a desire to have substantial control over program goals as central components of the model.

8
Others have claimed that this is illustrative of a broader shift in criminal justice practice which moves strategies away from trying to alter offenders and their environments in hopes of eradicating or significantly reducing crime rates and towards strategies of simply managing crime by keeping law-abiding citizens out of harms way and criminals incapacitated (see Simon 1993 and Feeley and Simon 1994). While these claims are beyond the scope of this research project, the proliferation of 'crime-avoidance' strategies is one possible indicator that this approach may be gaining popularity.

9
The Community's Stake in Crime Prevention: a citizen's action guide. Law Enforcement Assistance Administration, U.S. Department of Justice. 1979.

10
From 1970 to 1997, there were 132 articles in the category of Crime Prevention – Citizen Involvement. Of those 132 articles, the dominant theme of the article was identifiable in 104. Articles were coded in the following manner: Opportunity-reduction articles mentioned keeping property or person safe from crime; Order-maintenance articles mentioned community policing, citizens 'taking back their neighborhoods' from drug dealers, citizen patrols and neighborhood watch programs; Community-centered articles raised issues such as employment, education, health care and/or broader governmental agents and policies which have hindered development in urban areas; the Other category was used for articles involving cases of crime prevention programs in foreign countries, instances when citizens did not respond to cries for help, or other issues which were not directly related to crime prevention/control.

11   I am grateful to Andrea Simpson for encouraging me to explore these differences and for directing me towards the National Black Election Study. The Sourcebook on Criminal Justice Statistics is also a valuable source for understanding differences in the perspectives of blacks and whites on criminal justice issues.

3   Getting the Community Involved: Operation Weed and Seed

> The ultimate object of Operation Weed and Seed is to involve everyone in this effort to "weed out" crime and revitalize crime-ridden neighborhoods...together we can all reclaim our neighborhoods for the law-abiding men, women and children of America.
>
> Attorney General William Barr, 1992.

Weed and Seed was introduced as a general *strategy*, rather than a specific policy with a clearly identifiable implementation plan. The goals were clear but the tactics were listed as a menu of suggestions from which local authorities would select those most appropriate to the target neighborhoods. The description of the policy in this chapter presents the original program goals as they were articulated in Weed and Seed's early days, i.e., 1991-1993. Documents that detail the Weed and Seed strategy have since been revisited and revised and as a result, the program goals have been altered, including more of an emphasis on direct community involvement and control. For the purposes of understanding the community response to Weed and Seed and its impact on the future of the program, however, it is necessary to establish an image of the program that was projected in 1992 when funding for the first 16 cities was first announced. Therefore, the following discussion brings together Justice Department documents from the early stages of the program and interview data to accurately reproduce the program's initial goals.

Weed and Seed Policy History

Weed and Seed[1] was developed by the Department of Justice in the early 1990s in order to "demonstrate an innovative, comprehensive and integrated multi-agency approach to law enforcement and community revitalization for controlling and preventing violent crime, drug abuse and gang activity in targeted high crime neighborhoods across the country."[2] The Justice Department referred to Weed and Seed as a strategy for tackling these problems through the coordination and concentration of resources in specific geographic regions to eradicate the cycle of crime and drugs, promote community involvement and private sector investment. Weed and Seed's primary focus was to coordinate various criminal justice agencies in order to 'weed' out violent criminals and then 'seed' the neighborhood with social and human services. Community policing was the bridge between the two-pronged approach as officers were to "obtain helpful information from area residents for weeding efforts while they aid residents in obtaining information about community revitalization."[3]

Operation Weed and Seed was introduced at the Attorney General's "Summit on Law Enforcement, Responses to Violent Crime: Public Safety in the Nineties" in March of 1991.[4] The program first took place in three demonstration sites in 1991: Kansas City, Omaha, and Trenton, New Jersey. These sites were chosen because of the presence of existing programs and relationships that coincided with the goals of Weed and Seed to coordinate federal, state and local efforts.[5]

President George Bush then proposed Weed and Seed as a national strategy for crime control in January of 1992. Along with a number of other anti-crime and drug control strategies unveiled in the early part of the year, Bush touted Weed and Seed as a combination of strong law enforcement and much-needed help for inner cities in the form of social services and community development. "Key to the seed concept will be jobs-generating initiatives such as enterprise zones, to give people who call these neighborhoods 'home' something to hope for" Bush noted in announcing the program.[6] In 1992, there were 18 Weed and Seed sites and by 1998, the Executive Office for Weed and Seed (EOWS) was funding 176 Weed and Seed sites around the country. In addition, over 80 cities have modeled programs after Weed and Seed. These sites do not receive Weed and Seed funds but are eligible to apply once they have obtained official recognition.

According to the Deputy Director of the Executive Office for Weed and Seed, during the 1980s the Justice Department had two main "camps" with regard to addressing street crime: the "law enforcement camp" that believed more police and federal activity could reduce crime, and the "root causes camp" that believed those approaches would not sufficiently address the crime problem without addressing broader social problems.[7] Weed and Seed was an attempt to bridge the gap between these two camps by trying to do both. As the discussion in the previous chapter suggests, however, the seeding component was unlikely to be embraced by policymakers because it focused on funding broad social and economic programs that lawmakers have difficulty defending in connection with crime control strategies. Thus, the focus of the policy was more on law enforcement than on underlying causes of crime.

At an oversight hearing before the Senate Judiciary Committee in 1992, Attorney General Barr noted that Weed and Seed is "designed to revitalize communities in the inner-city by targeting high-crime neighborhoods and housing developments with efforts to weed out violent offenders, drug traffickers, gang members and then to seed these high-crime areas with comprehensive social and economic revitalization programs."[8] Barr also noted that serious crime contributes to poverty by creating an atmosphere of fear, contributing to the decline of neighborhoods, deterring investment and making it difficult for many projects to reach their full potential.[9] The key goal of Weed and Seed was to "eliminate violent crime, drug trafficking, and drug-related crime from targeted high crime neighborhoods; provide a safe environment, free of crime, *for law-abiding citizens to live, work and raise families.*"[10] The rationale for this strategy was that these problems could not be addressed by a single agency but rather, require a comprehensive and coordinated approach involving Federal, State and local agencies.[11]

Weeding

The United States Attorney assumed primary responsibility for supervising the law enforcement component of Weed and Seed The U.S. Attorney for the region that is home to the grant recipient city organizes a Law Enforcement Task Force. The Task Force consisted of local representatives from each of the following agencies: the State Attorney General, State District Attorney, local Chief of Police, Sheriff, District Attorney Chief Probation Officer, Special Agent in Charge of the Drug Enforcement Administration, Federal Bureau of Investigation, Bureau of Alcohol, Tobacco and Firearms and the United States Marshal.[12]   The Justice Department's emphasis on law enforcement was rooted in the belief that narcotics traffickers and violent criminals are often returned to the neighborhoods where they were arrested to continue their illegal activity.[13]   Federal, state and local authorities were to coordinate efforts through the U.S. Attorney in the local setting. Offenders arrested in the target areas would be subject to "pretrial detention, speedy trials, and mandatory minimum sentences."[14] Thus, offenders could be immediately removed from the target area and serve the maximum sentences allowed by local, state and/or federal law. Law enforcement efforts focused on targeting, apprehending and incapacitating violent street criminals who terrorize neighborhoods and account for a disproportionate percentage of criminal activity.

Tactics are to include identification and security of trouble spots, saturation patrols (extended/extra police activity in particular areas) with an emphasis on field interrogations (stopping and questioning suspicious persons), buy-busts (undercover operations where police officers pose as drug buyers in order to arrest drug dealers), identification and apprehension of probation/parole violators and felony fugitives, and aggressive use of search/arrest warrants (Roehl 1996).

One example of a law enforcement strategy which Weed and Seed sites were encouraged to use is Operation Triggerlock, a Department of Justice Initiative that targets violent offenders for prosecution in Federal court if they used firearms while committing a crime. Rather than applying local or state laws that may not impose lengthy incarceration, arrests made in the Weed and Seed areas were intended to be prosecuted under this federal law. Weed and Seed sites were encouraged to use federal sentencing for all crimes that could be charged under federal law and to coordinate with other federal law enforcement agencies including, the Federal Bureau of Investigation, Immigration and Naturalization Service, U.S. Marshals Office, and Bureau of Alcohol, Tobacco and Firearms.

Seeding

The U.S. Attorney, while not directly responsible for implementation of seeding, was directed to serve as chair or co-chair of the Neighborhood Revitalization Coordinating Committee. Members of that committee were to include representatives from public and private agencies and organizations that are able to bring resources to the project, such as: the Mayor, local Directors of the Department of Social Services, Health and Human Services; Housing Authority; the Superintendent of Education; the local director of the United Way; directors of community-based organizations; the State Criminal Justice Administrator; and representatives from private foundations and business leaders.[15]

Prevention, intervention and treatment activities were promoted to maximize family services, organized recreation, job and life skills development, mentoring, service projects, educational programs and counseling, and support programs. Coordination between law enforcement, social services, the private sector and the community was intended to maximize stability and keep crime from entering the community. These efforts could include youth services, school programs, community and social programs, support groups designed to develop positive community attitudes toward combating narcotics use and trafficking.[16] Neighborhood restoration, which consists of renovating and refurbishing housing, commercial establishments and open areas, was intended to create a solid economic foundation for entrepreneurship and job creation.[17]

Tactics included enhancing home security, developing long-term efforts to renovate and maintain housing, low-cost physical improvements, and providing educational, economic, social and recreational opportunities. An important aspect of Weed and Seed was fighting the apathy, fear and hopelessness that pervade high-crime areas.

Community Policing and Community Involvement

Weed and Seed's original fundamental principles were coordination and partnerships between various public and private agencies/organizations, including community groups. These partnerships would aggressively attack crime in the area, provide concentrated service delivery of social services to residents and mobilize residents to be "active participants in service delivery."[18] Each site was required to develop its own approach to suit the needs of that particular area but these basic principles were to be essential to each program (Roehl 1996).

Weed and Seed sites were encouraged to *build upon* existing relationships with community members and to develop or expand community-policing strategies. Community policing was intended to serve as the bedrock principle that connects weeding and seeding. The presence of police who have on-going relationships with members of the community was to provide security and stability for the residents and information and assistance for the police. As part of the Weed and Seed strategy, community policing involves residents in crime prevention and creates partnerships that will help neighborhoods solve drug-related problems. Increasing community-policing in Weed and Seed target areas would promote police visibility, develop cooperative relationships between police officers and community residents and support activities that will suppress criminal activity.

Community involvement in the program was intended to "empower residents to assist in solving the crime problems in their neighborhood."[19] That involvement in the program, however, was not to begin until the target area had been identified because "inviting community involvement prior to site selection could create an environment that encourages a political rather than an analytical approach to selecting the target neighborhood."[20] Since the extent and nature of the crime problem is most important, federal, state and local law enforcement officials were strongly encouraged to be the key persons involved in site selection. When the planning of the local program actually begins, a Weed and Seed Implementation Manual suggests that managers of the program should attempt to "fully integrate the needs and views of the target community into the process."[21]

Residents were encouraged to take responsibility for their neighborhoods through activities such as neighborhood watches, marches, rallies and neighborhood graffitti clean-up efforts.[22] "Enhanced public safety and reduced fear in the community make it possible for human services and economic revitalization activities to be implemented successfully."[23] Community policing efforts focused on suppression and containment activity and provided a bridge to seeding efforts by helping residents develop solutions to violent and drug-related crime and fostering a sense of responsibility within the community, which could serve as a mobilizing force for change.

Community policing tactics included foot patrols, problem solving, victim referrals to support services, nuisance abatement and police mini-stations which are small offices in target neighborhoods where residents can come to speak with officers. "The objective is to raise the level of citizen and community involvement in crime prevention and intervention activities to solve drug-related problems in neighborhoods to enhance the level of community security."[24]

> Community policing will increase police visibility and develop cooperative relationships between police and citizenry in target areas. This strategy will support suppression activities and promote a "bridge" to prevention, intervention and treatment, as well as to neighborhood reclamation and revitalization. Officers on foot patrols and meeting with residents, citizen neighborhood watches, and community relations activities will increase positive interaction between police and neighborhood residents and help continue reductions in drug use, trafficking and related crime resulting from weeding efforts.[25]

According to the manual provided to participants in the Weed and Seed Applicant Training Workshop held in Washington, D.C. on February 11 and 12, 1992, implementation of Weed and Seed in individual sites should consist of six steps:

1) *Organization of the steering committees* for Law Enforcement and Neighborhood Revitalization: these committees should include key federal, state and local law enforcement officials and social service agents;

2) *Selection of a Target Neighborhood*: the neighborhood should have high levels of gang-related violence, homicides/aggravated assaults/rapes and other violence crime, drug arrests, high school dropout rates, unemployment, public assistance and residents on parole or probation;

3) *Neighborhood Needs Assessment*: Information from selection of the target neighborhood should be used to assess the problems and needs of the target area;

4) *Select Resources*: Identify existing and new resources that are necessary to meet objectives identified in step 3;

5) *Identify Implementation Activities*: Program activities and human services that will be implemented should be specified along with who is responsible for administering, what it will involve, where the activity will be conducted, when it will be done, how it will be implemented and how much it will cost;

6) *Develop an Implementation Schedule*: A time-task plan should be developed to set a schedule for completion of major activities.[26]

Each of these components involved decision-making by federal and local officials, including federal law enforcement and prosecutors, local police, city officials and social service agents; neighborhood residents were noticeably absent from the process.

Funding for Weed and Seed

Adequate funding for the program has been a struggle since the outset. Initially, the proposal was for a $500 million program, $30 million of which would be for law enforcement and the rest would be for other federal agencies, such as Housing and Urban Development, to focus on the seeding side of the program. However, the 102nd Congress did not pass the bill authorizing funding so the Justice Department was needed to shift money from a variety of internal sources, such as the Bureau of Justice Assistance and the Executive Office for U.S. Attorneys, in order to fund the original sites. The money available was a fraction of what the Justice Department had requested. Originally, the Office of Justice Programs, through the Bureau of Justice Assistance, funded the pilot programs and the 16 original sites in 1992. In 1994, the program was able to acquire some funding from the Edward Byrne Memorial Fund for State and Local Law Enforcement Assistance Program, which is part of the Anti-Drug Abuse Act of 1998 (PL 100-690, Title VI, Subtitle C). The Program provides funds "to assist states and units of local government in carrying out specific programs that offer a high probability of improving the functioning of the criminal justice system and to enhance drug control efforts at state and local levels." The Fund emphasizes nationwide and multi-jurisdictional projects and programs that address the drug problem and advance national drug control priorities. Thus, the following types of programs are encouraged: community-based programs; crime and violence prevention; violence reduction programs; alternative dispositional approaches; intergovernmental coordination initiatives.[27]

A 1992 letter from Deputy Assistant Attorney General S. Ricardo Narvaiz in the Office of Justice Programs to the U.S. Attorney for Western Washington, Mike McKay, indicates the restrictions on funding.[28] The first sites to be funded (after the pilot sites) received funding from two sources. First, the Executive Office for U.S. Attorneys (EOUSA) provided over $9 million that was restricted to the investigation and prosecution of violent crime and drug offenses. These funds, according to the letter, *may not be used to support seeding activities*. The second source of funding was the Office of Justice Programs, which contributed $2 million dollars to the first round of Weed and Seed grants. This funding would be available for "any of the 21 statutorily authorized purpose areas set forth in 42 U.S.C. 3751." Those 21 areas include: demand-reduction education programs in which law enforcement officers participate; multi-jurisdictional task force programs; community and neighborhood programs which assist citizens in preventing and controlling crime; improving the operational effectiveness of law enforcement through the use of crime analysis techniques, street sales enforcement, schoolyard violator programs and gang-related and low-income housing drug control programs; providing programs which identify and meet the treatment needs of adult and juvenile drug-dependent offenders; innovative programs which demonstrate new and different approaches to enforcement, prosecution and adjudication of drug offenses and other serious crimes; addressing problems of drug trafficking and the illegal manufacture of controlled substances in public housing; improving the criminal and juvenile justice system's response to domestic and family violence; providing alternatives to prevent detention, jail and prison for persons who post no danger to the community; programs of which the primary goal is to strengthen urban enforcement and prosecution efforts targeted at street drug sales.

While some of these activities are broad-based and could be used to justify a range of seeding activities, they are focused primarily on law enforcement (in a variety of forms) as the key component of crime prevention. The letter to US Attorney McKay indicated that the Office of Justice Programs funds "may not be used to support pure "seeding" activities, i.e., *those activities with no direct connection to law enforcement.*" Despite the fact that both original sources of funding severely restricted the seeding possibilities, Weed and Seed guidelines continued to indicate that sites should craft their programs so that they have a balance of weeding and seeding and proposals that do not include a substantial seeding component would be regarded less favorably than those with a balance of both areas.

In 1993, the Executive Office for Weed and Seed was established and provided with a budget to assist with funding that is less restricted. Beginning in 1994, the program began receiving money from the Asset Forfeiture Fund. This fund allows state and local law enforcement agencies to use money and resources acquired by federal law enforcement seizure of goods purchased through illegal drug trade money to be used for "payment of overtime salaries, travel, fuel, training, equipment, and other similar costs of State of local law enforcement officers that are incurred in a joining law enforcement operation with a Federal law enforcement agency participating in the Fund."[29]

Table 3.1 illustrates the amount of funding for Weed and Seed and the source of the funding. In addition to the limitations on funding use, the EOWS decided to fund more cities at a lower rate because of the increasing number of sites requesting funds. Funding has not increased dramatically from 1996 when 88 sites were funded to 1998, when a total of 176 sites were funded.

Table 3.1 Weed and Seed Funding Sources, 1991-1998

Year	Amount	Number of Sites	Average Amount Per Site	Source
1991	$508,000	3	$169,666	Bureau of Justice Statistics (BJA)
1992	$11,507,334	16	$719,208	EOUSA and BJA
1993	$13,542,821	19	$712,780	Weed & Seed Program Fund (WSPF)
1994	$31,528,938	36	$875,803	WSPF, Edward Byrne Memorial Fund (EBMF), Asset Forfeiture (AF)
1995	$32,456,000	36	$901,555	WSPF, EBMF, AF
1996	$37,500,000	88	$426,136	EBMF, AF
1997	$37,500,000	118	$317,796	EBMF, AF
1998	$42,500,000	176	$214,477	WSPF, Violent Crime Reduction Fund, AF

Source: Executive Office for Weed and Seed.

Racial Composition of Weed and Seed Sites

The racial and ethnic composition of the sites varied, though the 1996 evaluation of 19 sites found that on the whole, the sites tended to have a high concentration of minorities, specifically African-Americans and Hispanics (Roehl 1996). The evaluation notes that African-Americans or Hispanics constituted more than 50% of the population in eight out of the twelve sites in which data was available. The remaining four sites had primarily white, non-Hispanic populations.

These numbers, however, *understate* the extent to which Weed and Seed was first implemented in predominately black and Hispanic neighborhoods. Seattle, for example, is listed among the 'white, non-Hispanic' sites but the targeted area in Seattle, the Central District, is 47% black and 35% white as compared to the rest of the city which is 75% white and 10% black (Asian-Americans make up most of the difference). Thus, despite the fact that the evaluation categorizes the Seattle target area as predominantly white, within Seattle the area is widely regarded as a 'black neighborhood' and the controversy about Weed and Seed was a direct result of conflict between minorities in the area and the Seattle Police. The true number of Weed and Seed sites that have substantial minority populations is probably higher than 75%.[30] On the one hand, this is not surprising since Weed and Seed targeted high-crime urban areas, which tend to have high concentrations of racial minorities. On the other hand, these areas also have high concentrations of poverty, joblessness, poor schools and other problems that quite possibly contribute to crime. That Weed and Seed was so heavily weighted towards law enforcement is an important indication of the willingness of policymakers to consider more community-building approaches to crime prevention in minority neighborhoods.

Weed and Seed and Community Crime Prevention

The original program goals, implementation plan and evaluation data raise several important points for this research. First, both weeding and seeding are narrowly conceived, focusing primarily on the opportunity-reduction and order maintenance models of crime prevention. Weeding emphasizes law enforcement strategies that give police broad discretion to remove suspects from target areas and encourage residents to fortify their persons and property against possible criminal activity. In addition, weeding was emphasized more than seeding in the program goals, in the funding possibilities and in initial implementation. As its name suggests, weeding activities also had a decidedly harsh ring to them: the program emphasizes arrest statistics and incapacitation efforts and promised big penalties for violent offenders by encouraging their prosecution in federal court which would be likely to carry stiffer penalties than those at the local level. The community-policing element emphasized encouraging community residents to provide police with information and to make their homes and persons less susceptible to crime. Key elements of Weed and Seed fall primarily into opportunity-reduction and order maintenance models.

While seeding activities were potentially broad-based, the direction of encouragement was in prevention and intervention for drug use and community beautification. Few economic development activities, employment programs, educational or health care strategies were discussed. Table 3.2 places the main components of Weed and Seed into the opportunity-reduction and order maintenance models outlined in Chapter two.

Table 3.2   Weed and Seed and Models of Community Crime Prevention

	Weeding	Seeding	Community Policing
Opportunity Reduction	Promote home safety, burglary prevention, better lighting, alarm systems.	Beautify area to make it less attractive to criminals.	Harden community as a whole to criminal activity.
Order-Maintenance	Remove offenders and suspects from area.	Restore order and stability to neighborhoods through more and better policing.	Build community trust in police; build informant relationship.

This table shows the main focus of each aspect of the Weed and Seed strategy and how each fits primarily with the opportunity-reduction and order maintenance models of crime prevention. Further, while economic development was encouraged, nothing in the program's original guidelines provided for how that would happen, other than making the target area more "attractive" to businesses.

As such, the weeding component of Weed and Seed was politically attractive to law makers because it promised tough law enforcement and big penalties for the worst offenders. Rather than focusing on broad social programs which are politically unpopular because of their cost and perceived inefficacy, Weed and Seed proposes a community-oriented approach to crime control which is aimed at increasing police visibility and community acceptance of police presence, while at the same time promoting responsibility on the part of neighborhood residents and other public agencies for maintaining order.

Second, community involvement was narrowly conceived, confined mostly to affirming police activity and assisting in identifying problem areas and people. While the implementation manual does suggest that the Steering Committee ought to consult community residents for input during the design stage, there is little indication of how that might be done or what kind of control community members might have over program planning. Furthermore, the implementation manual notes that citizens should not be involved in the site selection because they would inject a "political" element while law enforcement officials would simply look at the objective crime data and make determinations based on that information. As the Seattle experience will indicate, however, there is no reason to believe that law enforcement officials are any less subject to "political" influences than community members and leaving community members out of this part of the process assumes that the program will be well-received in any area. As a result, community participation is largely confined to serving as informants for the police and a community policing devolves to merely getting residents to better use the police as a resource and vice versa. As the Deputy Director of Weed and Seed noted, with community policing "you get better law enforcement because you have better information."[31]

In addition, while the Justice Department suggests that communities with existing community policing programs and/or strong community organizations will fare best with the Weed and Seed strategy, the implementation manual does not require those programs or organizations nor is there any recognition that communities most devastated by crime (which Weed and Seed originally targeted) may be the communities with the fewest resources to work with police. The program was originally designed to address violent gang and drug activity in some of the most blighted areas in the country through coordinated efforts, including the community, but communities that have few organizations, few leaders and few resources are not likely to be vocal participants in a partnership. Thus, Weed and Seed community involvement seems almost inevitably confined to basic communication and information-sharing.

Third, the funding situation has dictated much of the program's design. Originally, Congress funded only the $30 million law enforcement piece so the seeding funding was confined to very narrow crime prevention activities that could be justified in law enforcement terms. By 1994, funding from the Byrne Memorial fund provided somewhat more discretion because it specifically calls for community participation and prevention activities but this funding is still largely restricted to law enforcement-related activities. Early on, funding from the Executive Office for Attorneys and later Asset Forfeiture funding also severely limited the program's possibilities. As the next chapter indicates, Seattle needed to convince the Justice Department that some of their programs were in fact crime prevention programs. Indeed, the Deputy Mayor in Seattle stated that this was a major "sticking point" between the Justice Department and sites like Seattle that raised questions about the "further edge of seed programs."[32] There was some resistance among Justice Department officials to the idea that economic development could fit with law enforcement conceptions of seeding. This goes to the heart of differences between local community conceptions of crime and its causes and the national rhetoric on crime that is much more geared towards law enforcement. To some degree, then, local communities were on the receiving end of the national politics of law and order that confine public debate and policymaking about the crime problem and its solutions to narrow, individualistic terms that preclude broad structural efforts to revitalize urban communities.

Another point with respect to funding that will become important for Seattle's second target area is that funding per site had been reduced by 75% since the program began. Between 1995 and 1996, the number of sites funded jumped from 36 to 88 and then to 118 and 176 in subsequent years (see Table 3.1). Officials in the Executive Office for Weed and Seed wanted to encourage sites that were trying to implement a Weed and Seed strategy; however, funds were not sufficient to continue current sites at the existing level *and* increase the number of sites funded overall.[33] As a result, the EOWS reduced funding to each site, lowering it from $1,000,000 to $250,000, recognizing that the funding would not permit major changes but were hopeful that it could be used as leverage to bring people together, such as community groups, law enforcement and social service agents, who might not otherwise coordinate with one another.

Fourth, Weed and Seed does not contain provisions for dealing with the 'weeded' populations to avoid their return to criminality. Recall from chapter two that blacks are more likely than whites to want felony sentencing to include training, education and rehabilitation. During an oversight hearing before the Senate Judiciary Committee, this fact prompted Senator DeConcini to ask:

> Since most individuals released from jail return to their old communities, are there provisions in the Weed and Seed program to habilitate the 'weeds' while they are in prison? Don't you really need a 'weed, seed and mulch' program to make sure we don't create another revolving door of 'weeds' arrested, rearrested and rearrested again?[34]

Attorney General Barr responded that while the key to closing the revolving door was a high degree of coordination between federal, state and local officials, the social, educational and economic programs are also necessary to address this issue. And yet, the language about community development is aimed at creating communities in which criminals are deterred from committing crime not because they have been 'rehabilitated' or have alternative choices, but because the community is no longer a 'safe' place in which to commit crime. Thus, the displacement problem arises. The displacement of criminal activity becomes problematic only when other communities notice an increase in criminal activity and demand a response. Indeed, this has been the case in a number of sites where residents have expressed concern that Weed and Seed simply "relocates crime" rather than alters any criminal behavior.[35] As the next chapter indicates, such a problem is the very reason that the Planning Committee for the Weed and Seed site in Southeast Seattle citing for wanting to bring Weed and Seed to that area. This is further evidence of the emphasis on reducing the opportunity for criminals to commit crime in targeted areas, rather than inducing them not to commit crimes at all (in any area).

Fifth, race is an important component of the strategy as most of the Weed and Seed areas have sizeable minority populations. As mentioned in the previous chapter, this seems appropriate given that Weed and Seed was intended to address problems of violent crime, gangs and drug activity – problems that are more commonly associated with minority or mixed race neighborhoods in urban areas than homogeneous white ones. On the other hand, to the extent that the program goals originally emphasized law enforcement and crime suppression/containment, it is interesting and somewhat surprising that the Justice Department did not better anticipate the concerns those communities might have with respect to a heavy emphasis on law enforcement.

Finally, Weed and Seed justifies development of the inner-city solely in crime control terms. Seeding is primarily aimed at revitalizing the neighborhood so that criminals who have been 'weeded' will not return and/or providing residents of the target area with treatment and intervention so that they will avoid criminal activity. While this approach has residues of a 'root causes' strategy for addressing crime, the real thrust of Weed and Seed resonates more with the governing through crime control strategy. It projects an image of a strong state empowering police and federal law enforcement agencies, providing long and harsh punishments for offenders, and injecting police into a wide array of inner-city programs in an effort to identify and 'weed out' criminality. Furthermore, it justifies expenditures for inner-city development strictly and narrowly in crime prevention terms. The goal of Weed and Seed is not broad revitalization of the inner-cities, of which crime control and prevention is one component. The goal is crime reduction, with drug treatment, education and development as means to that end. Finally, while Weed and Seed contains provisions requiring the involvement of a vast array of law enforcement and detailing specific policing strategies, it merely suggests that economic development be a component of the program and weakly indicates that local businesses should take part in revitalizing the neighborhood.

Cross-site summary

In 1998, 176 cities in the U.S. were operating a Weed and Seed strategy. This included a heavy concentration of law enforcement, a wide array of possible social service activities and some form of community policing (Roehl 1996). A process evaluation that examined 19 official sites through the end of 1993 indicated that early Weed and Seed strategies closely followed the Justice Department model, emphasizing aggressive law enforcement activities involving arrests and police visibility/presence. Table 3.3 indicates the most common weeding activities.

Table 3.3   Reported Weeding Activities

Type of activity (in order of reported use)	No. of times ranked in top five (n=18)
1. Identification of "trouble spots"	7
2. High visibility/saturation patrols	12
3. Search/arrest warrants	11
4. Controlled buys by informants	10
5. Apprehension of felon fugitives	4
6. Buy/bust operations	13

Source: "National Process Evaluation of Weed and Seed." Department of Justice, Office of Justice Programs, National Institute of Justice Research in Brief. October 1996.

The most common weeding strategies through this period were: high visibility/saturation patrols, search/arrest warrants, controlled buys by informants and buy/bust operations (Roehl 1996, 5). Interestingly, while the program originally emphasized the reduction of violent crime, of the 32,459 cases brought before state courts during the evaluation period, only 9% of them involved violent crime charges. Table 3.4 shows the breakdown of prosecution charges for cases during the evaluation period.

Table 3.4   Crimes Charged Under Weeding Activities

Type of Crime	State (32,459)	Federal (3,064)
Violent Crime	9%	0%
Felony Drug	33%	1%
Possession of Drugs	19%	16%
Firearms	6%	4%
Continuing Criminal Enterprise/RICO	0%	38%
Other	33%	41%

Source: "National Process Evaluation of Weed and Seed." Department of Justice, Office of Justice Programs, National Institute of Justice Research in Brief. October 1996.

Seeding activities focused on prevention strategies for children and intervention for teens and adults.

Table 3.5   Most and Least Common Seeding Activities

Seeding Activities	Number of sites (n=19)
Prevention/education	19
Safe Havens	19
Boys and Girls Clubs	16
Cultural/entertainment activities	16
Community clean-ups	16
Self-employment programs	5
Rehabilitation of seized property	5
Farmers' Markets	4
TASC (Treatment Alternatives to Street Crime)	4
Scouting programs	4

Source: "National Process Evaluation of Weed and Seed." Department of Justice, Office of Justice Programs, National Institute of Justice Research in Brief. October 1996.

The most common seeding activities involved drug prevention and education projects, multi-service adult and youth programs such as Urban Leagues, Boys and Girls Clubs and Safe Havens, and community beautification and cultural activities (Roehl 1996, 5). Least common seeding strategies included self-employment programs and housing rehabilitation.

All of the sites conducted some form of community policing, though activities varied greatly. Some sites had community police officers focus exclusively on non-enforcement activities such as community contact, problem-solving and youth projects while others had them continue with regular enforcement functions but also develop community contacts (Roehl 1996). Community policing, broadly defined, is a key component of Weed and Seed but each site interpreted the meaning and mission of community policing in substantially different ways.

Reactions to Weed and Seed

When the Justice Department announced the first round of grants for Weed and Seed, it quickly became apparent that it had underestimated the concerns of urban minorities about implementing a tough law enforcement policy in their communities. Even with its seeding component, some community leaders immediately saw the program as a threat to young, black males and poor immigrants.

There were two main concerns expressed by people in these sites. First, there was some apprehension about the weeding program because of the perception that it would mean arresting people based on racial profiles. In Chelsea, Massachusetts, for example, Hispanic activists withheld support for the program because of the proposed involvement of the Immigration and Naturalization Service (INS).[36] Activists were concerned that the INS would conduct street sweeps that would gather up undocumented residents who were not involved in crimes and would further undermine existing trust between law enforcement and Hispanics. Similarly, in Los Angeles, the city succeeded in changing the name of the program because of fears that 'weeding' meant that too many young minorities would be swept up in law enforcement efforts.[37] And in Seattle, which is explored in detail in subsequent chapters, numerous community organizations mobilized to oppose the program arguing that it would allow federal law enforcement agencies to conduct street sweeps of young, black males who happened to live in the target area. Clearly law enforcement tactics were a serious concern.

Second, residents in other sites expressed concern that the program would focus too heavily on weeding and that the program would not address the needs of the community.[38] Most of these concerns had to do with a belief that the areas would never see the 'seeding' portion of the program and that this element was simply a way to make the 'weeding' portion more palatable to residents of the target areas. Indeed, in some of these areas, seeding never did materialize to the extent that city officials claimed it would and even community activists who supported weeding efforts expressed disappointment about the lack of funds for social and economic infrastructure.[39] Others also expressed reservations about 'seeding' activities in general, citing concerns that the programs would subject youth in target areas to greater intervention than similar youth in other parts of the city.

The response of the Urban Strategies Group in Los Angeles illustrates the specific objections expressed in more subdued form in other cities which originally applied for Weed and Seed funds. The Urban Strategies Group "is a multiracial anticorporate 'think-tank/act-tank' committed to building democratic internationalist social movements. The Strategy Center's work encompasses all aspects of urban life: it emphasizes rebuilding the labor movement, fighting for environmental justice, truly mass transit, and immigrant rights, as well as actively opposing the growing criminalization, racialization, and feminization of poverty."[40] The Group called for the rejection of the Weed and Seed program in its entirety, arguing that Weed and Seed would subvert what the Group called legitimate community concerns and needs by shifting the focus of attention away from social and economic problems in urban minority areas to simplistic law enforcement responses.

> Its primary approach is not to *solve* complex urban problems of racism and poverty, but rather, to *suppress* the symptoms of urban neglect - drugs, crime and violence - and in doing so, suppress the youth of the inner city. By "linking" funding for social programs with funding for police repression, it offers what amounts to community blackmail.[41]

The Urban Strategies Group argued that the money would go almost entirely for law-enforcement programs and, worse, that the program would create a two-tiered justice system which applied harsher federal penalties to crimes committed by blacks in the inner-city than to those whites who commit the same types of crimes in other areas. A similar concern was expressed in Seattle as a potential violation of the civil rights of minorities. The Strategies Group argued that what was really needed was social service assistance for health, education, etc., that was not tied to law enforcement. This was seen as a kind of fiscal blackmail that required community groups to support law enforcement efforts in exchange for funding for social and economic development.

In addition to the issues raised within the communities themselves, a black congressional representative, Charles Rangel of New York, also expressed concern about the emphasis of the program. Like his counterparts in urban settings, Rangel wanted the program to focus on seeding and worried about young blacks unnecessarily getting caught up in the criminal justice system. At a Congressional Hearing about Weed and Seed, Rep. Rangel noted that having the Justice Department as the central figure in the program is a concern to those interested in addressing the problem of the inner-cities:

I do not see Weed and Seed being a response to urban problems. I see it being a factor, *one* of the programs that can be put together to try to address the inequalities of the past, and that is why I wish this was coming from the Secretary of Education, the Secretary of Labor, the Secretary of Health and Human Services, Mr. Martinez or whomever, but I do not see or hear from them, and that is why you [Attorney General William Barr] are getting more than your share of the compliments in terms of addressing the problem.[42]

As demonstrated earlier, the Justice Department guidelines for Weed and Seed, with the emphasis on containment, apprehension and incapacitation of offenders, did not inspire confidence in the ability of law enforcement agents to respond to the concerns of urban minority communities about fear of harassment and profiling. Further, the assumption that community members would simply serve as the functional equivalent of informants and as 'partners' in conventional police activities, illustrates the disjuncture between crime prevention models in the Justice Department as compared to those at the community level. Nor was there any indication that seeding would be responsive to the community's ideas about what was necessary for revitalization and development; rather, it seemed to consist of preconceived ideas imposed onto communities without their input. Indeed, several programs, such as those in Las Vegas and Pittsburgh, experienced community opposition as a result of the program's emphasis on law enforcement and little, if any, attention to community development initiatives.[43]

The issues raised in these controversies around the country point to concerns that Weed and Seed would amount to little more than opportunity-reduction and order-maintenance. While this brief treatment of the controversies does not explicitly illuminate the community-centered model, the concerns expressed by community leaders in Weed and Seed target areas parallel the missing components of opportunity-reduction and order-maintenance, which are actualized in the community-centered model. The following chapters explicate this model further, drawing attention to Weed and Seed's absence of broad economic and community development programs and the centrality of law enforcement.

Notes

[1]   Weed and Seed is funded and administered by the Executive Office for Weed and Seed, which is overseen by the Executive Office of U.S. Attorneys and the

Bureau of Justice Assistance (BJA). The Executive Office for Weed and Seed focuses on "overall program policy, development and budgeting as well as enhanced law enforcement and prosecution coordination among federal, state and local agencies." The BJA monitors the discretionary grants that are provided to Weed and Seed sites through intensive, on-site monitoring (Executive Office for Weed and Seed, "Operation Weed and Seed Annual Report for 1994").

2 National Evaluation of Weed and Seed - Interim Status Report, 1993. Operation Weed and Seed arose out of several programs which were operating in Philadelphia in the 1980s and 90s: the Violent Traffickers Project (VTP), a joint Federal-State multi-agency task force developed in 1988 as part of the President's Organized Crime Drug Enforcement Task Force Project; the Federal Alternatives to State Trials (FAST) program, a collaboration between the Philadelphia District Attorney's Office and the Office of the U.S. Attorney for the Eastern District of Pennsylvania; a joint effort by residents of the Mantua neighborhood in Philadelphia and a Federal, State and local government project called Operation PEARL (Prevention, Education, Action, Rehabilitation and Law Enforcement) for which BJA provided a planning grant (DOJ, Operation Weed and Seed: FY 1993 Program Description) and the anti-drug effort by government agencies and citizens in the Spring Garden neighborhood (National Evaluation of Operation Weed and Seed Interim Status Report Nov. 1993).

3 Weed and Seed Training and Technical Assistance, "Strategy," March 16, 1998 http://usdoj.weedseed.org.

4 Weed and Seed Applicant Workshop manual, Office of Justice Programs, U.S. Department of Justice, February 11-12, 1992.

5 U.S. Congress. House of Representatives. Select Committee on Narcotics Abuse and Control. May 20, 1992. 102nd Congress, p. 12.

6 "Bush offers plan to save inner cities from crime" *Atlanta Journal and Constitution.* January 28, 1992. A6.

7 Interview 15: September 9, 1998.

8 U.S. Congress. Senate. Committee on the Judiciary. June 30, 1992. Oversight of the Department of Justice. 102nd Congress.

9 U.S. Congress. House of Representatives. Select Committee on Narcotics Abuse and Control. May 20, 1992. 102nd Congress.

10 Weed and Seed Implementation Manual: Draft #6. August 14, 1998. Section I, page 5, emphasis added.

11 Weed and Seed Applicant Workshop, Office of Justice Programs, Department of Justice, February 11-12, 1998, p. 2.

12 Id., p. 3-4.

13 Department of Justice, Operation "Weed and Seed, Reclaiming America's Neighborhoods." Executive Summary.

14 Weed and Seed Training and Technical Assistance, "Strategy," http://usdoj.weedseed.org. March 16, 1998.

15 Weed and Seed Applicant Workshop, Office of Justice Programs, Department of Justice, February 11-12, 1998., p. 5.

16 National Institute of Justice, Office of Justice Programs. "Research in Brief: National Process Evaluation of Operation Weed and Seed." October 1996.

17 Weed and Seed Training and Technical Assistance, "Elements," http://usdoj.weedseed.org. March 16, 1998.

18 Weed and Seed Training and Technical Assistance, "Goals and Objectives," http://usdoj.weedseed.org. March 16, 1998 (italics added).

70   *The Politics of Community Crime Prevention*

19   Weed and Seed Applicant Workshop, Office of Justice Programs, Department of
      Justice, February 11-12, 1998.
20   Weed and Seed Implementation Manual: Draft #6, August 14, 1992. Department
      of Justice, Office of Justice Programs, Section 2, Page 1.
21   Id., Section 4, Page 1.
22   Weed and Seed Training and Technical Assistance, "Strategy,"
      http://usdoj.weedseed.org. March 16, 1998.
23   Weed and Seed Implementation Manual: Draft #6, August 14, 1992. Department
      of Justice, Office of Justice Programs.
24   Weed and Seed Training and Technical Assistance, "Elements,"
      http://usdoj.weedseed.org. March 16, 1998 (italics added).
25   Weed and Seed Implementation Manual: Draft #6, August 14, 1992. Department
      of Justice, Office of Justice Programs.
26   Weed and Seed Applicant Workshop, Office of Justice Programs, Department of
      Weed and Seed, February 11, 12, 1998, pp. 6-9.
27   Bureau of Justice Assistance Fact Sheet – Edward Byrne Memorial State and
      Local Law Enforcement Assistance. FY 1995.
28   Letter from the Office of Justice Programs to U.S. Attorney for Western
      Washington, Mike McKay, dated February 5, 1992 and included in the Applicant
      Workshop materials.
29   "Use of assets forfeiture funds for state and local law enforcement expenses,"
      Justice Management Division, Department of Justice. December 9, 1994.
30   I was able to gather racial/ethnic composition data on 31 cities that are either
      receiving or trying to receive Weed and Seed funding. Of 31 target areas, 30 had
      Black and Hispanic populations of 45% or more and 19 exceeded 70%.
31   Interview 15: September 9, 1998.
32   Interview 23: March 29, 1999.
33   Interview 15: September 9, 1998.
34   U.S. Congress. Senate. Committee on Appropriations. June 30, 1992. 101st
      Congress, emphasis added.
35   Orange County Register, December 14, 1992. A1; Southeast Citizen Advisory
      Committee Meeting, February 19, 1998.
36   "Chelsea eyes aid for crime fight." *Boston Globe*, April 3, 1992.
37   "U.S. assents to name change for Weed and Seed program." *Los Angeles Times*,
      November 21, 1992.
38   "City gets grant to overhaul bad areas." *San Diego Union-Tribune*, April 7, 1992;
      "Bush in Pa. hears plea for social programs." *Boston Globe*, May 16, 1992;
      "Some fear Weed and Seed is just a temporary solution." *Orange County
      Register*, December 14, 1992.
39   "Santa Ana: anti-gang efforts criticized." *Los Angeles Times*, December 11,
      1992.
40   "A Call to Reject the Federal Weed and Seed Program in Los Angeles" Urban
      Strategies Group, The Labor/Community Strategy Center, p. 2.
41   Id.
42   U.S. House of Representatives. Select Committee on Narcotics Abuse and
      Control. Hearing on Department of Justice and The Drug War, Weed and Seed.
      May 20, 1992. p. 29.
43   National Institute of Justice, Office of Justice Programs. National Evaluation of
      Weed and Seed: Cross-site analysis. July 1999.

4 Weed and Seed in Practice in the Central District

> [The mobilization against Weed and Seed] wasn't like any kind of organizing I'd ever seen in my life. It was so easy! We got a copy of the grant proposal and started passing it around. It multiplied like rabbits...when we found out that the city was going ask the NAACP to sign [a memorandum of understanding], we found out about it and 50 people showed up. The NAACP refused to sign it.
>
> Sarena Johnson, Coalition to Oppose Weed and Seed.

Seattle has a long history of citizen pressure on local government to be attentive to the needs of local residents. The original Weed and Seed target area, the Central District (CD), has a particularly rich history of community organizing. Weed and Seed emerged after decades of community organization pressure on city government to address problems of economic development, housing, crime and police brutality. The ensuing story of citizen mobilization against Weed and Seed is best understood in the context of Seattle's rich history of citizen initiative. Thus, the following section provides some background on community initiatives and organizations in Seattle. Particular emphasis is on the CD in order to better understand the context in which Weed and Seed emerged and the range of concerns about community development that have been on the agenda of Central District organizations for some time.

Citizen Initiative in Seattle Politics: A Growing Contribution

In 1965, Edward Banfield noted that in Seattle, "the officials watch from the sidelines while citizens groups struggle to get more money for public services." This "do-it-by-citizen-committee" style, Banfield argued, was partly the result of the city's charter which distributed authority widely, thus making it difficult for any individual or group to take charge (Banfield 1965, 145). Changes in the city charter and the economic and demographic composition of the region over the past 30 years have produced an even greater role for citizens in controlling how local politics operate.

71

While Seattle politics was once controlled largely by the area's main downtown business interests and a weak, usually Republican mayor, in the past 25 years the city council and mayor have consolidated power and become more responsive to a wider range of citizens. When Banfield wrote that Seattle politics is dominated by "do-it-by-citizen-committee," he and others observed that citizen initiative came primarily from the business community (Banfield 1965; see also Gordon, et. al. 1991). In the late 1960s, however, citizens began pushing for a stronger mayor and city council and by the 1970s, a growth of interest in neighborhood issues helped shift the focus from business development concerns to equity and justice issues. "Minority and women activists became especially important. [There was a] Steadfast focus on the degree to which economic growth is or is not compatible with quality of life and environment" (Gordon, et. al. 1991, 224). The nine-member city council has become so powerful that the city's system of government is sometimes called "the 10-mayor system" (Gordon, et. al. 1991, 227). Further developments helped solidify Seattle's transition from a business-dominated local political climate to a progressive, citizen-focused one.

[The election of Mayor Charles Royer in 1978] seemed to personify the completion of the transition from the Big Ten dominance of city politics to the young, progressive, strong-mayor, strong-council form that has dominated Seattle politics ever since...Royer garnered national attention when he advocated national urban causes as president of the National League of Cities when it was struggling with Reagan's budget cuts and devolution of many federal programs to the states (Gordon et. al. 1991, 229-230).

Since then, a variety of citizen initiatives have focused on quality of life issues, including a 1% levy on all construction costs for city arts projects; a campaign to save the Pike Place Market which was threatened by developers interested in waterfront property; the creation of one of the country's first department of human resources and the enactment of a water-quality act that became a national model (M. Gordon et. al. 1991, 228). Seattle has become distinguished by its strong role for citizens in local political struggles and maintenance of this role over time (A. Gordon, et. al., 1998). The question that goes unanswered by much of this literature on citizen initiative, however, is whether minorities share in the privileges of city governance as much as whites. Seattle's population has changed over the past 35 years from 8.4% minority to 25% minority, with an unusually eclectic mixture of Blacks (10.1%), Asian/Pacific Islanders (11.8%), and Native Americans (1.4%) (Gordon 1998, 197). Research on Seattle politics, which emphasizes citizen participation, tends to gloss over some of the difficulties that minority groups, particularly those representing lower-income populations, may have had in successfully lobbying local officials on particular issues.

There is some indication that Mayor Norm Rice's tenure (1989-1997) helped create an atmosphere in which minority citizens' groups were given a voice in city government, and that the Rice regime made an effort to raise the economic status of the city's poorer black residents (Vega 1997; see also Gordon, et. al. 1998). Nonetheless, blacks in Seattle remain far worse off economically as a group than whites. In 1990, 22.1% of black families lived in poverty compared with only 3.5% of whites (Vega 1997). In addition, on-going concerns about police-community relations among black residents also indicates that the local political regimes have influenced those relations more positively with middle-class blacks than those in the lower socioeconomic strata where tensions remain high (see Vega 1997, 359-363; Lyons 1999). According to David Vega, the progressive regimes in Seattle did not shy away from helping poor blacks but their efforts do not appear to have been very fruitful (Vega 1997, 382-383).

Citizen initiative has clearly played a significant role in Seattle politics; however, while there is room for influence by actors from a wide socioeconomic spectrum, advocates for lower income minorities have not been particularly successful in influencing policy. Seattle's Weed and Seed story is an excellent opportunity for understanding the extent to which opposing community perspectives about policing, crime prevention and community development are incorporated into the actions of those traditionally responsible for crime prevention on the local level, including police administrators, city officials, social service agencies and businesses.

Community Councils in the Central Area

The Central Area provides a particularly rich illustration of the active history of citizen initiatives in Seattle, with some of the local community councils dating back to the 1940s. The Jackson Street Community Council, for example, was a coalition of Japanese Americans and African-Americans who organized in the late 1940s to support projects in the area such as a well-baby clinic and physical improvements, including street mending, traffic lights and a bulkhead to prevent mudslides (Taylor 1994, 174).[1]   The Council was, by some accounts, a   model of interethnic cooperation, with officers rotating between Japanese, Filipino, Chinese and African-American members.

In 1967, the Central Area Community Council, which had been formed by a group of black residents, merged with the Jackson Street Community Council to create the Central Seattle Community Council. The CSCC quickly developed into an umbrella organization that served as an advocate for community members becoming involved in local politics. The organization focused on issues such as decentralization of the city's police force, unemployment, police-community relations, education, community organization, and consumer protection. A sign inside the CSCC office read, "Power to the people and to the community," reflecting support for the black power movement and for community solidarity.[2]

The CSCC turned to community residents to involve them in politics, decision-making and civic identity activities that it believed would strengthen ties among residents. "The function of a community council is to provide a web through which individual citizens may influence actions on the most important level of a democratic government: the community."[3] The CSCC emphasized *community control* over decision-making that related to the Central Area. The CSCC and other community groups in the area also identified themselves as distinct from organizations that were formed with the assistance or support of local government, such as crime prevention councils and the Human Rights Commission. These organizations were 'bred in downtown' and did not necessarily adequately or accurately represent views in the community.[4]

The CSCC stayed on top of activities in the area and alerted community residents and city government to issues the council thought were important enough for community input. For example, an Urban Renewal Project in the Yesler-Atlantic area was planned in the 1970s without much community consultation. The CSCC expressed concern that residents were not provided with an opportunity to dispute the plans or advocate for an alternative renewal plan.   The CSCC was particularly concerned that the existing plan was "chaotic and hazardous" and would further undermine the area's stability.[5]   As other community councils formed around issues of housing and economic development, such as Yesler Terrace and Mann-Minor (which dissolved in 1974), the CSCC saw an opportunity to show residents of the Central Area "that they could have power and influence if they were organized and unified" (Gossett 1977).

The Central Area community councils emphasized housing concerns, education and economic development broadly. A 1977 survey of community households indicated that employment was by far the biggest concern of residents, with housing issues second and crime concerns third (Gossett 1977, 14).[6] These concerns seem to have been reflected in activities initiated by the community councils.

In 1975, the CSCC produced a scathing critique of banks in the area, accusing them of redlining the Central District, causing economic stagnation and making it difficult for residents to own homes. The report stated that "no conventional or FHA loans were granted in the last five years [1970-1975] in large parts of the Central Area by nearly all banks except to speculators or investors." Furthermore, it accused local banks of taking the residents' money and investing it outside the area:

> While Central Area branch banks loan out as little as 19 cents for every dollar they collect in deposits from the area, suburban branch banks invest up to $2.40 in loans for every savings dollar that originates in those communities.[7]

In the 1980s, some of the community councils became particularly energized around drug and gang issues, particularly the crack cocaine problems that rocked the city in the mid-1980s. A new community group, the Central Neighborhood Association, was formed just to combat drug-related problems in the area. Other community councils, such as Squire Park and Yesler Terrace, organized with the Central Neighborhood Association to combat drugs and to lobby the city for attention. Their frustrations emphasized the inattentiveness of the SPD to problems in the area.

Regarding the problem of drug dealing in the Central Area, a Squire Park Community Council member told the police: "You [the SPD] have known it's been there for a long time but you didn't come until people started rattling your cage."[8] In 1986, the Council organized a community meeting at a local cultural arts center to discuss drug and related problems in the area. Over 60 residents attended, including a representative from the Coalition for the Education of Black Children who later became an active opponent of the city's Drug Traffic Loitering Ordinance which was designed to give police more discretion in arresting drug dealers in the area. In this instance, he, like many others at the meeting, expressed anger and frustration at the police for not doing more to curb crime in the area.[9] A counselor at the Central Area Motivation

Program, a neighborhood resource center that began operating in the early 1960s, also noted police inattention to the problems. "The police have the attitude that 'since you live there, [drug dealing] is something you have to accept.' They seem to have decided that that's just where it's going to be."[10]

The Yesler Terrace Community Council, which represents residents of a federally-subsided low-income housing project, set up regular card games between 10:00 PM and 1:00 am to watch activities in their housing complex, write down license plate numbers and be prepared to call the police if trouble started.[11]   The Garfield Community Council, which formed in 1989 to "work on neighborhood beautification and instill community pride in children and people who work and live" in the Central Area, also joined the anti-drug campaign in the Central Area.[12]   Between 1986 and 1990, Spruce Park, Garfield and Yesler Terrace Community Councils along with the Central Neighborhood Association regularly garnered the attention of the local media in their efforts to combat drug and crime problems in the Central District.

In addition to the organizing around the increasing drug activity in their neighborhoods, however, these community councils also advocated for better development and planning and their attention to crime was not solely focused on increased police presence. In 1991, the president of the Squire Park Community Council complained that many of the people buying drugs in the Central District were suburbanites and that they ought to be targeted, arrested and their names published in local newspapers.[13] While on the surface it may appear that the calls for help were exclusively calls for a greater police presence, in fact, they were permeated by concerns with activities for youth, economic development of the area and fear that the area was regarded as a dangerous place to live and work. The underlying theme of the concerns about crime were that the city had long neglected the area, regularly made decisions about its future without consulting residents, and not provided sufficient incentive for economic development in the area.

Even during the 1980s the community councils were focused on a variety of concerns. The Squire Park, Judkins Rejected[14], and Garfield Community Councils joined with others to lobby the city so that the city's plans for a park in the area would change from a 'passive park,' which residents feared would end up as wasted space, to an 'active park,' which would include a much needed ballpark for the area. By the early 1990s, many of the councils were advocating for support for local businesses and broad economic development.   Some of this advocacy centered on complaints that the area had long been redlined by local banks, making it nearly impossible to sustain businesses in the area.[15] Coupled with this, however, were fears that businesses would begin to come into the area because whites were increasingly settling there and that this would result in long time black residents and low-income people being pushed out.[16]

More recent studies of community activity in the Central Area indicate that the community councils continue to be influential in the area and to represent a wide range of residents. A 1992 plan for the Central Area, which came out of the University of Washington's Urban Design/Economic Development Studio, suggested that the community councils in the Central Area enjoy influence and reflect the diversity of the area. This study also illustrates the shifting concerns in the 1980's towards increasing crime and drug problems:

> Yesler Terrace Community Council was ...[the] most influential Council in the Central District. Miller Park and Garfield Community Councils, formed [more recently], are developing reputations of similar stature. Their issues of concern generally fall into the categories of: crime, drug activity, and land-use. In addition, their sphere of influence is also much greater than the many other community councils in the District whose boundaries usually encompass a four to five block radius. Yesler, Miller and Garfield have the advantage of working through their respective community center, a factor that has contributed to their established role and respect by city officials. At present, the Garfield Community Council is most active, having recently initiated a weekly neighborhood picketing program to combat evening crime and drug-related activity in the Garfield area (Master Plan for the Central Area 1992, 11).

Crime Prevention Councils and Police-Community Relations

The history of crime prevention councils also provides insight into community concerns, particularly the differences between blacks and whites. In 1969, Mayor J.D. Braman proposed to city council the establishment of the City of Seattle Crime Prevention Advisory Commission, which would promote the development of local community crime prevention councils. The Advisory Commission advocated for the integration of city agencies, community members and public safety organizations. By 1971, there were 21 crime prevention councils scattered throughout the city. The city council, in approving Resolution #21805 on January 20, 1969, established the Advisory Commission and encouraged the development of crime prevention organizations. All community crime prevention councils that formed, whether emerging out of existing community organizations or formed independently, were required to get the approval of the Crime Prevention Commission, "including the approval of any programs initiated prior to the undertaking of any ambitious action."[17] The guidelines go on to suggest that Crime Prevention Councils should be organized for the purpose of helping citizens recognize the need for cooperation and understanding, providing opportunities for citizens to meet with law enforcement to discuss problems and activities, and for making recommendations to improve local protection and help law enforcement implement crime prevention programs.[18]

The Council-approved plan did not mention race relations or police-community problems. While Seattle did not experience the same kind of devastating riots that other cities in the U.S. did during the volatile and often-violent late 1960s, it certainly had its share. The assassination of Rev. Dr. Martin Luther King Jr., for example, was followed by three days of riots, burning vehicles and clashes with police that resulted in countless arrests and two black residents being shot by a white citizen (Taylor 1994).

The lack of attention to race issues did not escape the notice of the Central Seattle Community Council. In a letter to the Mayor from Edward H. Banks, the President of the CSCC, the CSCC encouraged the Mayor to enlist the support of a cross-section of people on the Advisory Commission.[19] In fact, Banks testified before the city council about the crime prevention council proposal and asked the city council to be aware of the fact that many in the Central Area were nervous about the idea. The concerns centered around fear that "anti-crime" would mean vigilante committees and that these committees would be legitimized by the city with the formation of the Advisory Commission. "There is a danger," Banks wrote in his notes for the meeting, "that the only ones who want [the] police-sponsored organizations would tend to be those not in touch with the community, those with a punitive or vigilante approach."[20] Banks further noted that "a community organization that is structured *from [the] top* is not coming from the people [and] will not be effective...involvement is needed from position of [the] population which is alienated, which may be on the borderline of criminal activity."[21]

The first action of the Advisory Commission, however, did not inspire confidence that the Commission was sensitive to the concerns that

Banks raised. Alfred J. Schweppe, an attorney who was appointed by the Mayor to chair the Commission, sent a letter to an array of community organizations and included a pamphlet from Los Angeles entitled, "Crime Can Be Stopped...Here's How." The pamphlet was substantial, containing at least five chapters of information about crime, its origins and ways in which community groups can help combat it. The letter that accompanied the pamphlet informed recipients that the first four chapters were not relevant for the Commission's purposes and should, therefore, "be ignored."

Those first four chapters, however, contained language and information that the CSCC found highly objectionable. In a letter to Mr. Schweppe dated June 25, 1969, from Ruth A. Brandwein, the Executive Director of the CSCC, Brandwein noted that the pamphlet contained many errors that would spread misunderstanding and resentment. For example, the pamphlet stated that "precious few Negro children have been raised in homes that are truly stable where love and respect and where discipline and character abound...[and] if there is a lack of a father figure in the home, obviously there is going to be a lack of control of young people."[22]

Schweppes's response was to point out that the letter that accompanied the pamphlet did ask recipients to skip the first four chapters and he felt "that our advice would be followed...it is my belief that when I tell someone to ignore a certain publication, that is not approving it."[23] The Crime Prevention Advisory Commission, however, decided that despite Schweppes's response, Brandwein and the CSCC's concerns should be taken seriously and so decided to forward only chapter five of the pamphlet to community organizations from that point on.

This incident is illustrative of the long history of tension between residents of the Central Area and the city government with respect to crime concerns. In fact, the Central Area was one of the last areas in the city to form a crime prevention council and it did so only after long deliberation and encouragement by the Commission. This is in part because of ongoing tensions between blacks in the Central Area and the police. The post-war period saw a rapid increase in the percentage of blacks in the Seattle area and police brutality was not uncommon. Quintard Taylor's rich, detailed history of the Central District provides a glimpse of these tensions:

> The legacy of police brutality in the rural South – a region where police power was blatantly used to maintain the political and economic dominance of whites – invariably meant black residents

(most of whom were southern-born) frequently feared and mistrusted police officers. The problematic relationship between the police and black community stemmed from low levels of police pay, which often attracted poorly educated and bigoted men, and the strident opposition of many white policemen to hiring or promoting more than a token number of black officers. But police brutality also emerged from societal stereotyping of blacks, which was further exaggerated by the daily, usually acrimonious contact between officers and distrustful community residents. In 1955, Mayor Allan Pomeroy appointed the Mayor's Advisory Committee on Police Practices to investigate charges of police brutality. The Committee, which police supporters hoped, and black community leaders feared, would exonerate the force, instead issued a harsh indictment of department practices in the Central District. The findings declared that the Seattle Police Department – like the Seattle white community – held essentially racist attitudes about black citizens, frequently stereotyping them as "criminal types." Some of the most common "facts," according to the report were that "All Negroes carry knives," "Any Negro driving a Cadillac is either a pimp or a dope-peddler," and "The bulk of the narcotic traffic in Seattle is among Negroes" (Taylor 1994, 177-178).

This report prompted the first of what would be many efforts to improve police-community relations. Tensions would only mount in the coming years, however, with police officers involved in shootings of young blacks, and local ministers and community activists accusing the police of not protecting Central Area residents but engaging in harassment.[24]

Police relations with the black community improved somewhat after a police corruption scandal in the 1970s resulted in a new police chief and a radical restructuring of policing activities that emphasized curbing officer discretion (see Scheingold 1991; Vega 1997). The appointment of Patrick Fitzsimmons as police chief also produced a greater effort to hire and promote minority officers and improve relations with the city's black residents. Ironically, however, some of the concerns over Weed and Seed stemmed from the belief among blacks in the Central Area that Fitzsimmons' police force would not implement the policy fairly but instead, would target minority youths for arrest. Sean Jeffries, an African-American male and president of the Garfield Community Council in 1992, and Tina Samora, a Japanese-American woman who was part of the Mayor's office during the Weed and Seed controversy, both indicated that the SPD under Fitzsimmons' command was regarded with suspicion because of the perception that Fitzsimmons was insufficiently attentive to concerns about racial harassment.[25]

Calls on the part of blacks in the Central Area and Rainier Valley for the city to establish a civilian-review board of allegations of police misconduct have not, to date, been heeded. Several organizations in the area, particularly Mothers for Police Accountability (formerly Mothers Against Police Harassment), continue to bring allegations of police brutality and to publicize events that they believe highlight police misconduct.

Contemporary Community Organizations in the Central Area

The Central Area continues to have vibrant and active community organizations. Community councils still operate and attract a wide range of members. There are eight community councils in the original Weed and Seed target area: Garfield Community Council, Jackson Place Community Council, Pratt Park Community Council, Spruce Park Community Council, Yesler Terrace Community Council, Judkins Rejected Community Council, Squire Park Community Council and the Central Neighborhood Group. These are small organizations formed by residents who live in the area chosen by the council.

More recently, the composition of the community councils may be shifting as whites find the Central Area to be one of the few remaining areas of affordable housing in Seattle. During the Weed and Seed controversy described below, Sarena Johnson and Bobby Ferris, two African-American members of the coalition opposing the program, charged the city with getting support from the community councils that are dominated by white interests, rather than addressing the broader range of councils in the area.[26] The opponents offered no evidence for these claims but, as the story below indicates, the community councils approached by the SPD were certainly more supportive of the SPD's tactics than some of the other councils in the area.

There is no question that the Central Area is changing. An article in a local weekly paper had a cover story entitled, "Honkies Invade the Central District," and described the fears of some black residents that the influx of whites will push out small, black-owned businesses, lower-income renters and long-time homeowners.[27] The corner of 23rd Avenue and Jackson Street, the center of the Weed and Seed target area, was once a hub of activity, with a plethora of clubs, shops, owned by blacks. In the 1980s, the area experienced serious decline and that intersection became symbolic of the deterioration and economic underdevelopment of the area. In the past few years, the area has once again been revitalized but the cornerstone of that effort was the arrival of a Starbucks coffee shop and a Hollywood video store.

Central Area residents are not of one mind on the influx of these businesses. Some residents charged the city with supporting the efforts of white-owned businesses in the area over black-owned ones and lamented the loss of small minority-owned businesses. Others see the changes as good for the neighborhood and are hopeful that it will change people's perceptions of the Central Area.[28] Ironically, inside the Starbucks is an exhibit of photographs from the area's glory days of the 1950s when jazz clubs lined Jackson Street and the 'after hours' scene was vibrant. A plaque describing the photographs notes:

> Imagine a time when Jackson Street was full of people walking up and down the sidewalk after midnight, ducking in and out of 34 nightclubs, between First and 15th Avenue…this was the rich, after-hours scene that peaked between 1937-51 and nurtured the early careers of Quincy Jones, Ray Charles and Ernestine Anderson. These photographs are a salute to the Jackson Street legacy.

The display says nothing about the rest of the community – a thriving black neighborhood with home-owners and black-owned businesses – which existed in the Central Area for decades and which helped create the Seattle music scene; nor does it mention that residents of the area have been struggling for years to have city officials recognize and respond to its troubles. This illustrates both the frustration of some residents of the area that whites in Seattle are unaware of the contribution blacks have made to the city, as well as the somewhat muted nature of racial conflict in Seattle.

In 1991, Mayor Norm Rice convened a Central Area Summit to bring people from the community together to discuss various concerns. The result was the Central Area Action Plan, completed in 1993 and involving approximately 80 Central Area leaders, along with representatives from the Chamber of Commerce's Urban Enterprise Project (Vega 1997). The Central Area Development Association (CADA), formed as part of the Central Area Action Plan, is a non-profit organization established to promote economic development, housing and general vitality in the area. CADA is deliberately focused on attracting new residents to the area, regardless of race, in an effort to build the base of residents who can support businesses in the area. The Director and Assistant Director, both African-Americans, argue that the area has suffered by not having a significant enough population to sustain local businesses.[29]

Despite the changing demographics of the neighborhood, there is no indication that any of the community councils in the Weed and Seed area are dominated exclusively or even primarily by white, affluent residents or business owners as opposed to middle or lower-middle income residents and blacks. And many of the councils continue to represent lower-income people and the African-American residents who have lived in the area for a long time. Of the eight community councils in Weed and Seed target area, at least two of the most active groups – Yesler Terrace and Judkins Rejected – have regularly lobbied for more economic opportunities for minority youth, more resources for low-income housing, and for preservation of existing minority businesses in the area. The Yesler Terrace Community Council is comprised of low-income residents from the Yesler Terrace Housing Project and has a history of advocating for more and better police services in that project. It also has a history of working with community police team officers to urge young people away from drug and gang activity without necessarily involving arrest.[30] The Judkins Rejected Community Council, which chose its name because of the feeling that it had been passed over by urban development programs in the 1960s and 1970s in favor of more affluent neighborhoods, is also a lower-income area with many homeowners who have felt that area residents are left out of the decision-making process with respect to policies and programs in their area.[31]

The Garfield Community Council, which became one of the most active groups in Weed and Seed, was formed in part to address drug dealing in the Central Area and the group worked actively with the police to increase police presence and activity aimed at reducing drug dealing. But many of the tactics advocated by the Garfield Community Council members were not typical police anti-drug activities. Instead, the Council advocated the use of reverse-stings, printing in the local newspapers the names of those arrested for coming into the area to buy drugs, and recording of license plates of taxis that were suspected of bringing drug dealers into the neighborhood. While the Council supported Weed and Seed from the outset, it was sympathetic to concerns of residents about excessive police presence in the community.

Nonetheless, the Garfield Community Council, along with the Central Neighborhood Group, seem to be the groups that have the most history of working with police and are most amenable to increased police presence in the community. As we shall see, this runs counter to the concerns of the Coalition to Stop Weed and Seed, which argued that an increased police presence would result in civil rights violations, harassment and abuse.

Just prior to the introduction of Weed and Seed, several other controversies surrounded police relations with the Central District. The ongoing struggle for greater police accountability culminated in the appointment of an independent auditor to review police procedures and charges of misconduct. This process left many citizens unhappy and, as a result, the civilian review board issue still resurfaces from time to time in the form of complaints that the auditor has no authority to require the police to do anything. In addition, the city had just ended a two-year struggle over a local policy entitled the Drug Traffic Loitering Ordinance that culminated in the Ordinance's renewal. This ordinance allowed police to arrest people suspected of being gang members and gave police discretionary authority that some believed would lead them to stop innocent youth. The original hearings on the Ordinance, as well as renewal hearings, were highly contentious.

Thus, the drug crime and economic development issues of the 1980s and 1990s were still fresh in residents'minds when the Weed and Seed program came into focus in early 1992. On the one hand, a large number of residents in the area felt that the police had ignored crime problems in the Central District because the area had and continues to have a high percentage of low-income blacks. They angrily charged the police department with neglect and, as one resident put it, practically "begged" the police to do more. On the other hand, a long history of tension between police and minorities, of redlining the area by banks, and of concern for economic development were also on the minds of many residents. The tensions between these perspectives played out in the Central Area itself and the Seattle community writ large. It was in this context that Weed and Seed make its untimely appearance in 1992.

Seattle's Weed and Seed Application

Seattle first applied for Weed and Seed funding in March of 1992. The area targeted for funding was the Central District (also called Central Area), which extends from E. Union to S. Dearborn and Martin Luther King Way to 12th Avenue. The population of the area is 47% African-American, 15% Asian American and 35% white, compared to the city as a whole which is 10% African-American, 12% Asian and 75% white.[32] The grant proposal noted that "the Central Area has been a concern to the city for some time and has the reputation as one of the "blighted" economically depressed and crime-ridden parts of the City."[33] Gang violence and drug activity, along with little economic development, troubled the area. Further, the proposal pointed out that the area has great potential for expansion and growth; its central location gives it proximity to downtown, Lake Washington and other popular areas of the city.[34] "The Central Area was chosen in part because of the nature of the problems impacting [sic] the residents and the business climate. However, more importantly, this area was chosen *because of its promise for improvement and growth*."[35]

The grant proposal is weighted towards law enforcement, a reflection of the Justice Department's guidelines and goals as well as the fact that the grant recipient was the Seattle Police Department (SPD). According to the grant writer Frank Daniels, the SPD tailored the grant application for the Justice Department but did not see the program playing out so punitively in Seattle.[36] Further, as recalled from chapter two, the Justice Department had to conduct the program under the constraints imposed by Congress (i.e., insufficient seeding funds), as well as the fact that its mandate is to use law enforcement agencies to address crime.

The details of Weed and Seed's policy history, however, were not widely known in the community and may not have mattered. Once Central Area community leaders[37] got a hold of the grant proposal, its emphasis on coordination between federal, state and local law enforcement struck fear into the hearts of many and generated widespread outrage. The proposal's role for the community suggests that the police would direct the program and tell community residents how to solve their problems, rather than the other way around: "Community residents need to be empowered to assist in solving the crime problems in their neighborhoods."[38] But it was not clear to community leaders of the Central Area that the SPD knew how to empower communities. A 1991 report on community policing in Seattle produced for the SPD makes suggestions for how police can be more responsive to community concerns and indicates that the department could do much to improve their record. Also, Lyons argues that community policing in Seattle has the potential to empower police as much or more than communities because police tend to respond to dominant voices in the community that already accept much of traditional police activity (Lyons 1999).

Controversy and Concern Erupt Over Weed and Seed

Seattle's original proposal for Weed and Seed emerged in a local government context consistent with many of Weed and Seed's principles. In fact, the city had been experimenting with community policing and other community-based programs for some time. The original grant proposal for Weed and Seed noted that Weed and Seed expands a "concept that Seattle has already embarked upon."[39] The concept of coordination between city agencies and a community-oriented style of policing had been in the works, at least in theory, for some time (Fleissner 1997; see also 1999).

The original grant proposal contained Memoranda of Understanding (MOU) between numerous local organizations and the city of Seattle in support of the concept of Weed and Seed. Sean Jeffries, who was president of the Garfield Community Council at the time and who lives and works in the Central Area, indicated that the Council supported the program from early on. The Garfield Community Council sits in the heart of the target area and residents of that area experienced the brunt of the drug trafficking and problems associated with that activity. Jeffries noted that the group held meetings and outside vigils to mobilize support in the community for the program.[40] However, while some community organizations did sign the MOU with the city in support of Weed and Seed, the vast majority of those memoranda came from city organizations. Table 4.1 illustrates the organizations and agencies that signed MOUs.

Involvement in the program was clearly weighted heavily towards government agencies, specifically law enforcement and social service programs. Note also that the three community groups consulted are three of the groups that had been critical of the police for not paying more attention to drug problems in the area. The criticism was borne more out of frustration at neglect, than of specific concerns over police tactics. Thus, while the groups were critical of the police, they had been working for several years with the SPD to bring a greater police presence to the area and tackle the drug problem through law enforcement tactics. They were not particularly critical of police tactics or police presence.

Table 4.1   Organizations and Agencies Signing MOUs in Support of Weed and Seed

Federal	City/County	Private	Community
U.S. Attorney for Western WA	Seattle Mayor	United Way	Central Neigh. Assoc.
Community Relations Service – USDOJ	Seattle Police Dept.	Greater Seattle Chamber of Commerce	Garfield Community Council
Federal Bureau of Investigation	Seattle City Attorney	Seattle-King Co. Private Industry Council	Spruce Park Neighbor Assoc.
Immigration and Naturalization Service	Dept. of Housing and Human Services	Alcohol-Drug Helpline	
Bureau of Alcohol, Tobacco and Firearms	Seattle Housing Authority	Seattle Emergency Housing Services	
Drug Enforcement Agency	Dept. of Neighborhoods	Pioneer Fellowship House	
Economic Development Authority	Dept. of Parks and Recreation	Seattle University	
Housing and Urban Development	King County Prosecutor		
Employment and Training Authority			
Job Corps - Dept. of Labor			
Small Business Administration			

Source: "Proposal for Department of Justice Operation Weed and Seed: Reclaiming America's Neighborhoods." Planning Section, Inspectional Services Division, Seattle Police Department. March 20, 1992.

Both the Central Neighborhood Association and the Spruce Park Community Council had been active with police in the area for some time. While the Garfield Community Council became somewhat more receptive to community leaders' concerns -- holding meetings to allow the growing opposition to express its concerns about the program, for example – Jeffries acknowledged that it had also been lobbying the police for more resources for several years.[41] That the SPD obtained MOUs from these community councils, then, did not appease community members who wanted the police to be receptive to a wider range of perspectives. Given the active role these three councils had played in advocating for more police resources in the years prior, they were logical targets of support for a program such as Weed and Seed. Indeed, when the Deputy Mayor, Lawrence Andrews, was handed the Weed and Seed project, within hours of taking the job, he noticed that the police were "approaching their friends" to sign-off on the program, rather than engaging the community more broadly.[42] The Deputy Mayor asked the police to involve more community residents in the process. This move may well have set the wheels in motion for the controversy that ensued.

In addition to the MOUs, several agencies sent letters of support, including the Pratt Park Community Council, the Washington State Department of Community Development and the Boys and Girls Clubs of King County. The letter in support of the program from the chair of the Pratt Park Neighborhood Council noted that the Council, "strongly supports the *concept* of the Weed and Seed Program. We eagerly await seeing the grant proposal."[43] The letter went on to note that:

> The Weed and Seed Program offers our community the opportunity to address the myriad of social problems endemic in our neighborhood. We are a community active in improving itself so any seed funds will surely ripen into fruitful endeavors far into the future. Pratt Park Community Council looks forward to working with other community organizations in its design and implementation."[44]

No mention of crime or 'weeding' is made in this letter and it is clear that the Council is interested in being involved in both the planning and implementation stages of the program.

It is worth noting that a controversy ensued over which of two Garfield Community Councils was the legitimate voice of the community. The original Garfield Community Council, which formed in 1989, was charged with being too cozy to business interests and as a result, a second group formed under the same name. Each group tried to claim legitimacy and it was the former group that negotiated with the SPD. The second group opposed Weed and Seed and charged the city with undermining their efforts to mobilize and gain support for the opposition to Weed and Seed. Sean Jeffries, then president of the original council, did advocate for alternative police tactics in the area and indicated his sympathy for the people, particularly black women, who testified at city council and other hearings around the area about their concerns for their young sons.[45] Thus, while the Garfield Council that worked with the city on Weed and Seed was less opposed to the program than the second group, it was still receptive to community concerns about police tactics.

A great deal of controversy ensued when neighborhood leaders were first informed of the city's proposal for Weed and Seed in the Central District.[46] Mothers Against Police Harassment, a group that had been focusing for some time on police harassment and brutality against blacks, joined with several area black residents to form the Coalition to Stop Weed and Seed. These organizations included the Central Area Planning Committee, the NAACP, the Rainbow Coalition, Church Council of Greater Seattle, The American Civil Liberties Union, the Seattle Federation of Community Councils, the King County Labor Council and the New Alliance Party.[47] Wendy Overton and Sarena Johnson, African-American women who lived and worked in the Central Area in the early 1990s, were two of the most active organizers of the Coalition to Oppose Weed and Seed. According to Overton and Johnson, the Coalition obtained a copy of the grant from the city and set out to publicize the program and educate the residents on what weeding could mean for their community.[48] They went door-to-door, organized community meetings and actively worked to inform area residents of the program and its potential consequences. The group then used that information and community opposition to focus the two key concerns mentioned earlier in conjunction with other programs (that the program would empower federal law enforcement and result in street sweeps of young, black males, and that there would be little seeding of the area), and also to emphasize the belief that Weed and Seed was simply a gentrification strategy that would move blacks out of a well-situated, underdeveloped area of the city.[49]

Weeding: First, community leaders' concerns were embedded in anger towards a police department that they believed had "overpoliced and underprotected" their area. The Coalition to Stop Weed and Seed charged the SPD with being unresponsive to concerns about crime in the area over a long period of time, thus allowing the area to fall prey to gang activity and drug violence. As previous discussion has illustrated, these concerns were not confined to a few disgruntled individuals. Numerous community councils in the area had been making the same charge for years. In a letter to Mayor Rice, Beatrice Jenkins and Wilma Harrison, co-chairs of the Coalition, claimed that many Central Area gangs formed because the SPD failed to protect young people in the area from the pressures of the more hardened gangs from Los Angeles that began infiltrating the Seattle area in the 1980s. Further, they argued that some young people identified as gang members were not, in fact, gang members and that some gangs do not engage in illegal activity. They did not trust the SPD to know the difference and they were concerned that police abuses would continue. With respect to policing strategies, the group suggested that community policing would not be effective until police abuse of young people in the area ceased. The letter warned that young people were very angry and that anger would eventually explode into violence if these abuses were permitted to continue.[50]

Thus, opponents of Weed and Seed feared that it would give law enforcement agencies license to stop the area's young people for no reason other than the fact that they were black or Latino, male and living in the target area. Even city council members joined the chorus of concerns. Margaret Paegler, the chair of the city council's public safety committee, noted "I'm a gardener and I know you can't always tell weeds from vegetables - especially when they're young."[51] Eventually, the mayor (the city's first black mayor who was obviously not anxious to alienate the city's minorities), though still advocating for Seattle's implementation of the program, acknowledged that it had some problems:

> When you look at a name like Weed and Seed, when you look at all the chest-beating rhetoric on public safety that politicians tend to speak these days, it's easy to see why communities might harbor some distrust for federal programs no matter how well intentioned.[52]

Second, the Coalition to Stop Weed and Seed raised fears about federal control over the program, noting that, despite city assurances that the program would be controlled locally and not by the Justice Department, the Congressional Record and the Justice Department documents relating to Weed and Seed "describe a policy committee overseeing the operation of the policing portion of the program that is chaired by the U.S. Attorney and whose members include all of the federal law enforcement agencies and some local law enforcement agencies."[53] This was a particularly harsh affront, according to the group, because of the long history of federal law enforcement agencies' confrontations with black activists.[54] The Coalition noted, in particular, that the weeding strategies would involve targeting of gang members and perceived gang members "in the same manner that the FBI targeted the Black Panther Party in the 1960s and 1970s with murders and framing of members." The term "weed" coupled with the program's goals of coordinating with federal and state law enforcement made many community leaders nervous that they would be harassed by federal agents and that federal laws would apply to arrests in their neighborhood but no where else in the city.[55]

Finally, like the Urban Strategies Group in Los Angeles, the Coalition to Stop Weed and Seed argued that weeding strategies would permit law enforcement agents to suspend constitutional rights for minorities. They were concerned that federal involvement in the program would provide the local police with authority to engage in activities that would never be tolerated in other areas of the city. The group demanded documentation that the structure of the program authority would be changed by Congress or the Justice Department to allow for the city to have control of the program. The lack of local control was seen by the Coalition as providing too much latitude for law enforcement agencies to engage in street sweeps and other tactics directed at minorities.

The group was also worried that the program would simply 'weed' out young black males and the result would be a lower crime rate but a highly destabilized community. Sarena Johnson noted:

> All the studies I've ever seen on crime show a direct correlation between the crime rate and the number of young males. Any program that removes young males reduces crime. But it also destabilizes the community and destroys community control.[56]

Seeding: With respect to seeding, community leaders feared that the seeding money would be too little to make a difference or that it would amount to coordination between law enforcement and social service in order to identify more petty criminals. They argued that law enforcement agencies should not have control over seeding, nor should there be any information sharing between law enforcement agents and social services. Further, they expressed concern that to the extent that money did materialize, it would go primarily to existing social service agencies rather than to the organizations in the community that were already trying to revitalize it.

Perhaps most importantly, the Coalition felt that Weed and Seed would deflect attention away from what they regarded as more pressing problems: jobs for youth; drug treatment; economic assistance for minority businesses; police harassment. The group also wanted police to engage in operations that would target whites coming into the area to purchase drugs. Sarena Johnson also suggested that Weed and Seed focused attention on law enforcement instead of economics because the area is largely black.[57]

Gentrification: Finally, opponents were concerned that the whole purpose of the program was to 'weed' out lower-income blacks and 'beautify' the area so that whites would be enticed to move in.   Bobby Ferris, whose wife Sarena Johnson was one of the founders of the Coalition to Oppose Weed and Seed, felt that the city council and mayor's office were interested in reducing crime in the Central Area so that whites would feel more comfortable buying homes.[58]   The letter to the Mayor noted that "new arrivals [to the Central Area] are pushing for the African-Americans to move out...intensifying policing in this area that already has a high level of police harassment and abuse will only hasten the out-migration of African-Americans." In the midst of the controversy, a group created a fake front page for the Seattle Post-Intelligencer (P-I) one morning and pasted it onto copies of the P-I in some street boxes.   The page headline read, "African-American community discovered" and claimed that Weed and Seed would "weed out local black youths, traditionally associated with drug activity, and seed the area with more law enforcement officials."[59]   Indeed, the site selection itself was controversial, with those opposed to the program noting that other areas in the city, such as the area around the University of Washington, had property crime rates and drug usage higher than that of the Central District.[60]

The Coalition to Oppose Weed and Seed also had the support of some church groups in the area.   Reverend Jeffries, a black minister at the New Hope Baptist Church, was concerned that Weed and Seed would respond to the concerns about crime that many Central Area residents had but would not respond to the fear of what that response would bring.   Reverend Jeffries, like others involved in the Coalition, disliked the sense that Weed and Seed was doing something *"for"* the community, rather than *"with"* the community.[61]   He did not have confidence that the SPD knew what strategies would most empower community residents, reduce crime and lead to revitalization of the area.

Opposition to the program was so strong that at one point a proposed seed site, The Garfield High School Site Council actually refused to take the

$30,000 that the city intended to provide with seeding money in order to fund the new Garfield Teen Clinic.[62] While the Council eventually agreed to take the money, the rejection symbolized the extent to which local organizations were frustrated by the proposal to implement the program.

The opponents of Weed and Seed had some evidence to support their points of opposition. First, with respect to weeding strategies, the Justice Department summary of the program did indeed call for U.S. Attorney to "play a central role in coordinating Federal, State and local law enforcement agencies to prosecute certain drug and/or violent felons," including the FBI, Drug Enforcement Agency (DEA) and Immigration and Naturalization Service (INS).[63] The city's grant proposal also had the U.S. Attorney and other federal agents playing central roles in the decision-making process. Furthermore, community leaders were not simply reacting out of an abstract fear of racism and heavy-handed law enforcement. Historically, the Seattle Police Department, like most professional police departments, had not responded well to community organizations that were critical of its activities. Weed and Seed raised new fears that community concerns would be ignored (Lyons 1999). Indeed, like many urban police departments, the SPD has had a troubled relationship with Seattle's minority communities, including charges that the lack of a citizen review board allowed racist incidents to go unpunished, that former police chief Patrick Fitzsimmons unfairly targeted minority populations and that police ignored explicit concerns raised by community members about aggressive police tactics in the Central Area. Several incidents involving black youths being arrested by police officers only served to reinforce concerns about police misbehavior.[64]

In 1992, the mayor formed a blue ribbon panel to examine police-community relations in response to a city Human Rights Commission finding of great hostility between the SPD and minority communities.[65] This Task Force issued a report in 1993 calling on the city to create a civilian review board.[66] Numerous minority groups have continued to pressure the SPD to institute such a board but to date no civilian review of complaints against the police has been created. Thus, the language of the Justice Department's guidelines for the program which included intimidating strategies with militaristic language such as street sweeps, sector integrity, directed patrols, only served to reinforce fears that the program would adversely affect minorities.

Second, the community involvement was minimal and it was unclear how much control, if any, the community would have over the program activities. The city had approached the community councils that were predisposed to increased police presence and asked them for their support of the program. Weed and Seed was not widely publicized in the community in which it was going to be implemented. Sean Jeffries indicated that his impression was that city representatives in general, and the SPD in particular, viewed the Central District as filled with criminals and "people who didn't care about their neighborhood."[67] Thus, the community-focus of Weed and Seed was less than appealing to many Central District residents precisely because they were unpersuaded that the SPD even knew what their community needs were, much less that it was prepared to actually respond to them.

Third, concerns that seeding money would not materialize were not unfounded as several other cities did in fact have trouble coming up with this funding, and the Justice Department had clear constraints on what kind of programs could constitute seeding. Area leaders also worried that this would be just another opportunity for the city to provide incentives for white businesses and homeowners to move into the area, thus displacing black businesses that had been in the area for years and were in need of bank lending practices that would allow them to continue or expand.

Finally, the gentrification charge was also not without merit. As suggested earlier, the Central Area is conveniently located near downtown, several popular shopping and entertainment areas, and has numerous older, charming homes that could be purchased for a fraction of the cost of homes in the adjoining, affluent neighborhoods of Madrona and Capital Hill. As the housing market skyrocketed in the mid-1990s, the Central Area has become an increasingly attractive area to purchase quality, affordable homes. Seattle has become nationally known for its crisis of affordable housing. The average price of a single-family dwelling went from $85,136 in 1981 to $172,825 in 1994 (Seattle-Everett Real Estate Research Report, 1994). In much of the Central Area, housing sales were infrequent and considerably lower than the city average in the early 1980's. By the mid-1990's, housing prices were keeping pace with the city mean and sales were much more common (Seattle-Everett Real Estate Research Report, 1981-1994).

Thus, rather than viewing Weed and Seed as the opportunity for community involvement in law enforcement in addressing crime in their neighborhoods and for community revitalization, many community leaders of the Central Area regarded it as an opportunity for further legitimating police practices which marginalized their concerns about the problems of crime, the problems of policing *and* other fundamental concerns about the area's development. The federal program vision of community was, for these residents, static and passive rather than dynamic and proactive and the emphasis on arrests and incapacitation raised fears about street sweeps and the reliance on profiles rather than a legitimate attempt to respond to crime.

The City Responds to Controversy

Mayor Rice, the city's first African-American mayor, had been under fire for some time for working with downtown business interests and not adequately representing black interests. Clearly, he did not want to let the opposition to Weed and Seed be used as evidence that he was more interested in business than in the black community that had nurtured his political career. According to the Lawrence Andrews, Deputy Mayor at the time and also an African-American, Mayor Rice also genuinely believed that the program had potential. "He believed in the concept – of marrying [different types of] services to prevent violence. He was really, truly focused on getting to know the neighborhood and seeing the police as helper."[68] In the years preceding Weed and Seed, the Mayor had spent considerable time working on development ideas for the Central Area and was stunned by the opposition to the program, particularly its vehemence. Andrews argued that the Mayor wanted to turn the program into a positive good for the community.

The Justice Department had incentives of its own to keep Weed and Seed going in Seattle. The SPD had numerous other Justice Department programs operating – including Comprehensive Community Programs, and the Youth Handgun Violence Initiative -- and felt that Seattle provided a good opportunity for the program to work. With 15 other cities also in line to receive grant money, Justice Department was not anxious to have it stall in Seattle.

In response to the controversy then, the city asked the Justice Department for greater funding for seeding and more of an emphasis on community policing in the hope that this would relieve some concerns that law enforcement in the target area would become hard-edged and linked to federal agencies. In fact, Mayor Norm Rice made a trip to Washington D.C. to argue for allowing Seattle to distribute the money more heavily towards seeding. Members of the Citizens Advisory Committee, Seattle Police Department officers who were involved in the initial planning and the US Attorney's Office for Western Washington claim that this trip, among other similar efforts, influenced national Weed and Seed strategy by bringing community concerns to the forefront.[69]

Initially, the Department of Justice rejected Seattle's request. The Deputy Director of the Executive Office for Weed and Seed indicated that the auditors had concerns about the department's ability to spend the money as Seattle wished.[70] In part, this had to do with the fact that all of the funding for the program came from the Justice Department, which is constrained by Congress as to how its money can be spent. However, the Department was anxious to see the program succeed in Seattle – which had a number of other popular Justice Department programs operating – and thus, eventually agreed to allow Seattle to spend a greater amount of money on seeding than the original Weed and Seed goals planned and to distribute some of the money to community groups that were already operating in the target area.[71] Seattle Police Chief Norm Stamper, who was working with San Diego's police department which was also an original Weed and Seed site, also noted that the Justice Department was under fire from other sites that wanted to use more of the money for seeding than weeding as well and did not want the program to face any more opposition.[72]

The extent to which the community controversy exerted pressure on the Justice Department is difficult to quantify. Certainly the organizers of the Coalition to Oppose Weed and Seed saw their role as vital to the programmatic shifts. In addition, Gretchen King, the Law Enforcement Coordinating Committee representative from the US Attorney's Office in Seattle, indicated that the Seattle experience was much more community-driven than she believes the Justice Department ever intended it to be.[73] Stephen Rickman, the Director of the Executive Office for Weed and Seed and Bob Samuels, the Deputy Director, both indicated that the controversies in cities around the country influenced the way the program was implemented and subsequent versions of the program goals.[74]

In addition to the funding distribution, the organizational structure and the composition of the weeding and seeding committees were altered to better reflect the needs of the community. Primary input into seeding programs and weeding activities would now come from a Citizens Advisory Committee (CAC) whose members would be appointed by the Mayor and would represent members of the community, primarily through the community councils in the area. In December of 1992, the Seattle City Council voted to accept the revised Weed and Seed grant.[75]

As we have seen, the community councils represent a range of residents in the area: groups like the Yesler Terrace Community Council and Judkins Rejected Community Council advocated for services for low-income residents, and emphasized concerns that existing police tactics might unfairly target minority youth; other groups, such as the Garfield Community Council and Central Neighborhood Association were more focused on and supportive of police practices. However, more radical critiques of the program that came from Mothers Against Police Harassment and church organizations, did not make their way into the decision-making process. This was partly because MAPH is a citywide organization that is not confined to the Central Area and some of the churches, such as the New Hope Baptist Church, are not in the target area. It was also partly by choice. Citizen Advisory Council meetings are open to the public and anyone can attend and express their views. Sarena Johnson, who was highly active in the Coalition to Oppose Weed and Seed and still opposes the program, felt that her work was finished once the program was adopted because "it would have been a much different program if we hadn't opposed it," indicating that she believed the program had been transformed at least in part as a result of the work of the Coalition.[76] Wendy Overton, who later became involved in the southeast Weed and Seed site (the subject of the next chapter), believed all along that the program would be accepted but felt that the opposition could and did make it more community-driven.

Many of the initial concerns seem to have abated over time and are now attributed, by both original supporters and some converts, as stemming from the language of the policy[77] and concerns that the police would not listen to the needs of the residents. During the grant review process, city officials declared that the program would deal with residents concerns and that it would not go forward if the concerns could not be addressed to the satisfaction of the community. Some of the program's initial opponents, including Wendy Overton, have become supporters and are actively involved in the original site and the new south Seattle site. These individuals cite the SPD's response to concerns and the lack of materialization of residents' fears of harassment as reasons for their change of heart.[78] One opponent noted after the city council vote to approve the program said: "Fortunately, the Weed and Seed passed yesterday is a better program than that which was first proposed to this city and the dialogue we've had had been beneficial."[79]

Mothers for Police Accountability (formerly Mothers Against Police Harassment)[80] remains uncomfortable with the program because of its law enforcement emphasis. The group maintains that Weed and Seed is essentially blackmail because it requires communities to accept unchecked police practices in return for funding for community development.

However, the founder of MAPH now takes a very active role in working with the SPD administration to improve relations between police and the black community. She sits on the African-American Advisory

Council to the Chief of Police and recently attended the Western Weed and Seed Regional Conference as a panelist in the police-community relations discussion. She continues to express concern about the program but at the same time, she and Chief Stamper developed a working relationship that has encouraged the department to look more closely at the way it handles relations with minority residents in Seattle.

Even some of the strongest opponents of the original program expressed some hope that the new target area in the Southeast can live up to the city's promise that the program will be community-based and more about revitalization than crime control. Sarena Johnson and Bobby Ferris expressed hope that the controversy in the Central Area had helped to make the program less punitive and more responsive to neighborhood concerns.[81] Any remaining opposition in the Central Area site tends to be muted both by the din of praise heard in most discussions of Weed and Seed as well as the responsiveness of police officers who attend these meetings.[82]

Implementation of Seattle's Weed and Seed Program

In January of 1993, Seattle's Weed and Seed program began. The goals, reflecting both local political struggles and federal policing initiatives, were:

- To control violent and drug-related crime through the full range of weed activities, including intelligence gathering and crime analysis, arrest, detention, prosecution, and incapacitation of offenders from the target neighborhoods.
- To enhance public safety and security by mobilizing neighborhood residents to work with police in solving and preventing violent and drug-related crime.
- To create a healthy and supportive environment by preventing and combating crime, drug use, unemployment, illiteracy and disease.
- To revitalize the neighborhood by providing adequate housing, a clean and attractive environment, and investment.[83]

The Seattle Police Department is the grant recipient and the lead agency for the project and "plays a major role coordinating among various City departments and with community and business groups."[84] Overall administrative coordination is assigned to the Planning Section Manager of the SPD, though the weed and seed coordinators do almost all of the planning and coordination. Seeding programs are under a full-time Seed coordinator, who works with the city's Department of Housing and Human Services. A lieutenant in the SPD is the weed coordinator. The original weed coordinator, Rosa Melendez, is now the U.S. Marshall for Western Washington. The weed and seed coordinators during the course of this research were Lt. Harry Bailey in the SPD and Walter Atkinson from the Department of Housing and Human Services. Both are African-American.

Weed and Seed in Seattle is overseen primarily by the Citizens Advisory Committee (CAC), a committee of community council members and representatives from social service agencies that operate in the target area. This differs sharply from the organization of the program as outlined in the original grant proposal that placed law enforcement agents, the US Attorney for Western Washington and social service agents in the prominent decision-making roles. Currently, the local US Attorney oversees only the Project Steering Committee that is comprised of federal and local agency representatives and meets rarely (Rolland 1997, 16). Both the seed and weed coordinators regularly attend the meetings, however, and their presence is formidable. They are well informed of federal, state and local grant possibilities, Weed and Seed conference agendas and programs that might help levy funds into the area. Thus, the CAC, while certainly the centerpiece of the program's implementation process, at times functions more like an advisory group that listens to the available options and decides among them, rather than taking the initiative and proposing implementation strategies. Table 4.2 illustrates shifts in control of the program.

The CAC, by far the most active committee, was established by mayoral appointment in March 1993. The Mayor approached each of the eight community councils in the target area and asked for a nomination to the committee. In addition to these council members, representatives were also appointed from local social service agencies and community organizations. Chair of the committee has rotated between leaders of a local vocational program and members of community councils. New members are appointed by approval of the CAC. The committee makes funding decisions for organizations and programs to receive seed money, and recommendations to the weed coordinator for law enforcement programs in the target area. The original CAC consisted of representatives from the eight area community councils, the Seattle School District, the Department of Housing and Human Services, the Rotary Boys and Girls Club, the Urban League, the Seattle Vocational Institute and a student at Garfield High School which is located in the heart of the target area.

Table 4.2   Central District Weed and Seed Controlling Interests

	Original Grant Proposal	Actual Implementation Strategy
Overall control	U.S. Attorney	Citizen Advisory Committee Weed coordinator (SPD) Seed coordinator (DHHS)
Weed	3 federal law enforcement agencies 3 local law enforcement agencies Mayor's office	SPD Lieutenant (Weed coordinator) Citizen Advisory Committee
Seed	2 federal agencies SPD Mayor's office Community councils Central Area Planning Comm. Other groups as identified	DHHS representative (Seed coordinator) Citizen Advisory Committee

Source   Seattle's Weed and Seed grant proposal; Interviews with weed and seed coordinators and CAC chair.

The first meeting of the Citizen Advisory Committee took place on March 10, 1993. There were 44 people in attendance including the Mayor who charged the committee with: a) choosing a new name for the program to distance it from the controversy b) allocating $164,000 in seed money and c) developing plans to address the future needs of the community. The first issue was dispensed with on April 8 as the committee voted 5-4 to keep the name; the majority decided that they wanted to transform the program into something other than what people feared it would be and the name recognition would promote visibility. The close vote illustrates that not all members agreed. The second issue was dealt with by issuing a Request for Proposals (RFP) on May 14, 1993 to organizations and agencies that might wish to submit program ideas for funding. Finally, the committee decided on three primary areas of focus for the seeding money: to provide services to improve middle and high school student skills in math and science; to support programs for adult education and apprenticeship; and to provide funding for youth and adult entrepreneurial training.[85] In order to promote strong proposals from community organizations, the CAC held a "bidders conference" on June 3rd to help smaller groups get assistance with the format and content of their proposals. [86]   Table 4.3 illustrates the original membership of the CAC.

Table 4.3   Organizations and Agencies Represented on the Citizens' Advisory Committee

Community Councils	Education	Social Service/Multi-Service agencies
Garfield	Seattle Public Schools	Urban League
Jackson Place	Garfield High School	Boys and Girls Club
Judkins Rejected	Seattle Vocational Institute	Department of Housing and Human Services
Yesler Terrace		
Spruce Park		
Pratt Park		
Central Neighborhood Group		
Squire Park		

Source: Citizen Advisory Committee Meeting minutes, April 1993.

Influence of the CAC on Weeding

The CAC is a central figure in the 'kinder and gentler' Weed and Seed that began to emerge in Seattle. As a result of the controversy, the Mayor promised to give the community a more central role in the program and the CAC has turned out to be the key player. The bulk of the seeding money is distributed through this committee and it also advocates for private investment in the area through a variety of channels, most notably the

Washington Insurance Council, a non-profit public relations and charitable organization funded by insurance agencies in the state of Washington.

Initially, CAC meetings were full. Crystal Parker, an African-American who represented the Seattle Vocational Institute on the CAC and was deeply concerned about educational issues in the area, noted that residents were angry and frustrated at how their neighborhood had decayed and placed much of the blame at the SPD's door.[87] Concerns ranged from anger at the police department for failure to close down crack houses and dangerous drug activity, to parents raising questions about how their children, particularly young black males, would be treated by police. The weed coordinator for most of the 1990s notes that he approached his first CAC meeting prepared to provide facts and figures about the number of drug dealing arrests and heavy law enforcement activities that were taking place - or about to take place - in the area. Instead, the heavy community presence "quietly and politely told me 'that's not how it's going to be.'"[88] These early meetings led to some strategy reconsideration for weeding.

One particular weeding operation was the direct result of meetings with the CAC and activity on the part of community council members who insisted that the police find out where the drug buyers were coming from. On at least three consecutive CAC meetings in 1993, Sean Jeffries repeatedly grilled the police representative about the possibility of conducting "reverse sting" operations. These operations target drug buyers rather than the more common operations (buy-busts) against dealers but, according to the original weed coordinator, are not conducted by the SPD because of the manpower needed and the liability issues involved (entrapment concerns). The members of the CAC, however, were convinced that most of the patrons of the drug dealers in the area were not residents of the area. The police, unpersuaded that this was the case and not anxious to spend a lot of resources on this, continued to resist. However, Rosa Melendez, a lieutenant in the SPD and the first weed coordinator, watched as the CAC members and community residents continued to pressure the department and other city officials by making phone calls to city council and the mayor's office.[89] The SPD finally relented, conducting several reverse stings and found that over 85% of those arrested did not live in the area; many were from Seattle's more affluent suburban communities.

The reverse stings were seen as an enormous victory for the CAC.[90] Not only did they persuade the SPD to conduct the operation (a victory in itself), but the results confirmed what community leaders had been telling the police all along: that many if not most of the drug buyers who were buying drugs in the area did not, in fact, live in the area. The reverse stings are frequently talked about in Weed and Seed circles as an important part of the weeding process and the original weed coordinator regards them as serving an important psychological function for the community; not only did they get the police to do what they wanted but the community turned out to be right and the police were wrong.

Other weeding activities In contrast to other sites reported in the National Process Evaluation (and noted in Chapter 3), the Seattle weeding experience included citizen-generated law enforcement activity: the two reverse stings in the first year which resulted in 23 arrests with 19 of those arrested residing outside the Central District. Nonetheless, most of the weeding money has gone to pay for overtime for officers. This primarily funds emphasis patrols, which consist of intensive police presence in specific problem areas. During the three-year period between 1993 and 1995, weeding operations resulted in 321 felony arrests, 478 misdemeanor arrests and 137 criminal citations.[91] Emphasis patrols included issuing traffic citations, checking business premises for criminal activity, executing search warrants and initiating contact with citizens. They also generated extensive field interview reports (FIRs) in which officers stop suspicious looking persons and talk with them about their activities. During a mere six-week period in 1995, patrol officers and community police teams (CPTs) conducted 289 FIRs. The following four-week period generated 424 FIRS.[92] Thus, the reverse stings did little to mitigate the presence of police addressing drug and crime problems in the Central District in more typical fashion.

The CAC also advocated different kinds of patrol. Some community leaders felt that bicycle or horse patrol would allow officers to see what was going on better, to be more connected to the community and to be able to respond to problems quicker. Some also encouraged a closer look at taxis in the area that some residents believed were shuttling drug buyers into the Central District. The SPD responded favorably to these requests and had CPT officers on bike patrol and encouraged patrol officers to keep a closer eye on taxis that might be bringing drug buyers to the area.[93]

Weeding activities also included developing programs to educate young people about the police, promote police as role models and connect youth and police officers. From October through December 1994, for example, the Community Police Team and Crime Prevention staff produced a video entitled, "Seattle Youth Involvement Network video" which instructs young people in appropriate interactions with police officers. They also produced a pamphlet entitled, "What to do when stopped by a police officer," to promote interactions between youth and police that would not escalate to violence.[94] CPT officers also developed the Explorers program that coordinated with the local Boys and Girls Club to provide young people in the Central District with opportunities to get out of the city and explore the environs that they might not otherwise have. CPT officers also routinely engage in "Knock and Talks" where they approach citizens in their homes to tell them of illegal activities and police operations in the neighborhood.

Collaborative efforts with other agencies included working with the Seattle Engineering Department to implement clean-up programs, with Harborview Medical Center Mental Health and other area hospitals to inform low-income senior citizens about crime problems in the area; with the Department of Licensing to address the use of fraudulent licenses; with the Department of Transportation and other SPD precincts to clean-up illegal encampments of transients; with Metro, the local transit authority, to remove benches and walls from bus shelters to make drug loitering less likely; and with the Liquor Control Board about local taverns and liquor stores that may be violating the law.[95]

Table 4.4 compares the different types of weeding activities during the first three years of operation. This is not an exhaustive list; in the course of regular CPT or emphasis patrolling, police engage in other activities and collaboration has likely occurred with other city agencies as well. But the table does illustrate how the bulk of police activities seem to be typical police approaches to gang and drug problems. The community-initiated activity pales in comparison. However, relative to the original Justice Department goals and to the SPD's original program plan for Seattle, community leaders at least have a place at the table.

No data on criminal prosecutions of arrests in the target area were collected, thus it is difficult to know how these cases were processed. A national evaluation that included Seattle noted that "all arrests were handled in state courts," but it is not clear how that can be known for certain, given that no data are available.[96] The interviews with law enforcement agents indicated that weed arrests were treated just like any other arrest for similar crimes in other parts of the city. This contradicts the original goals of weeding, which were to bring the whole array of federal, state and local law enforcement to bear on the gang, drug and violent crime problems. However, as the data cited above illustrate, much of the weeding activity consisted of extensive patrols that are likely to result in arrests for less serious crimes, rather than major drug dealing or violent crime.

Table 4.4   Summary of Police Collaboration on Weeding Activities, Central District, 1993-1995[97]

Typical police activities	City collaboration	Community-initiated
Emphasis patrols	Seattle Engineering Department	Additional bike and foot patrols
CPT patrols including premise checks, FIRS	Harborview Medical Center Mental Health	Reverse stings
Explorer Program	Department of Licensing	Attentiveness to taxis driving drug buyers into the area
Video and pamphlet	Department of Transportation	
Adopt-a-family	Metro	
Knock-and-Talks	Liquor Control Board	
Foot patrols	Department of Revenue	

Murals

Source: Seattle Police Department Quarterly Reports 1993-1995; Participant Observation at CAC meetings 1998.

While reverse stings have their role in empowering the community and, perhaps, reducing the numbers of people driving through the Central District to buy drugs, they are clearly not the preferred approach for law enforcement. The more conventional police methods – buy-busts, emphasis patrols, execution of arrest warrants, and FIRs – are a much more visible and speedy way of 'weeding' drug and gang activity from the area. The question for the community is whether such activities are more effective than the reverse stings; if not, a more balanced approach might provide the community with greater confidence in the police and less incidence of negative police-community interaction. Those involved in the CAC or the local community councils generally speak favorably about policing activities in the area, though it is clear that the reverse stings were most popular.

A recent evaluation of Seattle's original Weed and Seed site offers one area of contention worth noting. Teens who were surveyed in the target area claimed that, while criminal activity seemed to be down, police presence and harassment had increased.[98] Some of the CAC members interpreted this as a selection problem; those teens that were interviewed were 'loiterers' and not necessarily representative of the teens in the neighborhood and the evaluation team reported this as an education problem, rather than a police problem (that is, the teens needed more education about what Weed and Seed entailed and what the police were up to). It is quite possible that information about actual changes in police activity in the area have not trickled down to young people who are perhaps more likely to be suspicious and less likely to believe that something new is afoot. Crystal Parker noted that her son, a teenager, does not worry about being stopped by the police in his neighborhood (the East precinct) because he knows the police; the community police team officers come to his high school basketball games.[99]

Other evidence is more difficult to sort through. The emphasis patrols that took place as part of the weeding strategy involved extensive Field Interview Reports (FIRs), which involve stopping and questioning persons 'of suspicion.' And the survey of area residents conducted for the evaluations do not offer much evidence one way or the other for how people feel about police responsiveness. Thus, the teen perspective finding remains important; while the reverse stings were a victory for the CAC, weeding activities still involve routine police practices that run the risk of producing interactions with young people that community leaders were concerned about in the early stages of implementation.

Influence of the CAC on Seeding

While the Citizens' Advisory Council members accepted that weeding is a necessary part of the process, their approach toward seeding was to try to make such practices unnecessary by dealing with what they see as the root causes of criminal activity. Their primary role has been to determine which organizations would receive the seed money. The CAC sent out 207 RFPs,

20 agencies attended the bidders conference and 22 proposals were submitted for funding.[100] The Seed coordinator and the CAC agreed that money should be for enhancement of existing programs, rather than start-up costs for new programs. The committee wanted to ensure that programs would not start and then have to fold when funding was no longer available.[101] Thus, the initial funding went to already existing organizations, some of which proposed to use the money for new projects. The decision-making process consists of a sub-committee that reviewed all proposals for funding and made recommendations to the whole committee. The committee then voted on which programs it will fund. Some of the groups that requested funding were small, community organizations that were unaccustomed to writing grant proposals. Derek Richards an African-American who represented the Boys and Girls club on the CAC, and Stephanie Yarez, an Hispanic female who represented a social service agency, stated that the committee worked with various organizations to help them with this process and to get their proposals to a place that the committee felt was appropriate for funding.[102]

Seeding efforts emphasized youth programs in existing organizations that were located in the target area. The most recent evaluation of the Seattle site (and seven other sites) notes that some of Seattle's seed programs have only a tangential relationship to crime prevention.[103] Given the concerns about unnecessary intervention into youth's lives and the fact that the CAC made most of the funding decisions, this is not surprising. The seeding efforts were on community development in a broad sense, rather than a narrow focus on crime prevention as the language in the federal policing initiative suggested. The two programs funded by the Advisory Committee that have the most consistent and long-term funding are a job training program at Seattle Vocational Institute that targets adults in need of retraining to move off welfare rolls or out of part-time, low-paying positions, and a teen health clinic associated with a local high school. The Seattle Vocational Institute representative noted that while most crime prevention programs focus on at-risk youths, the CAC recognized that if the youth have no role models for regular, meaningful employment, the programs may be lost on them.[104] Table 4.5 illustrates the funding breakdown for seed monies from 1993-1998.

Table 4.5   Seed Grants, Central District, 1993-1998

Program	Amount Allocated	Percent of Total
Job Readiness/Skills Programs	$550,149	39%
Multi-service programs for adults and youth[105]	224,435	16%
Daycare/after school programs	182,820	13%
Education	155,000	11%
Drug/Alcohol Education/Treat	135,722	9%
Neighborhood Enhancement	80,000	6%
Administrative Programs	48,150	3%
Business Development	40,000	3%
TOTAL	$1,416,276	100%

Source: CAC meeting minutes; Dept. of Health and Human Services Seed reports.

In contrast to the evaluation of other sites, where social service programs involving prevention and intervention activities were the primary focus – typically drug and alcohol programs, health and nutrition services, personal and family development – (see Roehl 1996), Seattle concentrated its resources on job programs for youth and adults, providing multiple services such as enhancement of education or literacy skills, daycare and after school activities for children and educational programs to enhance the math and science skills of young people in the area. Because the CAC had direct responsibility for dispensing funds for seeding, this aspect of the program reflected deep concern about educational and employment opportunities for youth, health care accessibility and adult job readiness.

Seattle's Weed and Seed program has focused little on physical and economic development of the area. This is possibly because a good deal of development of this kind was already occurring in the area prior to the Central Area's designation as a Weed and Seed site. More importantly, the CAC has had few funds to work with (none of the programs funded by the CAC received more than $50,000) and the grant solicitation process resulted in social programs more than economic development or physical restoration programs.

In 1994, the Washington Insurance Council (WIC), a nonprofit consumer education and media relations organization representing insurance agencies in Washington State, developed the Seattle Neighborhood Action Program (SNAP), "a public-private partnership working to reduce crime and improve the quality of life in a neighborhood having significant challenges with crime and urban decay."[106] The city encouraged WIC to focus on the Weed and Seed areas and a $100,00 grant was awarded to the Jackson Place Community Council to:

- decrease crime
- improve the appearance of the neighborhood
- decrease non-resident auto traffic and increase foot traffic
- increase level of resident participation in community activities
- improve the quality of life for community residents.

The SNAP grant provided funding for programs such as home anti-theft devices, community social events, tree planting and P-patches, litter clean-up, new street lighting and traffic circles.   A board member of the Jackson Place Community Council in the East Precinct which received the $100,000 WIC grant noted that "Allowing us to use money to help ourselves, instead of funding professionals in a non-profit organization to do the work for us, is what made this grant unique...*it is frustrating and disheartening to have outsiders come into a community and tell residents what is best for them.*"[107]

After the first fiscal year, program funds continued for most of the programs funded in the first year. In subsequent years, funding was also provided for a variety of community development purposes including a farmer's market and neighborhood restoration projects, as well as a youth entrepreneurial training program and summer enrichment program. However, beginning in 1996, the Justice Department decided to fund each site at a lower rate in order to have the ability to fund more sites. As a result, fewer programs were funded in Seattle. In 1997-8, only four programs are being supported with Weed and Seed funds (Urban League Safe Havens, Girls, Inc., Garfield Teen Health Clinic and Midtown Commons Computer Training Project). Table 4.6 illustrates the changes in seed funding from 1993-1998. The 1994 and 1995 allocations do not correspond to declining funds because of underspent money in 1994, which was then allocated in 1995.

Clearly the enormous drop in funding has an impact on the programs that the CAC can fund and the low-level of funding seems at least partly responsible for the decline in attendance and interest in the program since its inception.

Table 4.6   Total Seed Funding in the Central District, 1993-1998

Year	Expenditures
1993-4	$492,412
1994-5	272,240
1995-6	416,749
1996-7	144,875
1997-8	90,000

Source: DHHS Seed Reports 1993-1998.

Expansion of the Target Area

In the 1994 Request for Proposals for funding continuation for Weed and Seed, the Justice Department required the original target areas to expand. Thus, in 1995, the original Weed and Seed area was expanded to include parts of the International District (ID), an area that is comprised largely of Asian-American immigrants and has a large array of countries and languages represented. Frank Daniels, the SPD grant writer, stated that the ID seemed like a logical expansion area since it is geographically connected to the original area (which is bounded on other sides by freeways and major thoroughfares) and because the SPD had been doing outreach with Asian community for some time and hoped that Weed and Seed might continue those efforts.[108]   In addition, Gary Chin, a Chinese-American member of an ID public safety committee, stated that community leaders in the International District were asking the SPD for more and better resources and Weed and Seed provided an opportunity to give community groups what they had been asking for without much difficulty.[109]

The ID community is made up of primarily Chinese, Japanese and Southeast Asian immigrants. Approximately 80% of the area is elderly and as a result, much of the focus is on securing housing and services for that group and ensuring public safety in the area. Gary Chin, who had served on the committees examining police-minority relations and who worked at the time with the area's Preservation and Development Association (PDA), as well as Christina Mao were invited to participate in the CAC. Both indicated that none of the concerns about the program that existed in the Central Area were present in the ID.[110]   There were several reasons for this. First, because the area housed primarily older residents, the crime problem was seen as one of outsiders coming into the area and making trouble, rather than one of young people living in the area. Activists in the

ID working with community development groups did not have the same concerns about 'their' youth being harassed by the police.[111] In fact, the PDA had been working with the West Precinct to get more policing in the area for some time. Second, the area had two long-standing community police team officers who were well liked and seen as a great contribution to the neighborhood. To the extent that Weed and Seed promised more of the same, the program was applauded. And third, the primary problems in the area had less to do with gangs than car prowls, thefts and public drunkenness. Thus, when the police approached community leaders and asked if they wanted more police walking a beat and additional patrols on weekends, they jumped at the chance. Community organizations in the area were anxious to have a greater police presence in the area to deal with those problems.[112]

Despite their on-going relationship with the SPD, however, the ID involvement in the CAC has been minimal. There are a number of reasons for this. First, as mentioned above, the original target area had more flagrant gang and drug activity than the ID. As a result, there were easier target spots and more for the community to complain to the police about. Second, the mandate of the CAC for seeding activities, which focused on youth, was established before the ID was part of the area. The ID's population is an aging one and, as such, it has only a few youth programs. Thus, there were few organizations that had appropriate programs to apply for funding. Only one ID program, a summer after-school project, received CAC funding.[113] Equally as important, the ID had been working with the Local Initiative Support Corporation, a private funding organization that provides support for community initiatives in urban areas, to develop the Community Action Partnership, which had some of the same coordination and community involvement principles as Weed and Seed. In fact, because CAP was almost entirely community-initiated, the community and coordination aspects functioned far more equitably than Weed and Seed initially proposed.

Third, the ethnic composition of the ID makes mobilizing that community difficult. There are over a dozen languages represented and many residents speak little English. Coupled with the aging population, this meant that few residents were in a position to advocate for particular services or programs. Fourth, the ID is in the west precinct of the Seattle Police Department, not the East, which contains the original target area. Thus, the police who were familiar with the program and had adapted to working with community members were not the same as those who would be working with the ID community. In addition, the ID had only one representative, which made lobbying the community for greater participation difficult.

Finally, and most importantly, the history of racial tension between the police and residents of the CD was a major factor in mobilizing the residents of that area against Weed and Seed. As this chapter has demonstrated, it was that opposition which brought many residents of the area into the program and got them involved in its implementation. No such controversy existed in the ID. In fact, the ID had a community team working with them for a number of years and those officers were appreciated by many in the community. Without the controversy to spark interest in the program, there was less community awareness of and involvement in the program.

Community Groups: Crime-focused vs. Development-focused

The Seattle case of Weed and Seed illustrates a more complex version of crime prevention than the one put forth by the Justice Department in the original program goals and one that is closer to the community-centered model of crime prevention. This discussion raises an important distinction between the three models of community-crime prevention discussed in the previous chapter. The opportunity-reduction model and the order-maintenance models are presented here as problematic for the community because they are police-centered crime prevention programs. Police-centered programs provide for citizen involvement in law enforcement that simultaneously legitimates existing crime control practices and allows the state to retain control over the direction of law enforcement and community development. It is centered on police activities and, though it encourages community responsibility for crime control, it does so primarily through community-assistance such as identifying trouble spots and informing police of criminal activity and criminal individuals. It does not provide substantial (if any) resources to the community with the power to control how those resources are utilized. This approach to crime control can redistribute responsibility for crime control to community organizations without challenging the basic assumptions of policing those communities. Finally, a police-centric crime prevention strategy emphasizes fear reduction through police visibility and contact with dominant voices in the community. As a result, it is appealing to national policy-makers and local law enforcement because it does not involve costly social programs and because it provides further authority to existing law enforcement agencies.

By contrast, a community-centered approach to crime control challenges existing police practices and advocates for departure from typical police activities. It sees crime *and* policing as problematic. It keeps the focus on state agencies to provide resources for community development but gives primary control over those resources to community members. In addition to the availability of these resources for the community to direct in the manner that it deems appropriate for crime prevention, community members also have a voice in the type of policing practices that take place in their neighborhoods. It demands that fear of police harassment be taken as seriously as fear of crime. Finally, a community-centered approach to crime control emphasizes community development independent of police activity and, as such, is much more likely to take seriously the needs of people living in conditions of poverty and social disorganization for greater inclusion in the economic, educational and social mainstream. As a result, it is likely to pose a serious challenge to national policy-making because it refocuses attention of root causes of crime.

Clearly, the original controversy over the program was aimed at creating a more community-centered strategy. The Coalition to Stop Weed and Seed and Mothers Against Police Harassment were *development-focused* organizations that saw Weed and Seed as diverting attention away from other concerns and as a means by which to increase aggressive police tactics in the Central Area. They objected to the emphasis on policing and advocated for greater funding for seeding and more meaningful economic development programs. The net result of the publicity that the Coalition generated about the problems with Weed and Seed was that it provided an opportunity for the community-centered crime prevention perspective to emerge and be folded into the implementation process. Table 4.7 notes the community-centered components of the program that stemmed from the controversy and community involvement.

The actual implementation of the program, however, diluted some of the Coalition's goals for several reasons. First, the most active community organizations – those that were originally approached by the police department – were more police-focused than those that actively opposed the program. The Garfield Community Council, Spruce Park Community Council and Central Neighborhood Association had all been actively courting police to spend more time and energy in their neighborhoods. While it is not wholly accurate to call these groups police-focused because they too had broader concerns about development and questionable police tactics, they were certainly more willing to accede to police discretion than most members of the Coalition to Stop Weed and Seed. They were more comfortable with greater police presence and were willing to allow police to serve as a central figure in crime prevention strategies.

Table 4.7   Components of Crime Prevention in Seattle's Weed and Seed Program

	Original Proposal Goals	Actual Implementation
Central Problems	Violent/gang/drug crime Insufficient social services	Education, employment opportunities, health care. Police power with insufficient accountability
Role of Police	Central and controlling	Dominant, but one aspect of many
Community Participation	Low	Moderate

Second, the most vocal opponents of the program did not participate in its implementation. This is in part because the privilege of voting membership for community groups on the CAC was restricted primarily to community councils but also because those most actively opposed to the program did not wish to participate in the program once the program had been redesigned. The local NAACP, which had been part of the Coalition to Stop Weed and Seed, was invited to participate on the CAC but sent a letter to the committee in April of 1993 declining the opportunity because the controversy had served to quell the organization's primary concerns about the program.[114]

Finally, the SPD was the grant recipient which meant that SPD agents – either police officers or civilians from the grants and contracts division – were necessarily involved in the implementation process and, therefore, in CAC meetings. While CAC meetings were open to the public and early meetings were filled with residents who expressed concerns ranging from problems with drug activity to the problem of few job opportunities for youth, groups that were downright antagonistic to police presence were unlikely to feel welcome at CAC meetings.

Despite the greater police-focus of some of the community groups involved in implementation, the controversy nonetheless provided an opportunity for community councils with less clout with the SPD – such as Judkins Rejected and Yesler Terrace – to air their views during the implementation process. Furthermore, the CAC's actions still, to some degree, challenged police authority (through reverse stings, primarily) and emphasized community development concerns such as education and employment. Recall that it was the Garfield Community Council – a group more sympathetic to police – that advocated most strongly for the reverse sting operations.

As Scheingold (1991) predicts, local level policy must respond more directly to the concerns of citizens. As a result, a policy such as Weed and Seed, that deliberately gives community residents a voice in crime control, may result in residents driving policy more than originally intended. In Seattle, this has taken the form of pressure on the police department to respond to crime and drug activity without undermining families and community trust of the police by engaging in seemingly wanton and indiscriminate arrests of area residents.

The Limitations of Community Empowerment in the Central Area

Though this chapter has highlighted the ways in which the community leaders in the Central Area were able to alter Weed and Seed's goals and implementation, there are several reasons to believe that the Seattle Police Department still controls the vast majority of the program. When conflicts arise, the power of the police department to maintain control appears to be formidable. For example, because the SPD is the grant recipient and the seed funding is administered through DHHS, the weed and seed coordinators have access to a great deal of information that community residents do not. When conferences or training sessions take place, the weed and seed coordinators are in the best position to know about them, inform a select group of people, and leave out whom they please.

This is illustrated in the next chapter by the feeling on the part of Southeast Seattle community leaders that the Central Area program was too controlled by the weed and seed coordinators and that the Southeast's version of the program was taking a backseat to the original site which has recently come into the national spotlight as a model Weed and Seed site. Several members of the SECAC recounted stories of having to ask repeatedly for information about conferences, funding availability and other resource aids that were coming from the Executive Office for Weed and Seed (EOWS) in Washington, D.C.

In the short-term, community leaders in the Central Area seem to have altered the original program goals of Weed and Seed considerably and many appear to be satisfied with the direction of the program.

Community involvement has taken place to the extent that residents have been able to participate, have their concerns heard by police officers and administrators and be recognized as an important part of the implementation process. With respect to actual *control* over the program, the CAC has been able to control the direction of seeding much more than weeding, though a few weeding programs did attempt to shift the balance of power away from an emphasis on young, black street drug dealing and towards the affluent whites who purchase drugs in the area.   Seeding funding has focused on education and employment but the limited funds makes any redistribution of economic power nearly impossible.

Whether the CAC can continue to exercise influence over Weed and Seed program goals is a more difficult question. Certainly the long-term prospects are not promising. The weed and seed coordinators continue to have a strong presence at every meeting and even active community members on the CAC acknowledge that since many of the visible crime problems have lessened and the CAC has control of the seeding funds, it is difficult to keep residents involved. Sean Jeffries noted that: "It used to be standing room only; now it seems like all we can do just to get a quorum."[115]   Joel Handler suggests that "there are strong tendency on the part of the less powerful to defer to the professionals. Participation on the part of the dependent person is difficult, often anxiety-producing, and sometimes time-consuming" (Handler 1996; 167).   This appears to be the case with residents in the Central Area, and Weed and Seed has not done much to help sustain community strength and power in relation to the SPD and DHHS. If a vacuum of community leadership exists, certainly bureaucratic agencies such as the police and social service agencies will quickly fill it. There is reason to believe that this is already occurring as the weed and seed coordinators bring information about upcoming conferences, grant opportunities and other funding sources to the CAC and make recommendations for how to proceed. The current CAC seems more willing to go along with these recommendations than earlier incarnations of the group, perhaps in part because serious crime problems in the area have diminished and there is a great deal of development and economic activity (most of which is not generated by Weed and Seed).

In addition, groups that did not get in on the ground level and challenge the program are likely to have difficult penetrating the happy contingent of community leaders, city, state and federal representatives who populate CAC meetings. At a meeting of the CAC in November 1998, a new participant identified herself as the new representative from the Yesler Terrace Community Council and asked questions about how weed and seed services are concentrated, who is eligible to apply for funding and for a summary of funding information from previous years. She also asked whether the CAC has written rules, how it does meeting minutes and which community council representatives are welcome.

To complicate matters, the old representative from the Yesler Terrace Community Council, who was not in attendance at the meeting, was then serving as the Vice-chair of the CAC and had made emotional public pleas for weeding and seeding activities, offering heartfelt thanks to the SPD for their efforts. The CAC members present at the meeting were not terribly sympathetic to the questions being thrown about by this new participant. In fact, the weed coordinator, the SPD lieutenant, fielded most of the questions and informed the participant that the politics of community councils is none of his business and that she was welcome to attend the meetings and they would do their best to answer their questions (if she put them in writing) but that the current Yesler Terrace representative would remain the Vice-Chair until her term expired.

Lt. Bailey later indicated that he does not allow his officers to get involved in community politics and that he did not want to become embroiled in a controversy about who best represented Yesler Terrace.[116] In this case, however, that was a convenient position to take because it meant that he continued to work with the representative who was sympathetic to the status quo and did not have to answer all the questions about how decisions were made and who was represented.

In his rich analysis of community policing in Seattle, Lyons' notes that a key component of any community-based crime prevention strategy is the development and maintenance of active, social relations with strong social capital which promote reciprocity between community groups and state agents (Lyons 1999, see chapter two). It seems unlikely that Weed and Seed can promote such relations if it encourages police and other city agents to respond primarily to those organizations which are, as Lyons notes, "afraid of crime and disorder, powerful enough to be heard, *and* cooperative" (Lyons 1995, 385).

Again, Handler is instructive. Powerful groups – in this case the SPD and DHHS – must have a stake in the involvement of grassroots organizations (Handler 1996). Otherwise the incentives to continue to promote cooperation will be minimal. In this case, the SPD and DHHS (particularly the SPD), which had a high stake in the community not reacting with vitriolic anger and frustration as it did initially, had little stake in the community playing a serious role in the actual implementation of Weed and Seed. Support from the community is certainly needed given the original controversy and the revised mandates of the Justice Department, which call for evidence that the community is involved, but meaningful participation, which provides community members with real control over resources and implementation, is not a necessary component of the program for either the SPD or DHHS.

The next chapter provides an opportunity to see how a more aggressive community is able to control the process and to assess the long-term prospects for success. It investigates the second target area in Seattle and builds upon the community-centered perspective by illustrating how residents in the second target area have taken further control over the program, emphasizing community development and directing weeding activities. It also explores some of the potential limitations of the community's ability to control the direction of the program.

Notes

[1]   See Central Seattle Community Council memoranda, May 13, 1971 (Manuscripts and Archives, University of Washington). Jackson Street runs east west almost the entire width of the city and the area that the Jackson Street Community Council was concerned with included a steep grade. A similarly steep road just several blocks to the south, Yesler Street, was the original 'skid road,' named for the process of skidding the logs down the hill to the mill.

[2]   "Power to the 'little' people," *Seattle Times*, January 18, 1971.

[3]   Central Seattle Community Council, memorandum. May 13, 1971 (Manuscripts and Archives, University of Washington).

[4]   "Pulling Your Weight: And Keeping the Neighborhood in Good Condition," memo by Junius Rochester, Central Seattle Community Council, October 20, 1970.

[5]   Letter from Central Seattle Community Council to Arthur Lamphere, Chair City Council Planning Committee. November 18, 1970. (Manuscripts and Archives, University of Washington).

[6]   The survey consisted of 1141 household interviews conducted by a team of survey collectors who went door to door to ask individual residents of the area for responses. Oddly, the study does not break down the respondents by race. However, the report is clearly focused on issues of concern to the black community in the Central Area and, given the large percentage of blacks in that area, one can assume that a substantial portion of respondents are black.

[7]   Central Seattle Community Council Federation. July 1975. *Redlining and Disinvestment in Central Seattle: how the banks are destroying our neighborhood*, p. 2.

[8]   "Councilman Says Crime, Not Curfew, is a Grave Problem," *Seattle Times*, September 5, 1986.

9   "Suggested drug, prostitution weapons: baseball bat." Seattle Times, July 13, 1986.

10   "Losing the War on Drugs: Complaints up as residents say police aren't doing their job," *Seattle Times*. April 26, 1987.

11   "Central Neighborhood Girds to Fight Drugs, Gangs," Seattle Times. December 12, 1988; "Vigils Against Drugs Nominated for Award," *Seattle Times*, May 8, 1990.

12   "New Group plans a block party." Seattle Times, September 28, 1989.

13   "Murdered Youths: perceptions must change." Seattle Times, September 4, 1991.

14   The Judkins Rejected Community Council was originally named because residents of the area felt that they had been neglected (rejected) by the city when the federal government handed out substantial urban renewal grants in the 1970s. At the Western Regional Weed and Seed Conference in Seattle in April 1999, one of the founders of the council told me that residents felt that affluent, white neighborhoods were given the benefit of federal funding while poorer, black neighborhoods were overlooked. Under pressure from the city, which pointed out all of the recent funding and support the area has received, the Council recently dropped the word "rejected" from its name. The founding member I spoke with said that she and one other old-timer were the only two to vote against the decision.

15   "Central Area gets chance to speak out: city invites residents to a day long summit." Seattle Times, October 24, 1991; see also Central Seattle Community Council Federation. July 1975. *Redlining and Disinvestment in Central Seattle: how the banks are destroying our neighborhood.*

16   "Following the dream: Central District's developing racial mix raises new issues for residents." Seattle Times, January 18, 1987.

17   In the copy of these guidelines that made its way into the hands of the CSCC, someone had circled the word "ambitious" and written "ambiguous?" beside it, possibly reflecting concern that the crime prevention councils would undertake activities that were of questionable legality. City Council of Seattle, Suggested Guidelines for Establishing a Crime Prevention Council. April 3, 1969. Central Seattle Community Council (Manuscripts and Archives, University of Washington).

18   Seattle Crime Prevention Advisory Commission Guidelines, April 30, 1969. (Manuscripts and Archives, University of Washington).

19   Letter to Mayor Braman from Edward H. Banks, President of Central Seattle Community Council, January 16, 1969 (Manuscripts and Archives, University of Washington).

20   Personal notes of Edward H. Banks. "Notes on my testimony to city council re: crime prevention councils." Central Seattle Community Council (Manuscripts and Archives, University of Washington).

21   Personal notes of Edward H. Banks, italics added.

22   Letter to Alfred Schweppe from Ruth Brandwein, June 25, 1969. Central Seattle Community Council (Manuscripts and Archives, University of Washington).

23   Letter to Ruth Brandwein from Alfred Schweppe, June 26, 1969. (Manuscripts and Archives, University of Washington).

24   Seattle Times, June 18, 1970.

25   Interview 1: January 10, 1998; Interview 11: May 1, 1997.

26   Interviews 17 and 18: November 11, 1998.

27   "Honkies Invade the Central District," *The Stranger*.

28   Interview 26: April 1, 1999.

29   Interview 26: April 1, 1999.

30   "Officers capture Yesler Terrace Spirit," Seattle Times, December 14, 1989.

31   "Black leaders quibble with mural project," Seattle Times, June 19, 1989; also discussions at Western Regional Weed and Seed conference, Seattle, WA, May 4-6, 1999.

32   *Proposal for Department of Justice Operation Weed and Seed: Reclaiming America's Neighborhoods.* Planning Section, Inspectional Services Division, Seattle Police Department. March 20, 1992.

33   Proposal for Weed and Seed, March 20, 1992.

34   Most recently, the south Seattle precinct of the Seattle Police Department has applied for and received its own Weed and Seed funding. The police and residents of the area argued that criminal populations in the Central Area were displaced and moved south, causing crime in the southeast part of Seattle to rise. Thus, Seattle has two Weed and Seed sites, the first consisting of the Central Area and International District and the second consisting of a portion of Southeast Seattle, largely the corridor along Rainier Avenue, a wide five-lane street that runs from just east of downtown straight through the southeastern part of the city and is a popular area for drug activity. This second site will be the subject of the next chapter.

35   *Proposal for Department of Justice Operation Weed and Seed: Reclaiming America's Neighborhoods.* Planning Section, Inspectional Services Division, Seattle Police Department. March 20, 1992, emphasis added.

36   Interview 19: March 1, 1997.

37   I use the term community leaders here to make it clear that my interviews and archival research on this controversy involved primarily those who led the opposition to Weed and Seed and those who subsequently became involved in the program implementation through their community councils. However, the vast majority of these individuals are not people with long histories of community organizing or with citywide political ties and/or influence. They are, by and large, long-time residents of the communities they represent, involved in small, organic neighborhood groups such as community councils, and unconnected to broader political organizations. It is possible, however, that people who become involved in community organizations have substantively different perspectives on crime issues than those who do not get involved. This story, then, could misrepresent residents' views by focusing on people who voluntarily become involved in community organizations. A serious problem would arise if the respondents cited here were more contentious and less willing to work with the city and police than the area's residents as a whole. That nearly all of the respondents ended up working with the police and city agents to implement Weed and Seed suggests that they are probably not *less* willing to work with police than other area residents. Similarly, that so many accounts of the controversy cited community meetings and general opposition by residents of the Central District suggests that the opposition ran deep. Nonetheless, the interview data and participant observations present a limited perspective; further research is required to obtain a substantial household survey that identifies individual perspectives.

38 *Proposal for Department of Justice Operation Weed and Seed: Reclaiming America's Neighborhoods.* Planning Section, Inspectional Services Division, Seattle Police Department. March 20, 1992.

39 *Proposal for Department of Justice Operation Weed and Seed: Reclaiming America's Neighborhoods.* Planning Section, Inspectional Services Division, Seattle Police Department. March 20, 1992.

40 Interview 1: January 10, 1998.

41 Interview 1: January 10, 1998.

42 Interview 23: March 29, 1999.

43 Letter to Dan Fleissner, Seattle Police Department from Mark Peterson, Pratt Park Community Council. March 9, 1992. Emphasis added.

44 Letter to Dan Fleissner, Seattle Police Department from Mark Peterson, Pratt Park Community Council. March 9, 1992.

45 Interview 1: January 10, 1999.

46 Interviews 1: 1/10/98; 3: 1/30/98; 6: 3/4/98; 10: 1/28/98; 11: 5/1/97; 15: 9/9/98; 17: 11/11/98; 18: 11/11/98; 20: 2/2/99: 21: 11/18/98; 23: 3/29/99; 24: 4/7/99; Seattle wins grant for Weed and Seed program." *Seattle Times*, April 6, 1992; "Federal Grant still drawing protesters." *Seattle Times*, May 25, 1992; "Rice Hits Weed and Seed," *Seattle Times*, July 1, 1992; "Fake Front Page Attached to P-I." *Seattle Times*, July 1, 1992. See also Lyons, 1999.

47 Coalition to Oppose Weed and Seed pamphlet.

48 Interview 5: May 15, 1998; Interview 17: November 11, 1998.

49 Interview 17 and 18: November 11, 1998; Interview 5: May 15, 1998.

50 Letter to Mayor Rice from Beatrice Jenkins and Wilma Harrison, Co-chairs, Coalition to Oppose Weed and Seed, August 12, 1992. (Referred to hereafter as Letter to Norm Rice, August 1992).

51 "Weed and Seed: a problem or a solution?" *Seattle Times*, April 14 ,1992.

52 "Rice Hits Weed and Seed." *Seattle Times*, July 1, 1992.

53 Letter to Mayor Rice, August 12, 1992.

54 The Black Panther Party was fairly active in Seattle during the 1960s and 70s and some residents of the area still remember the breakfasts they would serve to school children. The violent confrontations around the nation between the Panthers and the FBI were in the not-too-distant memory of some Central District residents. (Interview with Crystal Parker, January 30, 1998). See also Taylor 1994).

55 "Fake Front Page Attached to P-I." *Seattle Times*, July 1, 1992.

56 Interview 17: November 11, 1998.

57 Interview 17: November 11, 1998.

58 Interview 18: November 11, 1998.

59 "Fake Front Page Attached to P-I." *Seattle Times*, July 1, 1992. No one in the Coalition would say who was responsible for this.

60 Interview 18: November 11, 1998.

61 "The Empire Turns Within." American Studies Association roundtable discussion with Reverend Jeffries, Prof. Bill Lyons, Assistant Chief Harv Ferguson (SPD) and Lisa L. Miller. November 20, 1998. Seattle, WA.

62 "Weed, Seed Aid for Clinic rejected." *Seattle Times*, June 11, 1992.

63 "Department of Justice Operation "Weed and Seed" - Reclaiming America's neighborhoods." Executive Summary. Department of Justice.

64   "Gang Crackdown or harassment? Police sweep in park draws criticism." *Seattle Times*, April 25, 1991.

65   The particular controversy that prompted the creation of the panel was the renewal of a Drug Traffic Loitering Ordinance that gave police more discretion and authority to arrest loiterers who the police believed were engaging in drug activity.

66   While prior to the task force report the mayor had created a new police auditor position to improve civilian oversight of the SPD, there has been no action taken on the question of civilian review since this report came out.

67   Interview 1: January 10, 1997.

68   Interview 23: March 29, 1999.

69   Southeast Seattle Weed and Seed Planning Committee meeting, February 19, 1998. Also, Interview 4: March 5, 1998.

70   "Department of Justice Approves Weed and Seed." *Seattle Times*, March 16, 1992.

71   Interview 15: September 9, 1998.

72   Interview 27: April 7, 1999.

73   Interview 4: March 8, 1998.

74   Interview 25: April 8, 1999; Interview 15: September 9, 1998.

75   *Seattle's Weed and Seed Program Final Evaluation Report.* Gambrell Urban, Inc., July 1997, p. 12.

76   Interview 17: November 11, 1998.

77   Christina Mao, a member of the CAC from the International District, was working at the SPD when the proposal for Weed and Seed came through. She noted that many in the department lamented the name of the program and wondered, "just what those DOJ boys were smoking when they came up with that name." Interview 10: January 28, 1998.

78   Interview 5: May 15, 1998.

79   "Council and Critics OK Weed and Seed." Seattle Times, December 15, 1992.

80   Mothers Against Police Harassment became closely involved with the Seattle Police Department on reforming specific police tactics after a mentally ill man was killed by police as they tried to carry out an eviction. MAPH met with Police Chief Norm Stamper and strongly urged him to consider training police officers in crisis intervention techniques to avoid comparable situations in the future. As a result of this urging, the SPD trained several dozen officers in a crisis intervention program that had been successful in Portland, Oregon. Chief Stamper hopes to train all of his officers in crisis intervention. Recognizing that they had forged a relationship with the SPD that could continue in the future, MAPH changed its name to Mothers for Police Accountability.

81   Interview 17: November 11, 1998.

82   Mothers Against Police Harassment did not made an appearance at any of the Southeast Seattle Advisory Committee meetings during its first two years in existence.

83   *Seattle's Weed and Seed Program Final Evaluation Report.* Gambrell Urban, Inc., July 1997, p.6-7. (Referred to hereafter as Final Evaluation Report, July 1997).

84   Final Evaluation Report, July 1997, p. 17.

85   Citizen Advisory Committee meeting minutes, April 6, 1993.

86   Citizen Advisory Committee meeting minutes April 2, 1993 and May 14, 1993.

87 Interview 3: January 30, 1998. Also South Seattle Weed and Seed Planning Committee meeting, February 19, 1998.

88 Southeast Weed and Seed Planning Committee Meeting. February 19, 1998.

89 Interview 1: January 10, 1998 and Interview 6: March 4, 1998.

90 I have no hard data to suggest that the reverse stings had a positive impact on community relations with the police department, but the interviewees who mentioned it spoke about it positively, regarded it as a victory for the community and were pleased with the police for finally acquiescing to their demands. Also, the original weed coordinator, when asked if reverse stings really have any impact on the drug trade, noted that, while the operations may not have made much of a difference in the crime in the area, they were worth the effort and resources because of the empowerment that they offered the community.

91 Draft of National Evaluation of Weed and Seed, Final Impact Evaluation, Seattle case study. Abt and Associations, February 24, 1998.

92 Calculated by author using internal Seattle Police Department memos of Weed and Seed quarterly activity reports.

93 Interview 1: January 10, 1998; also Southeast Seattle Advisory Council Meeting, February 19, 1998.

94 Weed and Seed quarterly report, February 1, 1994.

95 Weed and Seed quarterly reports, February 1, 1994.

96 Draft of National Evaluation of Weed and Seed, Final Impact Evaluation, Seattle case study. Abt and Associations, February 24, 1998.

97 This table was compiled from Quarterly Weed reports internal to the SPD. It is not an exhaustive list of the weeding activities undertaken by the SPD since the program's inception; rather, it reflects the activities specifically recorded in the 1993-1995 reports.

98 The question was posed as: "Please check whether you think each issue is getting better than [sic], the same or worse in the Central Area...police harassment" - 12% responded better, 16% responded same and 72% responded worse. *Seattle's Weed and Seed Program Final Evaluation Report.* Gambrell Urban, Inc., July 1997.

99 Interview 3: January 30, 1998.

100 Citizen Advisory Committee Meeting Minutes

101 Interview 1: January 10, 1998.

102 Interview 2: February 24, 1998. Also Interview 9: March 6, 1998.

103 Draft of National Evaluation of Weed and Seed, Final Impact Evaluation, Seattle case study. Abt and Associations, February 24, 1998.

104 Interview 3: January 30, 1998.

105 Multi-service programs, such as Safe Havens at the Urban League, are programs that provide a variety of enrichment programs for youth and adults. In Seattle, this includes: employment workshops, GED preparatory classes, SAT classes, on-line financial aid information, homework assistance, parent education classes, family outings, support groups, family literacy service, health services, housing assistance, science fairs and social and recreational activities (Rolland 1997, 25).

106 *Seattle Neighborhood Action Plan, Final Evaluation*, Washington Insurance Council, March 1996.

107 *Seattle Neighborhood Action Plan, Final Evaluation*, Washington Insurance Council, March 1996.

108 Interview 19: March 1, 1997.

109   Interview 22: March 24, 1999.
110   Interview 10: January 28, 1998; Interview 22: March 24, 1999.
111   Interview 22: March 24, 1999.
112   Interview 22: March 24, 1999.
113   Interview 10: January 28, 1998.
114   Citizen Advisory Committee meeting minutes, April 2, 1993.
115   Interview 1: January 10, 1998.
116   Interview 21: November 18, 1998.

5 Striving for Control in the Rainier Valley

My concern, personally, is for the youth and to help them -- if they have dreams – to help develop those dreams. And those that don't, who feel that they can't achieve dreams, to show them or create a possibility, a way for them to have [dreams]. Because you know, a kid can get in trouble but if someone takes time with particular youths and really hears what they have to say and really show a genuine concern for them...if we could take [a youth who has been in trouble] under wing and help him turn his life around and then have a way of acknowledging him – that's the kind of stuff I'd like to see.

Edith Norton, Southeast Seattle Citizens' Advisory Committee.

When we think about crime prevention our automatic response is more police, blockwatches...[but] we really need to redefine for ourselves what crime prevention is. It includes prevention, community service, economic development, [holding] judges and prosecutors accountable, getting youth involved. This is really what Weed and Seed is all about...people who are involved in Weed and Seed know this - we need to keep redefining for ourselves what crime prevention is.

Captain, South Precinct Seattle Police Department.

While the protests of residents in the Central District were strong enough to alter the program's implementation on the local level and filter back some of their views to the national program, as noted in chapter four, Weed and Seed in the CD remains only partially community-controlled and still has the SPD at its core. This chapter suggests that the experiences of the Central District helped to create a foundation of community involvement that community leaders of the southeast target area have used to build an even more community-centered program that incorporates residents' perspectives in a fundamental way. The Southeast Citizen Advisory Committee has taken steps to untangle itself from the local governmental organizations to which Weed and Seed has been tethered since its inception, namely the Seattle Police Department and the Department of Housing and Human Services. As a result, the citizens of the area are striving to have a program that is under the direct control of community organizations and is implemented in a manner quite different from the original program goals. However, this disentanglement may come at a price: as the groups involved become more community-centered and push for greater community control, state agents,

125

particularly the police, resist this move and may make it difficult for the Citizens' Advisory Council to maintain control.

Southeast Seattle in Context[1]

In March of 1998, a new Weed and Seed site was established in Southeast Seattle. This target area is located in the Rainier Valley, which is home to a high percentage of the city's racial minorities, including blacks, Hispanics and a growing number of southeast Asian and Filipino immigrants. In 1990, the area was approximately one-third black (30%), one-third white (33%) and one-third Asian and Hispanic and other (36%) (Lyons 1999, 64).[2] Aptly named "the valley," the area is located between two hills, the affluent Mt. Baker area that overlooks Lake Washington, and Beacon Hill, a middle-class racially mixed area that runs parallel to Boeing field and Puget Sound.[3] Many residents in the Rainier Valley feel that city officials have long neglected the area because of its high percentage of African-Americans.[4] A recent series of events illustrates this point well.

Seattle is in the process of implementing a new Regional Transit Plan which will take 10 years to complete, and includes a 1.8 billion-dollar light rail system. Some areas will have underground transit while others will have elevated or ground level rail. When the transit committee held public hearings in the Rainier Valley to hear from residents, they get an earful about concerns that the Valley was once again being neglected: the current plan is to put the rail underground on Capital Hill, a predominantly white, affluent area and to have elevated or ground-level rail along Rainier Avenue. Residents of the area are concerned that a surface route would result in property loss and divisiveness among neighborhoods. The transit committee's response was to say that looking into an underground rail in that area would slow down the process and jeopardize funding for the whole project. Residents think the committee is simply "saving money on the south end, like usual."[5] In a second meeting in the Rainier Valley, residents expressed concern that the area was being neglected because of its racial composition and economic deprivation:

> We are less economically advantaged, we are minority, we are of color, we are elderly, we are poor and we know that our voices do not carry as much weight as voices on the North End. And we want to be heard.[6]

Save Our Valley, a group that describes itself as "a broad based community organization of Rainier Valley residents and business owners" has formed to mobilize residents in opposition to the transit plan. Residents of the South End, they argue, will get less service and pay a higher price in terms of displaced businesses and disrupted intersections. Table 5.1 illustrates these differences. While the reasons behind structuring the plan in this way are beyond the scope of this book, it is not difficult to see why residents of the area feel slighted. The same flier that included this table also noted the following, under the heading of Environmental Justice: "Under Presidential Executive Order 12898, all Federal Agencies must determine whether projects have a disproportionate distribution of high and adverse impacts on minority and low income populations."[7] The flier also said, "Sound Transit should not be allowed to build a train system down the middle of Martin Luther King Way at the expense of the poor or communities of color." Save Our Valley illustrates the on-going tensions between the Rainier Valley and the rest of the city.

Table 5.1   Impact of Sound Transit Plan on Rainier Valley as Compared to Rest of Seattle

Impact	Rest of Seattle	Rainier Valley	% of Adverse Impact
Miles of track	11.4 miles	4.6 miles	
Businesses lost or impacted (sic)	31	169	85 %
Single family homes lost or impacted (sic)	0	127	100 %
Multi-family units lost or impacted	12	48	80 %
Cross streets blocked	4	40	67 %
Proposed cost *per mile*	$129 million	$47 million	

Source: Sound Transit's Draft Environmental Impact Statement of 11/30/98 to U.S. Department of Transportation, Pages 4-28, S-16, S30-S44, in the *Save Our Valley flier*, January 1999.

In addition to issues like the transit plan, which bring to the fore concerns about the Valley receiving the short end of the economic and social development stick, residents have long felt that the police have neglected their concerns about crime. This feeling is not without justification. The South Seattle Crime Prevention Council had been in conflict with the SPD for many years about crime problems in that area. Sarah Malano, a white female who is a member of the Southeast Citizen Advisory Council and organized a neighborhood group to address drug trafficking, talked about witnessing a shooting in the new target area. When asked why it was not reported on the local news, she replied sarcastically, "You know, it's just another shooting in the valley."[8] Her statement reflects a sentiment among many residents that crime in the area is not taken seriously by the city. As a result of these feelings of neglect, area residents have strong ties to their community organizations and neighborhoods. Lyons' study of community policing in Seattle illustrates a vibrant, active community that sees itself continually battling for its share of resources and for the voices of its residents to be heard by the police and other city agencies (Lyons 1999).

Racial conflict is also a palpable part of life in the southeast. In addition to the feeling of some residents that the Rainier Valley is neglected because of its diverse racial composition, tensions between white and minority residents have existed for some time. Lyons' notes that the South Seattle Crime Prevention Council (SSCPC), which was originally formed to address a wide range of crime from a number of perspectives, has become far more responsive to the concerns of white homeowners and businesses than the less affluent members of the community who are often racial minorities. As the Valley has increased in diversity, this has only deepened the sense that the SSCPC is more responsive to whites than people of color.

Edith Norton is an African-American woman who served as the first chair of the SECAC. She has also worked with a number of grassroots organizations in the Rainier Valley, including the South Shore Community Council and Mothers Altogether Raising Our Sons. Norton worked for the SSCPC for a year and felt strongly that the organization, while having the appearance of diversity, is controlled largely by whites whose main interest is in gentrification and moving out businesses and groups they see as less desirable – namely lower-income people of color. "There are still a lot of racial issues in the valley," she noted. "Actually, it's certain groups that keep the community separated...the Rainier Chamber [of Commerce, a business development group] and the SSCPC have undercurrents of being racist groups."[9] She talked about her own experiences being involved with and working for the SSCPC and her discomfort with raising issues of about race.

I had gone to a meeting years back but I thought it was not the place for me to be because when I walked in the room there were all

Caucasians there and I thought it was not the place to bring any concerns for African-Americans. To a certain degree, I still feel that way about the Crime Prevention Council. They do certain things – I won't say [to] just African-Americans but I will [to] say people of color – there are some biases there.

She noted that the Regional Transit debate brought out some of these issues when an SSCPC board member stated that some of the businesses that objected to being displaced were unwelcome anyway. "I don't care about those little shops," she quoted the board member as saying, "those nail shops [small, family or individually owned businesses which provide hair, make-up and fingernail polishing services], they need to leave anyway."

As a result of some of these concerns, she and several members of another community council organized the South Seattle Community Council (later renamed South Shore Community Council to avoid confusion with the SSCPC) to address public safety and community development concerns with a more diverse group. They were particularly interested in identifying the concerns of residents and, to that end, conducted a survey of residents by setting up tables outside markets and libraries, talking to people at bus stops, and going door to door to talk to residents. Their surveys revealed that residents were highly concerned about public safety but were also interested in identifying more activities for youth and in broad economic development. In addition, they learned that young people felt intimidated and harassed by the police and that older youths were particularly upset at not having a place to congregate together independent of younger children and/or adults.[10]

The southeast of Seattle, then, has a long history of racial tension as well as community organizing, both of which are important for how Weed and Seed develops.

Weed and Seed in Southeast Seattle

Development of the Southeast Citizen Advisory Committee

In late 1997, Ginny Kramer, director of the Seattle Neighborhood Group, a city organization that helps communities respond to public safety and community development concerns, Captain Nicholas Metz, captain of the SPD South precinct, and members of the South Seattle Crime Prevention Council began talking about bringing Weed and Seed to south Seattle.[11] Captain Metz felt that many of the people who had been engaging in drug activity in the Central Area had now moved south, as a result of the activities of Weed and Seed in that area. He also had grown weary of repeatedly arresting the same people or having those people simply be replaced by another group; "just law enforcement isn't enough," he noted.[12] This group, working with officials from the police department, Department of Housing and Human Services, the Seattle Office of Education, and the Seattle/King County Health Department developed a Citizens' Planning Committee in order to select the new site and get community members involved. Police in the south precinct felt that Weed and Seed in the Central Area had displaced some crime to the south and were concerned about gang and drug activity being on the rise again.

The grant proposal stated that the controversy in the East Precinct taught police and city officials that "residents must be given meaningful decision-making and advisory responsibility about the scope of law enforcement and neighborhood assistance efforts, *and not be simply viewed as a "rubber stamp" of approval for programs that others devised.*"[13] Thus, the planning committee approached community groups in southeast Seattle, including boys and girls clubs, senior centers, religious institutions, community councils, crime prevention councils, educational organizations and a variety of small, neighborhood groups and asked them to sign a Memorandum of Understanding in support of Weed and Seed. In addition, the planning committee conducted meetings involving over 600 hundred people which were designed to allow community members to express concern and ask questions. A videotape was made to inform residents of the specifics of the program and to provide them with contacts in the police department and community. If community groups in the area supported the program, they were asked to sign a memorandum of understanding in support of bringing Weed and Seed to the southeast.

The Southeast Seattle grant proposal noted that the development of the Weed and Seed program in the Central Area "has created a growing awareness that the crime problem can be reversed and that neighborhood revitalization is possible." It also noted that police officers and some residents of the area believe that crime has been displaced south, away from the weeding activities of the Central Area and towards the south end of the city. Finally, it pointed to the "lessons learned" from the original target area and indicated that a "problem-solving approach with analysis of specific targets and input from the neighborhood residents has proved effective and will be strengthened with the establishment of the new Southeast Seattle Weed and Seed." Table 5.2 illustrates the organizations that signed MOUs for the southeast program.

Fourteen government agencies or social programs signed the MOUs compared with 24 community groups. Recall from chapter four that

19 government agencies and only three community groups signed MOUs in the grant proposal for the original Weed and Seed site in Seattle. While not all of the community organizations that signed MOUs have become active in the new site, the shift in emphasis is dramatic and a good indication of the strength of commitment to a community-based policy in the southeast. It is also important to note that many of the community organizations are small groups that target particular ethnic minorities for assistance and support.

As word spread about the program possibly coming to the southeast, members of the South Shore Community Council (then the South Seattle Community Council) expressed concern that the program might empower police to a greater degree than they wanted and might result in harassment of youth. However, the process of contacting community organizations and providing them with voting membership on the committee calmed some of those fears.[14] The Planning Committee organized the initial meetings of the Southeast Seattle Citizens' Advisory Committee (SECAC) in January 1998. Attendees included representatives from a variety of local organizations and agencies shown in Table 5.3.

In order to provide information about the program and its implementation in the original target area, the CAC's weed and seed coordinators also attended the meeting. The SECAC quickly established by-laws that provided for membership on the committee to be restricted to "representatives from the community, community councils, churches, neighborhood businesses, and agencies located within the designated Weed and Seed area."[15] Noting the need for effective community-wide coordination of services, the SECAC included service providers as non-voting members. The original voting members of the SECAC included representatives from the organizations listed above.

After reviewing the history of Weed and Seed in the original target area and the events leading up to the development of the program in the southeast, the Planning Committee turned the meeting over to the two co-chairs of the Southeast Citizens' Advisory Council. The co-chairs, both female, one black and one white, represented their community councils and had expressed an interest in chairing the committee and agreed to get the Advisory Council off the ground by serving as co-chairs. Edith Norton, an African-American, had a lot of reservations about Weed and Seed before becoming involved. She had heard about the controversy in the original target area and had reservations about working with the police department.

Table 5.2   Organizations and Agencies Signing MOUs for the Southeast Seattle Weed and Seed Program

Federal	City/County	Private	Community
U.S. Attorney for Western Washington	Seattle Police Department	Cederstand Apartments	Refuge Women's Alliance
DEA	DHHS	Homesight	Southeast Effective Development
ATF	SPD Civilian Crime Prevention Coordinators	Rainier Vista Boys and Girls Club	Vietnamese Senior Center
U.S. Customs Service	King County Drug Court	Quality Food Center	Residents (4)
FBI	Rainier Community Center	Washington Insurance Council	Columbia City Revitalization Committee
DOJ	South Shore Middle School		Holly Park Merchants' Assoc.
HUD	Franklin High School		Union Gospel Mission
			Kubota Garden Foundation
			Single Mothers Altogether Raising their Sons
			Southshore Parent, Teacher, Student Association
			Southeast Senior Center
			Genesee Merchants Association

Federal	City/County	Private	Community
			SE Community Council
			Columbia Pl. Revitalization Council
			Rainier Chamber of Commerce
			Brighton Neighborhood Council
			Afr-Am Advisory Council to Seattle Police
			Seattle Neighborhood Group
			SSCPC
			Jubilee Christian Center
			Vietnamese Friendship Association
			Vietnamese Resident Council of Holly Park
			Khmer Community of Seattle
			Southeast Arts Council

Source: "Proposal for Department of Justice Southeast Seattle Weed and Seed Program." City of Seattle and Office of the United States Attorney, Western Division of Washington; Division of Family and Youth Services, Seattle Housing and Human Services Division; Research and Grants Management, Seattle Police Department. December 1997.

But she was also determined to help change her neighborhood and after meeting with people involved in Weed and Seed, she concluded that the program could be beneficial to the community if the community genuinely had control. The captain of the south precinct assured the co-chairs that this is "your program" and that the Council would set the agenda for the program in the southeast.[16]

Table 5.3   Agencies and Organizations Represented on the SECAC

| Crime Prevention Councils | Community | | | Private |
	Orgs.	Centers	Councils	Development Business
SSCPC	South Seattle Pastors' Assoc.	Rainier	Holly Park	Genesee Merchants' Assoc.
		Rainier Beach	South Shore	Columbia City Revitalization Committee
			Brighton	Southeast Effective Development
			Rainier Vista	Rainier Chamber of Commerce

Source: Planning Committee Meeting, Southeast Seattle Weed and Seed, February 2, 1998.

At this first meeting to establish the Advisory Council in Southeast Seattle, members of the Freedom Socialist Party read a statement to the group expressing their opposition to the program based on fears of police abuses, opposition to the connecting of social service money with police presence in the community, and the belief that police-community relations would not improve until a Civilian Review Board was established. A Gay and Lesbian organization also expressed concerns about policing and law enforcement in the area and opposed the program on most of the same grounds that the original opponents argued.

These were the only voices of opposition during the development of the Advisory Council. The Planning Committee noted that there were no outright objections to Weed and Seed when they met with community groups and explained the role that the community would play. Edith Norton indicated that that the South Shore Community Council was the last group to sign the MOU because members were concerned that the program would be too top heavy with law enforcement and wanted to be certain, before signing on, whether the program would indeed be community-driven. With respect to any opposition that they program may have received, she noted:

> I'm not aware of anyone who is opposed on the south end but that's not to say that people aren't watching to see how we're doing and that's why we have to constantly keep an eye on the police, constantly remind the police that we are partners, that we are community driven...so that there isn't the perception that we are a police initiative.[17]

While only members of the SECAC are permitted to take part in voting, many more members of the community than just the voting members have frequently attended the meetings. In 1998, the voting membership consisted of 13 individuals. Across six meetings during a seven-month period between April and October 1998, the average attendance for meetings was 18, with a high of 25. At any given meeting, at least one voting member is usually absent; there is clearly interest in participating in the program even in the absence of voting membership.[18] Guests at the SECAC meetings include community police team officers, members of the CAC in the East Precinct, Gretchen King, the Law Enforcement Community Coordinator with the U.S. Attorney's Office and members of the community interested in the program.

The fact that the original Advisory Committee is comprised primarily of community councils, business/merchant groups, and crime prevention councils is worth exploring, given the comprehensiveness of the MOUs, the goals of the Planning Committee of including all ethnic groups in the valley, and the outreach that the committee did to many small organizations. When compared to the list of organizations that signed the MOUs, original voting members of the Advisory Committee included few of the small, grassroots organizations (in fact, only the South Seattle Pastors' Association would qualify as a small organization with a specific, narrow constituency). At that original meeting in January, the Planning Committee discussed ways to encourage some of those organizations to become involved in the program and it became clear that it would be difficult to incorporate small organizations that represented some of the more isolated ethnic groups, such as Vietnamese and Filipinos.

The level of commitment to bringing in these groups provides an important illustration of the desire of the SECAC to become ethnically diverse and representative of the valley as a whole. At a more recent meeting, representatives from the Jubilee Christian Center, which has a primarily southeast Asian constituency, were in attendance, as was a representative from the Filipino Youth Center, which was the recipient of a seed grant.

Program Plan

The SECAC's responsibilities are detailed in the proposal for funding:

> The SECAC, as proposed, will oversee the establishing of priority funding needs for the Seed programs and make decisions about which agencies are best qualified to provide the program or service. This committee will also be responsible for requesting periodic progress reports, and for a final assessment of the program's impact and effectiveness....The SECAC will also be responsible for identifying law enforcement targets that the Seattle Police and/or joint SPD/FBI operations will be expected to investigate and resolve. The Weed Coordinator is expected to be the primary contact for the coordination of such targets, and will serve as the liaison with federal law enforcement agencies if their participation is appropriate. The SECAC will also search for private sector funding for needed activities, and will prepare a plan to expand the Weed and Seed program initiatives throughout the area.[19]

The proposal also provided demographic information on the area and included charts which noted differences between the target area and the rest of the city on issues such as: leading cause of death; chronic disease mortality; leading cause of hospitalization; rate of communicable diseases (including sexually transmitted diseases); injuries and violence; mental health and substance abuse; environmental health; and maternal and child health.

Weeding activities focused primarily on the drug problem. The objectives included a reduction in street-level sales, especially to youth and more rapid and effective prosecution of offenders. Building on the perceived success of the reverse stings in the Central Area, the Southeast proposal included an effort to "structure 'sting' operations to interrupt the expected transient nature of drug buyers. Special attention will be paid to the residence of origin of the buyers."[20] Seeding activities were aimed at improving educational outcomes, health care, business development and transportation and to work with the Washington Insurance Council and the Local Initiative Support Coalition.

The community-policing component emphasized good working relationships between the SPD and the SECAC and a more cooperative approach to working with the neighborhood's youth. In June of 1998, the following goals were identified for the first phase of seeding:

- Reduce youth violence
- Reduce violent victimization of youth
- Reduce drug and alcohol crimes and related health problems
- Improve accessibility to health care
- Improve academic achievement
- Improve job availability for youth and families of the Weed and Seed areas.

It is worth noting that a resident survey of the southeast, which asked people about their concerns for the area, indicated that almost as many people identified jet/air traffic noise as a problem (19.9%) as identified violence as a problem (22.5%). This is particularly interesting given the Justice Department's original focus on gang and drug violence as the primary target of weeding and seeding activities. While the south precinct has justified its Weed and Seed program in terms of the increased criminal activity that has been displaced from the Central District, the residents appear equally as concerned about community development as violent crime.

Implementation and Community Control of Weed and Seed

Seeding

At the January 6, 1999 meeting of the SECAC, the grant recipients of seeding money were announced.[21] Two Safe Havens sites were identified.[22]

- *Filipino Community Center/Filipino Youth Empowerment Project*:
  The funding was provided for the "Youth and Family Support

Network" which is "designed to reach out to low income families and offer a comprehensive package of services to include youth sports tournaments, parenting classes, leadership skills development camps, academic counseling, youth mentoring, culturally appropriate classes on arts and crafts, dancing, ethnic games, and intergenerational activities with senior citizen population of the community."

- *Southeast Youth and Family Services*: "The program will provide community residents with a variety of educational, cultural, family support and recreational services, as well as linkages to mental health and employment services."

The rest of the seeding funding was allocated in the form of community support programs. Two programs were funded:

- *Seattle-King County Department of Public Health/Columbia Health Center*: "Youth Substance Abuse Outreach Program." This program is designed to provide primary care, substance abuse and youth intervention services.

- *Rainier Beach Community Center*: "Technology 2000 Video and Computer Program." This program is intended to provide at-risk youth with "opportunities to gain insight into the video and computer industry and develop skills they can use for growth. The youth will get hands on training in script writing, producing, set design, directing, camera use, editing and other skills related to this field. The youth will also gain proficiency on software applications such as Work, Powerpoint, Excel, and Adobe Photoshop."

The funding process was a long and difficult one. The SECAC initially sent out a request for proposals to 200 organizations in and around the Weed and Seed area. They also held a proposers' conference that was designed to help smaller organizations submit proposals that would be acceptable. The initial round of proposals submitted for Safe Havens sites were problematic in two ways: 1) they focused too heavily on youth and 2) they did not involve partnerships with agencies in the Weed and Seed area. The seed committee requested additional information from the agencies that submitted proposals.[23] Despite this added information, the committee still felt that it did not have proposals that were proper fits with federal guidelines and the mission of the SECAC, which was particularly concerned about funding agencies that operated in the target area and that worked extensively with other organizations in the area. As a result, the seed committee decided to reissue the request for proposals and created a new deadline of December 3, 1998. Because of the holidays, after the seed committee made its recommendations, a vote of the entire SECAC was taken by telephone to officially approve the seed committee's recommendations.

This created some frustration among those who had submitted proposals and, when the seeding awards were finally announced, the Rainier Community Center, which was not funded, sent a letter of protest to the SECAC. The letter noted that the holidays made the process more difficult than usual but nonetheless expressed frustration at the lengthy and indeterminate nature of the process. Further, it expressed concern that this process, particularly the lack of written ballots, would cause some community organizations to be less involved in the program in the future. The SECAC replied in writing and encouraged representatives from the Rainier Community Center to sit down with members of the SECAC to discuss the process.[24]

The funding decisions for seeding money reflect two basic concerns of the SECAC. First, the SECAC wanted to ensure that a wide array of residents have access to services, including communities that are typically not involved in community development programs, such as the quiet but growing Filipino population in southeast Seattle. Second, the funding decisions indicate the SECAC's interest in addressing a range of concerns for the area, including education and job opportunities for youth (Video 2000 Project) and health concerns which many residents believe contribute to crime and overall neighborhood decline (Columbia Health Center Substance Abuse Program).

Weeding

Weeding activities have included a number of traditional policing activities, such as emphasis patrols and buy/busts. There has also been an attempt to conduct reverse prostitution stings where male pimps are arrested, rather than (or in addition to) female prostitutes. One such effort resulted in just one male pimp and five female prostitutes being arrested.[25] It is unclear whether this reflects a greater interest on the part of police officers in arresting female prostitutes or whether there are other obstacles (such as manpower, resources and know-how) to arresting pimps. Edith Norton also noted that the committee might push the police to arrest "johns," those seeking services from prostitutes, rather than the prostitutes themselves.[26] Finally, community police team officers have conducted numerous walks through the target area to get to know business owners, restaurants and other establishments in the area.

At a recent SECAC meeting, one community police team officer announced a plan for the SPD to invite residents to meet in several locations in the target area one evening and walk through the area with police officers. This would provide officers with the opportunity to "talk with community people and hear from them about crime and other problems" in the area.[27] While this announcement surprised and angered some SECAC members, which will be discussed more fully in the next section, it nonetheless indicates a willingness of the part of police officers in the southeast to hear from residents about their primary public safety concerns.

Weeding and Seeding in Perspective

The seed decisions illustrate an important aspect of Weed and Seed in its current form: the amount of money available is quite limited, restricting seed programs to small, specialized programs rather than broader economic development or job-generating initiatives. The SECAC has begun looking for additional funding sources that might allow them to pursue larger projects.

Weeding activities in the southeast also raise important differences in perspective within the target community. Some members of the CAC, particularly those from the SSCPC, Chamber of Commerce and the Columbia Revitalization Committee, seem content to have the police listen to their concerns and act on them using traditional police techniques. As was the case in the Central Area, the fact that police often did not take residents' concerns about crime seriously appears to have been the root of much of the conflict between the South Seattle Crime Prevention Council and the SPD (see Lyons 1999). These organizations tend to be more police-focused because they are primarily interested in having the police respond to their particular concerns about specific types of crimes and specific problem areas.

Other members, however, specifically those from lower-income and minority populations, expressed concerns not just about *whether* the police deal with crime in their area but *how* they deal with it. These smaller, more marginalized organizations, such as the South Shore Community Council, Single Mothers Altogether Raising Our Sons, and Rainier Vista Community Council, are more community-centered and as such, are concerned about how policing of their neighborhoods takes place and are more interested in community development that will make policing less necessary.

In contrast to the Central Area, the community organizations represented on the SECAC seem to be a greater mix of police-focused and development-focused groups. The CAC members from the community originally came from the community councils, at least three of which were somewhat police-focused. The SECAC, however, has more community groups that have not had much interaction with police officials, such as the South Shore Community Council and the Filipino Youth Center, and are more interested in community development. To some extent, as long as the former group does not oppose the latter group's goals, there need not be a conflict. None of the meetings observed revealed any effort on the part of the police-focused groups to hinder those who were interested in alternative policing strategies. And the development-focused groups were also interested in more responsiveness so there has been no resistance to increased police presence so far. Needless to say, however, should these two perspectives clash, the outcome could have a significant impact on whether community members who support alternative strategies have the opportunity to promote and enact those programs.

The controversy in the original target area prompted organizers in the southeast to approach community groups from the outset, thus providing a broader range of community organizations to be involved. Those who initially took charge were groups with a strong interest in changing the economic and educational disadvantages of the southeast and making the area a better place to live and raise children. The police-focused groups seem content with this, so long as it does not clash with efforts to police crime-intensive areas. So far, this has not been much of a problem but there have been a few occasions in which the development-focused groups were more willing to be critical of the police than the police-focused groups. This primarily took the form of some members insisting on the police informing the group prior to taking action as opposed to after the fact.[28] The police-focused groups did not object but they conceivably could raise objections if the criticism interferes with policing problem areas.

Establishing Strong Community Control

The SECAC was self-conscious about the need for vigilance in establishing and maintaining itself as the centerpiece of control over Weed and Seed. Four issues in the development of the SECAC indicate the desire on the part of participants to ensure that the community retains control over the direction of both weeding and seeding and that the program's primary focus be on serving the community through development, education, employment and youth activities.

First, the composition of the SECAC reflects a range of community groups. This includes mainstream organizations like the SSCPC, which has been criticized for being too responsive to white homeowners and white businesses in the area, as well as small, neighborhood organizations such as the Brighton Neighborhood Council and the South Shore Community Council. In addition, community organizations that target particular populations, such as the Filipino youth organization, are becoming involved with the Weed and Seed through seeding grants and outreach to have representatives sit on the SECAC. Two community centers in the target area that target minority youths are also involved on the SECAC. These groups have different agendas but their common ground is a desire for community control over Weed and Seed.

The Sound Transit problem provides an excellent illustration of how maintaining agreement about the community control of Weed and Seed takes precedence over other disputes in the neighborhood over which groups on the committee are likely to take different sides. As mentioned earlier, there is currently a great deal of controversy about whether the rail tracks should be above or below ground. Since the organizations on the SECAC represent a wide range of perspectives on that issue, and the transit issue becomes highly controversial precisely at the moment when the SECAC is beginning to settle into an established routine, the committee agreed not to take a public stance on the issue. Instead, the chair of the SECAC suggested that the group issue a press release stating the need to take public safety into consideration during the planning of the transit system. This proposal resulted in a lengthy discussion in which members proposed that the group also remind transit planners of the need for jobs in the area and of the potential ways in which youth might become involved.

A second important illustration of the desire of the SECAC to have the community in control is that, as the proposal and initial goals indicate, the SECAC is at pains to retain a balanced focus on public safety concerns as well as broad economic, health and educational concerns. It would like to continue the tradition of reverse stings in order to identify targets for arrest and prosecution in the drug war other than local residents, particularly young blacks. Furthermore, the committee is committed to economic, social, educational and health care development of the area. The committee set an agenda for helping residents of the area build their lives and community so that criminal behavior itself is reduced.[29]

Third, in several meetings, members expressed concern about the city using its Weed and Seed grant status to leverage other federal government funding sources without consulting the community on how those funds would be used. At a September meeting, after the committee was well established and was preparing to review proposals for Safe Havens sites, a discussion ensued about how the SECAC could be certain that community members had sufficient input into weeding and seeding activities. The SECAC's Executive Committee expressed concern that, because the grant agency was the Seattle Police Department and the seeding funding came through the city's Department of Housing and Human Services, citizens were excluded from decision-making processes. Indeed, Sarah Malano, the white female who eventually became the staff member of the SECAC, felt that the East Precinct CAC allowed the police department to control too much of the activities and to make decisions about additional funding sources that did not include citizens.[30] She also noted that much of the discussion about crime control and community development occurs among police officials and city agencies without the involvement of the community and suggested that the SECAC needed to position itself to be a player in those discussions.[31] The group is particularly aware of its second-class status in comparison with the on-going relationships and consistent contact that city agents such as police and social service administrators have with one another and with federal agents.

Similarly, at a January 1999 meeting of the SECAC, one of the new community police team officers in the south told the committee that the SPD would soon start asking residents to come out in the evenings and join officers for long walks through the neighborhood to create a presence of people mingling in the evening and to identify any problem areas. An uncomfortable silence permeated the group, though no one objected.[32] Later, Edith Norton noted that some members of the committee, herself included, were uncomfortable with the officer's remarks, not because they disagreed with the plan but because the committee had not been consulted first. She raised concerns about the police department making decisions about activities without first consulting the SECAC. "No one had talked about that - we knew nothing of it. So we had to call them and say, 'wait a minute now, that's just not how we do things.'"[33]

Finally, two recent developments illustrate most powerfully the desire of the SECAC to uncouple itself from the city agencies which have had control over the funding and had the most contact with the Justice Department and other agencies since Weed and Seed's inception. First, the SECAC has recently received Weed and Seed funding for a staff person for seven months (until the end of the fiscal year). The person hired is a community resident who has been active for some time in creating a neighborhood council in her area and mobilizing residents to deal with crime and development concerns. In the East Precinct site, the SPD and DHHS did most of the staff work, which allowed those agencies to retain a certain amount of control over meetings and decision-making. In the southeast site, the addition of a community staff person allowed the SECAC to set up offices in the Holly Park Community Council office, which is located in the target area, further solidifying the locus of control with the community.

Perhaps most importantly, the SECAC is quietly taking steps to incorporate to non-profit status in order to allow the funding to come directly through that organization.[34]   SECAC members are aware that, as Sarah Malano put it, "it's no secret that power is where the money is."[35]   If the funding could come through the SECAC, the group would have more complete control over how it is used. Perhaps because the funding for the new site is so much smaller than the original grants, the SECAC feels particularly pressed to make sure that they have control over where it goes and that they have the credibility and authority to leverage funds from other public and private sources. The chair of the SECAC noted that gaining non-profit status will legitimize the committee as in control of the program and will allow residents to promote their own program of community development and public safety that is less pressured to involve traditional agents of criminal justice policy with whom SECAC members may disagree. In addition, several SECAC members indicated that they believe the weed and seed coordinators in the Central District have too much control.

The locus of control has experienced a clear shift from the original Justice Department goals to the original target area to the southeast area. The original program guidelines focused heavily on the US Attorney, federal and local law enforcement; the controversy in the original target area resulted in the CAC having considerable influence over a number of programs, though still serving as subsidiary partner with the larger and more experienced Department of Housing and Human Services and SPD; in the new target area in the southeast, the SECAC is endeavoring to maintain control over nearly the direction of nearly all weeding and seeding activities.

These examples illustrate an important point that will be discussed at greater length in the next chapter: community residents and the crime prevention professionals who are typically responsible for implementing crime prevention programs have substantially different definitions of community control, particularly with respect to policing.   To the community, this means having a voice in how their neighborhoods are policed, not simply being informed of policing strategies after the fact or not simply informing the police of the location of trouble spots. If weed funds come directly through the SECAC, the organization will be in a much better position to direct how those funds are used.

The Limitations of Community Involvement in the Southeast

Community organizations and leaders were involved in Weed and Seed in the southeast Seattle from its inception.   This is primarily because relevant city agents (namely the south precinct captain) were receptive to community control, and community groups were able to get in on the' program at the ground level, and establish by-laws and goals for the SECAC.   In contrast, community leaders in the CD had to begin with a program whose goals and implementation strategy had already been established.   Community involvement in the southeast seems clear: community organizations are participating in the SECAC, voting on weeding and seeding activities, enjoying their status as decision-makers and are so far pleased with the role of the SECAC in the program.   Community leaders also exercised more extensive control early on than in the east precinct because the SECAC is farther removed from the original controlling group, the south precinct commander was willing to give the SECAC a wide berth, and the SECAC itself has taken steps to have greater over day-to-day activities (with the staff person) and over the funding (with incorporation).

Again, however, the extent to which community leaders can maintain control is more ambiguous.   Certainly the SECAC has had lively, interactive discussions that promote mutual understanding and can strengthen existing community organizations in relation to one another and to city agencies.   The group has gone through numerous difficult decision-making periods – such as the decision to reissue the RFP for seeding proposals -- and has weathered those storms well.   But the SECAC is still heavily dependent on the East precinct professionals to provide information about Weed and Seed programs and on the south precinct officers to be willing to take direction on weeding activities.   And as mentioned in chapter four, the seeding money is now so small that it is difficult for those programs that are funded to produce long-term, sustainable projects that increase community solidarity and strengthen community ties.

Justice Department Reconsideration

Seattle's experience with Weed and Seed has also had an impact on the Justice Department's conception of the program.   The community component, originally conceived as finding a way to help communities work with existing police and social service practices, has evolved from what appeared to be a last-minute addition into a central feature of the program: it requires sites to make clear how the community's perspectives will be taken into account. The problems of local implementation forced the Justice Department to reconsider the community role. Furthermore, while the original goals were intended to deal with the urban areas facing the most difficult gang violence and drug activity, the community component of the program has made it most likely to be successful in areas where the community is somewhat organized. The Deputy Director of the Executive Office for Weed and Seed acknowledged that most urban areas plagued by hardened drug and gang activity do not have organized community groups with strong ties to residents and the ability to work effectively with city agencies.[36]   As a result, the EOWS now gives preference to areas that have pre-existing community organizations that can take part in the implementation of the program.

Changes in the way the community component is conceived can be seen in the requirements for demonstrating what role the community will play in the program when sites first propose a Weed and Seed area in their city. As chapter three demonstrated, the original implementation manual from August 1992 includes provisions for community involvement only *after* the target area is chosen; it does not specify how that involvement should happen, nor does it require the site to demonstrate that the community has been consulted other than providing memorandum of understanding. The Official Recognition process, which was developed in 1992 as a means to recognize and reward communities which employed a comprehensive, collaborative Weed and Seed strategy, now requires resident input as a condition for recognition.[37] Specifically, the application for Official Recognition, issued in May of 1998, asks the following questions:

Did residents of the target neighborhood participate in the resources and needs assessment? How?   If you had community meetings to gather input, please provide dates and the number of attendees.
Describe the participation of residents in formulating and implementing the Weed and Seed strategy.   At minimum, please describe:

- How the community is a clear partner with the community police officers in identifying and solving problems
- The role which residents will play in prevention, intervention and treatment efforts.
- The role which residents will play in the neighborhood restoration efforts.

- How will you promote your Weed and Seed efforts to area residents, i.e., how will residents learn about Weed and Seed and ways to access its programs and services? Describe the outreach program you plan.[38]

Furthermore, the national evaluation of eight Weed and Seed sites initiated by the National Institute of Justice concludes that:

> Weed and Seed sites that employed a *bottom-up grassroots approach built trust among residents and community organizations*...the clear lessons from this experiences were the importance of involving residents early in Weed and Seed planning, providing residents with substantial program authority, and earning their trust. The seeding component was typically the means through which community trust was built and participation fulfilled. Citizen willingness to participate in law enforcement was sometimes contingent on the trust built and demonstrated through the investments in seeding.[39]

The current director of the Executive Office for Weed and Seed (EOWS) is a former resident of the Washington D.C. Weed and Seed site. Stephen Rickman, an African-American male, is particularly concerned about community development beyond narrow law enforcement strategies. When he became director of the EOWS four years ago, he instituted a policy *requiring* at least 51% of the funding to go towards seeding. At a recent site visit to Seattle, Rickman noted that community members must be allowed to participate in designing programs that will affect their neighborhoods; he also advocated altering the economic equation so that residents had more of a stake in their own neighborhoods. He lamented the fact that the federal government is giving the Weed and Seed program "$40 million to build community while it also gives $600 million to build new prisons...but if we invest in young people at the front end, we won't need to build so many prisons on the back end."[40]

Rickman is also aware of the ambivalence that racial minorities have with respect to police in their communities:

> There are some crimes that are committed in the community that residents don't see a need for the police to respond to. Or, they don't necessarily need to have the police drag them [offenders] off to jail. But they do want open-air drug markets shut down, they

do want crack houses shut down, they do want the guns to be gone.[41]

This paralleled the words of the chair of the SECAC when she stated that she didn't always want the police handcuffing people or breaking doors down.

Finally, a 1998 conference entitled, "What Can the Federal Government Do To Decrease Crime and Revitalize Communities?" and sponsored by the Executive Office for Weed and Seed addressed a variety of community development issues under the auspices of the Weed and Seed Program. The panel papers included discussion of the relationship between public health problems and crime, the changing demographics of inner cities and the problems of highly concentrated areas of poverty, the need for long-term building of assets and knowledge about finances for poor communities, and the role of communities in combating crime and revitalizing communities.[42]

It is difficult to assess the precise impact that Seattle's local politics had on the way Weed and Seed evolved in the Justice Department. As mentioned in chapter three, other sites had controversies as well and SPD Chief Norm Stamper, who was with the San Diego police at the time, stated that the San Diego police chief simply told the Justice Department that they would not accept Weed and Seed funding if the city could not spend more of the money on seeding.[43] But by the accounts of the EOWS and the US Attorney's Office in Seattle, Seattle's controversy was particularly protracted, city officials were especially interested in calming community fears and providing a meaningful voice for residents, and Justice Department agents took the complaints seriously.[44] Thus, it is likely that Seattle's experience at the very least played a role, perhaps a definitive one, in how the Justice Department reconceptualized Weed and Seed.

The controversy generated by residents' concerns in the original target area created a program which takes at least some community input seriously, considers community needs in both the planning and implementation stages, and shifted focus from managing crime to addressing its underlying causes. Wendy Overton, one of the original members of the Coalition to Stop Weed and Seed, who ended up working to bring the program to the southeast, said that police and city officials learned a lesson: "They can't say it's a community project without involving the community."[45] To some extent, residents have indeed exercised control over the direction of both weeding and seeding activities. The original target area residents succeeded in having a direct say in how both would be implemented. Further, the southeast advisory committee was created with the specific intent of controlling weed and seed activities.

The control exercised by community residents runs counter to both the programmatic intentions of Weed and Seed as crafted by the Justice Department, as well as broader policing strategies espoused by the Seattle Police Department's own community policing bureau which promotes a policing strategy which centers activity for community development around policing both minor and major criminal offenses and uses police resources to direct citizens to other state agencies for assistance. A policy such as Weed and Seed, which deliberately gives community residents a voice in crime control, may result in residents driving policy more than originally intended.

The next chapter reviews survey data of participants in both the East Precinct CAC and the SECAC. It calls attention to the subtle distinctions in perspective between traditional agents of criminal justice policy who were to be responsible for Weed and Seed's development and implementation -- police officers, city officials, social service agents and business leaders -- and community residents. In particular, it notes how community residents see community members as central decision-makers and broad community development issues as central to their concerns.

Notes

[1] I use the terms 'southeast Seattle' and the 'Rainier Valley' interchangeably throughout this section. The Rainier Valley neighborhood is in the southeastern section of Seattle.

[2] When asked about the composition of the crowd at a recent meeting in southeast Seattle, a Rainier Valley dweller responded, "Oh, you know, the usual Valley crowd - a third, a third, a third," meaning one-third black, one-third white and one-third Asian.

[3] The racial composition of the area appears to be changing in several ways. First, African immigrants from Eritrea and Ethiopia, and Southeast Asian immigrants from Vietnam and Cambodia are settling in the Rainier Valley in increasingly large numbers. At the same time, the area is becoming more popular for middle-class whites who cannot afford homes in other parts of the city.

[4] For a comprehensive description of the development of the area and the on-going disputes between residents of the Rainier Valley and the city, particularly the police department, see Lyons 1999. See Taylor 1998 for a history of the Central District.

[5] "Rainier Valley interests want tunnel for light rail." *Seattle Post-Intelligencer,* October 29, 1998. C1.

[6] "South End demands voice in rail route." *Seattle Post-Intelligencer,* December 16, 1998. B1.

[7] Save Our Valley flier, January 1999.

[8] Interview 16: November 11, 1998.

9   Interview 20: February 2, 1999.
10   Interview 20: February 2, 1999.
11   Interview 7: February 26, 1998.
12   Southeast Citizen Advisory Committee Meeting, February 19, 1998.
13   *Proposal for Department of Justice Southeast Seattle Weed and Seed Program*.
     City of Seattle and Office of the United States Attorney, Western Division of
     Washington; Division of Family and Youth Services, Seattle Housing and
     Human Services Division; Research and Grants Management, Seattle Police
     Department. December 1997, p. 12. (abbreviated in future notes as Southeast
     Seattle Grant Proposal).
14   Interview 20: February 2, 1999.
15   Interview 20: February 2, 1999.
16   Southeast Citizen Advisory Committee Meeting, February 19, 1998.
17   Interview 20: February 2, 1999.
18   The percentage of black participants over the same time period averaged 43%
     with overall minority participants being 55% of the total.
19   Southeast Seattle Grant Proposal, p. 3.
20   Southeast Seattle Grant Proposal.
21   Weed and Seed Citizens Advisory Committee, Southeast Seattle. Monthly
     Meeting Agenda and Seed Funding Awards. January 26, 1999.
22   Recall from chapters three and four that the Justice Department requires a
     percentage of the seeding funding to go to a Safe Havens site, a multi-service
     center that offers a variety of youth and adult services. Currently, the Justice
     Department requires that $40,000 of the Weed and Seed grant be allocated to a
     Safe Havens site.
23   Southeast Citizen Advisory Committee Meeting, January 26, 1999.
24   Southeast Citizen Advisory Committee Meeting, January 26, 1999.
25   Southeast Citizen Advisory Committee Meeting, February 19, 1999.
26   Interview 20: February 2, 1999.
27   Southeast Citizen Advisory Committee Meeting, January 26, 1999.
28   Southeast Citizen Advisory Committee Meeting, January 26, 1999.
29   Southeast Citizen Advisory Committee Meeting, February 19, 1998.
30   Interview 16: November 11, 1998; Southeast Citizen Advisory council meeting,
     September 22, 1998.
31   Southeast Citizen Advisory Council meeting, September 22, 1998.
32   Southeast Citizen Advisory Committee Meeting, January 26, 1999.
33   Interview 20: February 2, 1999.
34   Interview 16: November 11, 1998.
35   Interview 16: November 11, 1998.
36   Interview 15: September 9, 1998.
37   Memorandum. From Stephen Rickman to 1998 Applicants for Weed and Seed
     Official Recognition. May 18, 1998. Executive Office for Weed and Seed,
     Department of Justice. p. 4; Fourth Quarterly Report on Operation Weed and
     Seed - 1992.
38   Weed and Seed Application for Official Recognition. Executive Office for Weed
     and Seed and the Office of Justice Programs. May 15, 1998. Pages 7 and 14.
39   National Institute of Justice, Office of Justice Programs. *National Evaluation of
     Weed and Seed: Cross-site analysis*. July 1999, emphasis added.

40   Opening Remarks, Stephen Rickman, Director Executive Office for Weed and Seed. Luncheon for Mr. Rickman, Seattle Vocational Institute, Seattle, WA, December 15, 1998.
41   Interview 25: April 8, 1999.
42   "What Can the Federal Government Do To Decrease Crime and Revitalize Communities?" National Institute of Justice and the Executive Office for 'Weed and Seed. October 1998.
43   Interview 27: April 7, 1999.
44   Interview 15: September 15, 1998; Interview 4: March 8, 1998.
45   Interview 5: May 15, 1998.

6 Communities in Control: Perspectives on Crime Prevention

> A community is a place that cares about you – that wants to know how you're doing. The community is geographic but it's also an identity.
> Harriet Walden, Mothers for Police Accountability.

The previous three chapters examined the stark differences between the conception of community crime prevention that was crafted by the Justice Department (and limited by Congress) and that which community leaders in Seattle envisioned. These chapters also explored some of the changes to the Weed and Seed program as a result of those differences. In this chapter, I draw out more explicitly the tensions between those who are typically involved in implementing crime prevention strategies, such as city officials, local police, and social service agents, and resident/leaders in the local neighborhoods. I refer to the former group as *local crime prevention professionals* (or simply professionals). While the crime prevention professionals were more in tune with community needs with respect to development issues and more sympathetic to concerns about policing, they nonetheless tended to support existing policing practices, view crime and public safety as central issues in these neighborhoods, and marginalize community development issues, particularly when punitive crime control strategies are popular at the national level. Public safety and crime reduction is seen by this group as, in large part, a precursor to community development and revitalization. While community development concerns are present (to a far greater degree than we might expect among federal law enforcement agents, for example), they are far more difficult to address than the short-term policing strategies that are popular in national discourse. Community leaders, on the other hand, tended to see crime reduction and public safety as, at least in part, the result of long-term community development.

The chapter begins with a detailed discussion of the three components of community-centered crime prevention that emerged from the intensive interviews and participant observations. Interview data from the previous chapters is summarized to bring into sharper focus each component of the model. This chapter also examines data from a National

Institute of Justice Weed and Seed evaluation that examined eight Weed and Seed sites across the country in order to contextualize the Seattle story. The evaluation, published in 1999, includes information that can be used to compare Seattle to other sites on several important variables: crime rate in the target area, residents' perspectives on crime concerns, police responsiveness, and social service availability. These comparisons will illustrate that there is little reason to believe that residents' views in Seattle are substantially more community-centered than residents' views in other Weed and Seed target areas. Furthermore, these comparisons suggest that the Central Area and Rainier Valley residents may represent a muted version of the community-centered crime prevention model, rather than a heightened version thereof.

Community-centered Crime Prevention

The three primary components of the community-centered model of crime prevention outlined in chapter two are:

- *Community revitalization for its own sake.* The community-centered crime prevention perspective is concerned with creating a vibrant living environment in which citizens have an array of viable opportunities for employment, housing, health care, recreation and social activity. This includes using law enforcement activities to address specific crime problems but does not regard those activities as the most central component of crime prevention and community development. Furthermore, it is expressly wary of connecting law enforcement activities and community development programs.
- *Challenge to existing police practices.* Concerns about existing police practices that might undermine community solidarity rather than strengthen it. This perspective is attentive to concerns of racial minorities and immigrant populations that may be particularly vulnerable to law enforcement activities. It is fearful of strategies that provide police with additional power or that do not provide communities with the ability to have some control over policing strategies.
- *Communities in control.* This perspective does not see police or other law enforcement agencies as the central controlling figure in crime control strategies, but rather, as one component of many. It

is more likely to advocate for direct community control over or serious community input into strategies for addressing crime and revitalizing communities.

The interview and archival data of the past two chapters illustrate key aspects of these components.[1] With respect to the first component, the controversy over the original program centered partially around concerns that seeding money would never materialize or, if it did, would serve only to further empower agencies outside the target area and encourage them to share information with law enforcement agents. But genuine seeding – in all possible forms – is precisely what many target area activists wanted. This was illustrated by the respondents that pointed to the lack of job opportunities, the community council representatives who drew attention to economic development concerns, the Coalition's efforts to emphasize seeding, the SECAC's clear focus on development, and the long history of community organization focus on economic issues in both the Central District and the Rainier Valley. Wendy Overton, the member of the Coalition to Stop Weed and Seed who ended up supporting the program in the Rainier Valley, echoed these sentiments by saying that the program ought to be about "equality of life issues," not simply attacking criminal activity.[2]

An important finding of this research is that the concerns about seeding that came from community leaders contrasted sharply not only with the Justice Department's conception of Weed and Seed but also with local crime prevention professionals. Community leaders were more likely to discuss crime problems as primarily the result of poor economic and opportunity conditions than the professionals were. This is consistent with Scheingold's claim that crime tends to be more of a latent public concern than an active one (Scheingold 1984, 44). That is, when asked whether crime is a problem, the public in general tends to respond in the affirmative or, when given forced choice questions about major social problems, crime is often chosen as important. But when given more open-ended questions or a broader range of problems to choose from, crime recedes into the background and is not consistently identified as a priority. Of course, both the community leaders and the local professionals in this study saw crime and development as important in the two target areas. The primary difference was in terms of priority and causality. Will reducing crime result in greater economic development or will greater economic development result in crime reduction? One's perspective on these questions helps dictate policy design. The local professionals focused quickly on the crime problem. This was true not only for those whom we would expect to focus on crime – law enforcement officials – but for city council members and other city officials as well. The resultant policy focus was to attack crime aggressively with most of the resources directed toward crime reduction. Local community leaders, however, wanted the largest share of the resources to be aimed at community/economic development from which crime reductions would, they believed, eventually result.[3]

The second component of community-centered crime prevention -- challenges to existing police practices -- is manifest in a myriad of forms in the Seattle experience. For the Coalition, even seeding programs were suspect because of their link to law enforcement. A frequent comment during the interviews was recalling that the controversy revisited on-going concerns that law enforcement strategies in the area were mostly about harassing young blacks. As noted in Chapter four, Crystal Parker, the African-American female who represented the Seattle Vocational Institute on the CAC, said that a lot of people feared that the FBI would swarm the area and that there was a great deal of mistrust of the police chief, Patrick Fitzsimmons.[4] This raises questions about the centrality of the police to urban crime prevention programs. From a policy perspective it is almost incomprehensible to imagine a crime prevention program that does not have law enforcement at its core. And yet, this seems to be precisely what community leaders are looking for: police involvement without police domination of an entire program.

The remarks of leaders in the Central District echoed concerns around the country that seeding was too intimately linked to weeding and, as a result, would focus all activities on crime control rather than broader community development. The Urban Strategies Group in Los Angeles argued that "...the Federal Weed and Seed program will endorse an approach to federal law enforcement that will ... create an unethical linkage between federal social welfare programs and federal military and police programs."[5] Related to this concern is the fear of increased policing activities that would continue to harass and intimidate minorities, particularly youth. This is an inescapable theme of nearly every interview with community residents and leaders. Sarena Johnson, the member of the Coalition to Stop Weed and Seed who remained opposed to the program, related concerns that some of the whites who were moving into the area were simply afraid of black youths and that they were projecting criminal activity onto all minorities, independent of any actual crimes being committed.[6]

Garfield Community Council president Sean Jeffries also noted that during the controversy when the Council held public meetings about the program, numerous mothers of black teenagers said that they were just as fearful of their children being the object of intense policing practices as they were of their children becoming involved with gangs.[7] This put residents in a difficult dilemma: oppose more policing and potentially relinquish their children to gang violence or support more policing and potentially subject them to abuse or harassment by the police. Edith Norton, the chair of the SECAC, stated that "sometimes what the police think is a crime isn't really a crime" and that the police "need to find different avenues [for getting the job done] other than kicking in doors and handcuffing people."[8]

These fears led to advocacy for policing practices that support, not undermine, community development and relations with police. The most prominent example of this is the reverse stings described in chapter four which are still conducted occasionally and which were regarded as a significant victory for the community. While arresting buyers rather than dealers is seen by some as misdirected because it does not deal with underlying addiction issues, at least a community other than a low-income minority one is being made to pay a price in the drug war.

Finally, consistent with the third component of the model, community leaders and activists in Seattle wanted far greater a role for themselves in design and implementation of Weed and Seed than they were originally given. Members of the community tended to view the police as heavy-handed in their response to crime and, while they wanted to address violent crime, they were fearful that encouraging police to do so would result in more harassment, abuse and possibly even deaths. Edith Norton noted that "there are always a few bad apples but that doesn't mean you have to throw them to the ground, handcuff them and drag them off."[9] Thus, even when residents acknowledged criminal behavior that needed to be addressed, they were not sure they wanted the police to use the degree of force that they have at their disposal. Furthermore, a common theme of the interviews with residents was the concern that police officers arrest or harass young people who are not doing anything wrong. "Sometimes the police think that something criminal is happening when it really isn't." In the Rainier Valley, the most dramatic illustration of the desire for control is happening with the SECAC in its efforts to incorporate so that it can control all the weed and seed funding and insinuate itself into police activity so that it maintains control over weeding. Rather than attack criminal activity on narrow law enforcement terms, the SECAC (and to a lesser degree the CAC) is striving to achieve a style of policing that encourages community-building and partnerships, rather than the adversarial relationships that police frequently have with minority communities.

Respondents from the community seemed particularly interested in having a say in how drug crimes were addressed. Community members were concerned that strategies to address drug crime focused too heavily on law enforcement and that policing strategies target young blacks. Since drug enforcement activities tend to focus on street dealers, who tend to be lower-income minorities, it makes sense that they would want to participate in how those enforcement activities take place.

Of course crime prevention professionals, particularly the police, have reasons to limit the amount of community control in policing. This group tended to see opponents of police tactics as the result of either misinformation or as coming from a small but vocal minority that dislikes all police activity. Thus, they were not anxious to allow too much community control that might permit the misinformed or radical community elements to gain control.[10] Respondents from the professional group indicated that concerns about policing were largely the result of misunderstanding and misinformation and once proper information was conveyed, those concerns would, or should, evaporate. The Deputy Mayor at the time of the controversy, Chief Norm Stamper and Margaret Paegler of the city council's Public Safety Committee all indicated that they believed a great deal of the controversy to be about misunderstanding.[11] The city council member stated:

> My sense was that a lot of it was perception. The funding could be used for good or for ill…we needed to get beyond the language but that was difficult because of the fear and hysteria.[12]

Paegler, who was responsive to Central District community leaders' objections to Weed and Seed nonetheless operated under the assumption that the concerns were largely unfounded and once everyone recognized this, the controversy will go away. The Deputy Mayor indicated a similar concern: while the residents' concerns were justified on some level, the intensity of the opposition to the program was the result of a few noisy community members who wanted to make a show of how little Mayor Rice had actually done for blacks in Seattle.[13] Similarly, Harry Bailey, the police lieutenant in the east precinct who served as the weed coordinator said that there are "still pockets of people that don't like it [Weed and

Seed] – no matter what we [the police] do, they won't like it. They have a fixed attitude."[14]

The main theme of this book, however, has been that community leaders were not simply misinformed or disgruntled with the police. On the contrary, many of the original opponents of the program are now involved in its implementation. Rather, their concept of crime prevention was substantially different from national and local policy makers. A comparison between the Justice Department's original Weed and Seed program and Seattle's implementation reveals substantial differences in control and objectives, suggesting that the opposition's goals went far beyond simple misunderstanding.

Seattle in Context

Throughout this book, I have argued that the case study in Seattle has provided an opportunity for rich analysis of perspectives on crime prevention. I have explored variations in those perspectives between local communities and crime prevention professionals on both the local and national levels. In addition, the case study allowed for the development of an analytic framework that can be used to explore the Weed and Seed experience and other community crime prevention programs in areas around the country. The three-tiered model of community crime prevention strategies provides, I believe, a necessary, if not sufficient, framework with which many community-crime prevention strategies can be analyzed.

If, however, Seattle differs substantially from other Weed and Seed target areas on key variables – crime rate, confidence in the police, dissatisfaction with community services – then the usefulness of this framework may be undermined because Seattle's target area could produce findings inconsistent with the vast majority of other inner-city urban communities. If Seattle's crime rate in the target area is substantially different from other areas, for example, this could have an impact on the views of local professionals and community residents. Lower crime rates might signal a greater skepticism on the part of community residents for increased police presence (less need) and a greater interest in increased social services, thus skewing the findings more towards the community-centered model than might be the case in other areas. Higher crime rates might suggest greater frustration with police for lack of service or responsiveness. Both of these scenarios could be seen as indicators that the Seattle experience does not translate well to other urban areas.

In this section, I compare Seattle's original target area and other Weed and Seed target areas in the country on several key variables: crime rate, residents' perspectives on how big the crime problem is, and residents' attitudes towards police and the availability of social services in the target area.[15] These comparisons illustrate that Seattle is *not* substantially different from other Weed and Seed sites on these key variables. Indeed, it may be the case that the Seattle's experience understates the strength of the community-centered crime prevention model.

Crime Rates

As Table 6.1 indicates, Seattle's Part I crime rate for the year preceding Weed and Seed is not among the highest for the areas in the 1999 study, nor is it substantially lower than other areas. While the rate is considerably higher than Akron or N. Manatee, three other sites have higher rates (Pittsburth, Hartford and Shreveport). Furthermore, when compared to rates in the rest of the city, Seattle is again unremarkable.

Table 6.1   Part I Crimes in Target Areas and Rest of City per 1,000 Residents One Year Prior to Weed and Seed

Site	Target Area	Rest of City	Ratio of Crimes in Target Area to Rest of city
Akron, OH	69.5	77.3	0.90
N. Manatee, FL	73.9	70.3	1.05
Las Vegas (West LV site), NV	118.0	72.6	1.62
Seattle, WA	**172.6**	**123.0**	**1.40**
Pittsburgh, PA	181.8	81.6	2.23
Hartford, CT	199.2	130.2	1.53
Shreveport, LA	211.6	122.9	1.72

Source: National Institute of Justice, Executive Office for Weed and Seed. National Evaluation of Weed and Seed: Cross-Site Analysis. July 1999. Exhibit 3.3, pg. 34. Salt Lake City is excluded from this table because only partial year data was available.

Thus, the opposition of Central District community leaders to the prospect of aggressive policing in the form of 'weeding' activities, does not seem to result from an unusually *low* level of crime, relative to other troubled urban areas. That is, community leaders were not reacting out of concern that weeding was an over-reaction to the problem; the interviews and participant observations also bear this out. Nor can it be said that an unusually *high* level of crime may have produced excessive animosity towards the police for lack of protection. The interviews illustrated that some community leaders were angry at the police for a perceived lack of attention to crime in the Central District but, given the history of community mobilization and police-minority relations in Seattle, it seems unlikely that this is more true in Seattle than in urban areas with higher rates of crime.

Table 6.2 illustrates that Seattle target area residents see street drug dealers, drug sales and drug use as a bigger problem than most residents in other areas; in addition, burglary and violent/gang activity appear to be less of a concern. This is a somewhat ambiguous finding. On the one hand, the higher level of concern about drugs might lead Central District residents to be *more* inclined to support programs aimed at addressing those problems, including drug treatment and rehabilitation programs. Concern about drugs may lead indirectly to a concern about social conditions that give rise to drug addiction, thus inflating the first component of community centered crime prevention. On the other hand, concern about drugs might also lead residents to be more sympathetic to greater police presence than they would be otherwise, thus understating the objections to police presence in communities with less concern about drugs. There is more evidence for the latter explanation, than the former. The Citizen Advisory Committee did not spend a significant portion of its seed funds on drug education and treatment (only 9%; see Table 4.3 in chapter four). But residents of all kinds had been clamoring for years for more police protection because of serious drug problems in the neighborhood. Thus, the greater concern about drugs in Seattle is not necessarily indicative of a proclivity towards broader community development and social service availability.

The fact that Central District residents seem less concerned with violent and gang activity presents a similar dilemma. On the one hand, this could indicate that these residents less interested in a strong police presence as residents in other target areas because they do not see as great a need. In other words, residents in other target areas that are more concerned about violent crime and gang activity may welcome a greater police presence.

But as we have seen, violence and gang activity are seen by many community leaders as a function of economic disarray and lack of opportunities. In this sense, residents who have greater concerns about violence and gangs may promote the first component of community-centered crime prevention even more than residents in Seattle. These findings do not present clear evidence one way or the other and further research is needed in order to determine whether violent crime rates have an impact on the strength of the community-centered crime prevention model.

Table 6.2   1995 Survey of Target Area Residents, Percent Indicating 'Big Problem in the Neighborhood'

Site	Street drug deals	Drug sales	Burglary/ Property	Violent crime	Gang activity	Drug Use
Akron	19	21	10	13	7	23
Las Vegas	38	29	20	32	27	38
N. Manatee	56	25	32	28	9	50
Salt Lake	14	17	28	40	44	20
Seattle	**45**	**35**	**15**	**12**	**14**	**48**
Pittsburgh	44	22	9	28	32	47
Hartford	78	60	45	74	62	84
Shreveport	17	17	22	21	15	17

Source: National Institute of Justice, Executive Office for Weed and Seed. National Evaluation of Weed and Seed: Cross-Site Analysis. July 1999.

Table 6.3 illustrates residents' perspectives on how good a job the police are doing at controlling drug crime and how responsive residents believe the police are to community concerns. Here, Central Area residents in Seattle appear to be somewhat *more* likely to think that the police are doing a good job and are responsive to community concerns than residents in other target areas.   Only Shreveport residents responded in greater numbers that the police were doing a good job of keeping order and being responsive to community concerns.   A slightly higher number of Shreveport and Hartford target area residents indicated that the police are doing a good job of controlling the sale of drugs.

This comparison is particularly important for our purposes. If Central Area leaders in Seattle are somewhat *more* satisfied with the job that the police are doing in their neighborhood and yet they are still troubled by the prospect of increased police presence, this would indicate that residents in areas with lower levels of confidence in police might have even greater concerns about centering crime prevention strategies around law enforcement. It also indicates that the target area residents in Seattle might be *more* willing to work with the police than residents in other target areas, since they perceive the police to be responsive (i.e., willing to listen). This demonstrates that the second component of the community-centered crime prevention model is probably not overstated.

Table 6.3   1995 Survey of Target Area Residents, Attitudes Towards Police

Site	Police doing good job controlling drug crime	Police are responsive to community concerns
Akron	38	76
Las Vegas	43	67
N. Manatee	38	78
Salt Lake	39	79
Seattle	**45**	**81**
Pittsburgh	34	78
Hartford	55	51
Shreveport	52	89

Source: National Institute of Justice, Executive Office for Weed and Seed. National Evaluation of Weed and Seed: Cross-Site Analysis. July 1999.

The last set of comparisons, Table 6.4, shows fairly low levels of satisfaction with the availability of social service programs in all the target areas. In Seattle, residents attitudes towards the availability of social services are not substantially different than attitudes in other target areas, with the exception of the higher satisfaction with sports and recreation opportunities. The high number of schools and after-school programs in the Central Area may account for this satisfaction. If residents in Seattle were less satisfied with the availability of social services in their area, that might explain the emphasis that community residents placed on community development initiatives. Once again, however, comparisons with other sites suggests dissatisfaction with community development programs; an interest in increased social service and community development programs does not appear to be unique to Seattle.

With respect to participation by residents in neighborhood clean-up efforts, anti-drug rallies, citizen patrols, and block watches, Seattle did not have higher levels of participation in any of those areas. In other words, Central District residents were no more likely to participate in community programs than residents in other target areas. Thus, the third component of the model, which focuses on the interest community residents have in having some control over the direction of crime prevention and community development, is not likely to be exaggerated in Seattle. This does not mean that community leaders in other target areas would be as successful as Central Area leaders in getting the police and city's attention; as argued in chapters four and five, the long history of community organizations and pre-existing community policing program were important components of the way Weed and Seed took shape in Seattle.

Table 6.4   1995 Survey of Target Area Residents, Availability of Services

Site	Sport/ recreation	Drug Treatment	Job opportunities
Akron	33	25	25
Las Vegas/West	50	34	29
N. Manatee	48	35	34
Salt Lake	53	14	19
Seattle	**73**	**21**	**29**
Pittsburgh	36	24	9
Hartford	57	32	39
Shreveport	28	35	33

Source: National Institute of Justice, Executive Office for Weed and Seed. National Evaluation of Weed and Seed: Cross-Site Analysis. July 1999.

These comparisons serve two purposes. First, they illustrate that the Seattle situation is not especially unique in that crime rates are consistent with rates in other areas, residents views about crime are not out of the ordinary, and their attitudes towards police and the availability of social services in their communities are not sharply different from other target areas.   This would indicate that the perspectives that Seattle community members brought to the Weed and Seed implementation process in Seattle were not substantially skewed towards the community-centered model of crime prevention.   In fact, as suggested by attitudes towards the police and social services, there is some evidence that Central Area residents may be somewhat *more* willing to work with police and address crime issues than residents in some other areas, thus providing the community control component of the community-centered model with even more weight.

Taken together, these comparisons provide some clues as to how well the community-centered model would fit with the perspectives of residents in other urban areas.   If Seattle represents a unique context, it is likely to be unique in the extent to which it understates, rather than overstates the model. Clearly more research is needed in order to ascertain the consistency of this model with inner-city perspectives, particularly those of minorities, as well as to draw out nuances that might make some components more important than others in different contexts.

The Future of Community-centered Crime Prevention

The research presented in this book suggests that while federal crime control policy making tends to be punitive and symbolic, city-level crime politics is more nuanced and likely to focus on structural explanations for crime. The findings of the interview and participant observation indicate that, while federal actors seem to miss the mark with respect to what community priorities are, local actors seem to miss the mark with respect to how best to achieve the community's priorities. Local actors were much more likely to anticipate the community's desire for seeding programs and to understand the concerns about police misconduct. However, they were clearly off target with respect to how the program goals should be achieved and did not recognize the "left out" feeling that many community leaders had with respect to decision-making about public safety and development in their neighborhoods.

Though the message highlighted in this book is that community members in Seattle were able to gain control over some aspects of Weed and Seed, the overall prospects for community-centered strategies remain in doubt; the community's ability to direct some law enforcement activities was hard fought and came only after intense public pressure. In addition, the seeding component, while more prominent than initially intended, is insufficiently funded to provide long-term solutions to urban problems. Furthermore, Seattle is regarded in Weed and Seed circles as an exceptional site where community, law enforcement, social service and private groups are working well together and where the police department has been remarkably receptive to the community's initiatives. Thus, a community-centered approach is both difficult to arrive at and equally as difficult to difficult to sustain.

While the locus of control over funding decisions and particular weeding strategies lies with the CAC, the community's control over the long-term goals for the area is still rather small. There are several reasons for this. First, the SPD and DHHS remain at the center in terms of the future of the program because they are in direct contact with the Justice Department, the US Attorney for Western Washington and because the seeding funding is all distributed through DHHS. The weed and seed coordinators are hooked into a network of people that are informed of other funding opportunities related to Weed and Seed and to broader city-wide strategies for community development and crime control. Second, Seattle has been designated a training site for newer Weed and Seed sites and, as a result, the weed and seed coordinators have been thrust into the national spotlight for their role in Seattle's program. While CAC members have attended conferences and been a part of the Justice Department's celebration of Seattle's successes, the turnover among community members on the CAC is higher than among the state and local agencies and therefore their presence and control is diluted in these activities. Finally, the amount of money being distributed is rapidly declining. As noted in chapter three, the funding is moving away from high-level resources for new programs and towards mere incentives for different groups to work together. If and when there is no more money to distribute, the role of the CAC as simply a strategizing body is questionable. This appears to be less of a problem in the southeast where residents are taking steps to ensure that they, not the SPD or DHHS or any other government agency are responsible for the direction that Weed and Seed takes in the future. But again, future funding remains an issue.

The important point from this story, however, is that an alternative vision of crime prevention exists on the community level and that this vision was able to work itself onto the local agenda, creating a modest impact on the national program. The argument is that the dominant rhetoric and practice associated with crime prevention strategies on the national level is not hegemonic; local actors can take control of some aspects of the program and alter its original conception so that it incorporates community views.

Notes

[1]   Research for this project also included a survey of participants in the Weed and Seed program in Seattle, including community leaders, social service agents, city officials, police officers and administrators, and business representatives. A comparison of responses between community residents/leaders and the other participants confirm the significant differences in perspectives described in this section. However, the low response rate (n=44) makes the usefulness of the survey results open to question. Nonetheless, the findings do lend further credence to each aspect of the community-centered crime prevention model that was fleshed out by the interviews and participant observations.

[2]   Interview 5: May 15, 1998.

[3]   This is consistent with recent research on the relationship between attitudes towards crime and justice and neighborhood structure. See Sampson and Bartusch for an interesting review of this literature (1998).

[4]   Interview 3: January 30, 1998.

[5]   "A Call to Reject the Federal Weed and Seed Program in Los Angeles" Urban Strategies Group, The Labor/Community Strategy Center.

[6]   Interview 17: November 11, 1998.

[7]   Interview 1: January 10, 1998.

[8]   Interview 20: February 2, 1999

[9]   Interview 20: February 2, 1999.

[10]   One can also imagine that the police are not anxious to have citizens know too much about their activities, particularly as they involve undercover operations. At an SECAC meeting, after one of the CPT officers had finished telling the group about some prostitution and drug sting operations they had done, the precinct captain reminded everyone that the nature of such activities – police officers posing as taxi drivers, for example – could not be widely publicized or it would endanger the safety of officers.

[11]   Interviews 23: March 29, 1999; Interview 24: April 7, 1999; Interview 27: April 7, 1999.

[12]   Interview 24: April 7, 1999.

[13]   Interview 23: March, 29, 1999

[14]   Interview 21: November 18, 1998.

[15]   The data are derived from a National Institute of Justice evaluation of Weed and Seed sights around the country published in 1999. The evaluators collected data on crime rates and conducted surveys of local residents in Weed and Seed target areas about their perspectives on crime, violence, social services and police responsiveness.

7 Community Development, Public Safety and the Future of Crime Prevention

> The people who are working on police accountability issues are usually outsiders. But it's a new millenium. We have to all sit down at the table.
>
> Founder, Mothers for Police Accountability

In April 1999, Seattle hosted its first Western Regional Weed and Seed conference, entitled "Power of Partnerships." Attendees from all over the country were treated to a showcase of Weed and Seed Northwest, with the east precinct in the center of the spotlight. Tacoma's Weed and Seed site was also highlighted. The program featured notable guest speakers such as EOWS director Stephen Rickman, the director of the Executive Office of U.S. Attorneys, and a diversity trainer who diligently reminded conference attendees that their project was a multi-cultural one.

The conference presented a successful Weed and Seed program in Seattle and presenters from all elements of the program praised Seattle for its efforts in bringing community members into the process. During the opening remarks, numerous speakers reminded those in attendance that Seattle's Weed and Seed began mired in controversy and that it was through the determination of community members, city agents and SPD officers to take seriously those concerns that the program survived. "We did not become this strong *despite* these struggles," noted Kate Greenquist, the local Law Enforcement Community Coordinator, "we became this strong *because* of our struggles." The Director of the Executive Office for Weed and Seed noted:

> Seattle is an awesome Weed and Seed site…looking out at the audience, there's America out there – Blacks, Latinos, Asians, Protestants, Catholics, Jews. Weed and Seed only works as well as the people who are working it. Here in Seattle there are some real champions.

During the opening remarks, Gretchen King from the U.S. Attorneys Office noted that she is currently working with the Seattle

167

Police Department to develop a long-term strategy for sustaining Weed
and Seed on the local level and for expanding the program city-wide. The
program goals include a power structure which has weed coordinator, seed
coordinator and citizens' advisory council on equal footing, with the
Police Chief and US Attorney as overseers. Programs to be implemented
include: special anti-drug program, problem-solving projects, employment
and computer training, teen clinic, safe haven, special problems-solving
and enforcement operations, health programs, and educational programs.
The proposal was warmly received. By all the accounts of speakers,
Seattle is a model Weed and Seed site.

The Weed and Seed story told over the past six chapters, however,
is more complex. It has highlighted the ways in which the original
program reflected the priorities of national crime control agendas and local
law enforcement goals more than a genuine interest in community
revitalization and involvement. While the citizens of the original target
area were able to insinuate themselves into the program implementation,
the community-centered crime prevention model that is more compatible
with the views of community leaders in Seattle's two target areas is still
heavily watered-down. A quick review of the keynote speakers for the
Regional conference illustrates the continued top-heavy nature of Weed
and Seed in Seattle. Opening remarks were made by the Mayor, Chief of
Police, Local Law Enforcement Community Coordinator, Human Services
Director, and the Director of the Executive Office for Weed and Seed. In
order to hear what community members had to say, one needed to attend
the breakout sessions that took place after the opening event. While the
lunch prayer on the first day was conducted by a local black minister, the
lunchtime speaker was the Director of the Executive Office for U.S.
Attorneys.

Interestingly, the lunch prayer was led by an African-Methodist
Episcopal minister who stated that he had only recently moved to Seattle.
Ministers at the two black churches in the Central District which have
traditionally been active in politics – Mt. Zion Baptist and New Hope
Baptist – expressed grave reservations about Weed and Seed during the
controversy. Reverend McKinney, from Mt. Zion, has since retired and
has not been involved in Weed and Seed. Reverend Jeffries, however, still
believes that Weed and Seed, even with its alterations, emphasizes too
much law enforcement. Thus, it is significant that the minister who
offered the prayer was someone new to the area and appears to have been
favorably disposed to Weed and Seed.

The story related throughout this book is about what citizen-sponsored crime prevention might look like if citizens were given meaningful opportunities to "sit at the table." It illustrates tensions between residents of urban crime-ridden areas and the governmental agents that are responsible for designing and implementing crime prevention and urban revitalization projects. The interviews and participant observations all point to deep cleavages between community residents and local agents of criminal justice with respect to the meaning of crime prevention, the importance of economic development and the proper role of the community. Racial politics exacerbates those cleavages and places them in sharp relief.

The primary thesis of this book has been that community leaders representing residents of the target areas in Seattle, particularly African-Americans, conceived of crime prevention and community development in strikingly different ways than those responsible for crafting crime control policy at both the federal and local levels. Furthermore, I have argued that when crime control policies specifically encourage community input, the differing goals will clash, with the potential to afford residents the opportunity to craft programs that better conform to their visions. These opportunities, however, appear to be narrow and short-lived, with more probable outcomes resulting in strengthened police agencies and minimal community control.

In this final chapter, I summarize the findings of the research and explore the meaning of community involvement in Weed and Seed by using the definitions of community involvement outlined in chapter one. I argue that Weed and Seed in Seattle falls short of a meaningful role for the community that can be sustained over the long-haul, but also that the experience leaves 'residues of reform' that can serve to provide groundwork for future community involvement, and offers modest transformations in crime prevention practice that have the potential to strengthen the economic and political power of crime-ridden communities.

I conclude the book by returning to the notion of 'governing through crime control' and exploring the implications of this strategy for high-crime area residents.

Summary of Findings

The research has generated four primary findings. First, the community-centered crime prevention perspective outlined in chapter two appears to represent fairly and accurately the goals of community leaders of the target areas in Seattle. Local residents involved in the Coalition to Stop Weed and Seed emphasized issues beyond narrow law enforcement concerns, and the CAC and the SECAC have tried to concentrate their efforts on seeding programs, with a particular emphasis on employment, education, and youth activities. Both advisory councils also attempted to control policing activities in their area and the SECAC in particular expressed a desire to exercise the majority of control over weeding. Both groups had extensive control over seeding activities, with little interest in police involvement in seeding programs.

Given the nature of interactions between local police and residents of crime-ridden areas, however, there is also a deference to police agents who approach meetings with lists of police activities that had taken place or were planned for the target area. In chapter five, we saw how unwelcome that approach was in the Southeast but it remains to be seen whether the police will heed the SECAC's warning and approach the council *before* making decisions about how to conduct crime prevention activities in the target area. Furthermore, community residents understand the phrase "community control" in substantially different ways than the police and social service agents responsible for responding to that control.

Second, community level crime control perspectives in Seattle are less punitive and more oriented towards crime's root causes than those that were presented in the original Weed and Seed program goals originating with the Justice Department. Similarly, while the original plan for Seattle framed the program in more localized terms, which included participation from a wider range of actors, it nonetheless perpetuated the federally-prescribed focus on law enforcement and minimal role for the targeted community. The original Weed and Seed program goals were heavy on law enforcement, light on community involvement, and tied many of the seeding programs to policing. The SPD did approach several community groups but, as chapter four illustrated, they were groups that were already working with the police on drug problems in area and were likely to be in favor of increased police presence.

Third, implementation struggles can modestly reconfigure national level policy. Weed and Seed is more community-centered as a result of some of the controversy, particularly Seattle's. Nationally, Weed and Seed has put seeding in the center of the program's mission. The director of the Executive Office for Weed and Seed rarely talks publicly about the virtues of policing and chooses instead to focus on the hope that the program offers for community development and revitalization in the form of seeding activities. He also talks freely about the ambivalence that some urban minority groups have towards the police and the legitimacy of those concerns. The program now requires that communities be consulted from the beginning, community advisory councils must be representative of the target areas and must be given substantial input into the program's implementation.

In the southeast target area, dozens of community groups and hundreds of residents in the area were consulted as part of the preparation for organizing the program in that area. Whether the community groups that got involved in the program will be able to exert substantial control over it remains an open question and, as chapter five illustrated, there is some question as to whether SPD officials will permit the group to exercise the control that it wants and that it was led to believe it had. In that area, in contrast to the Central Area, where the some of the community groups involved were already working with police on crime issues, the community groups are more balanced in their police- and development- focus which, I believe, explains in large part the greater push towards more community control. However, this could also mean less influence in the long run because the police are less likely to respond to community groups that are critical of police tactics or advocating alternatives to police-centric programs.

Finally, Seattle's community-oriented policing program, the long history of community organizing and strong community organizations in both target areas, seem important for the ability of the community-centered crime prevention perspective to make its way into the implementation process. Since there are no dramatic differences between the east and south precincts with respect to these external variables (with the possible exception of the weed coordinator in the east who was not originally in favor of community involvement and the weed coordinator in the south who was), it is difficult to ascertain whether and to what extent those external factors might play a role in the ability of community groups to insinuate themselves into the implementation process. At the very least, however, some formalized organizations seem necessary in order to counterbalance the formidable organization and power of state agents such as police and social service organizations. Similarly, a police organization that is favorably disposed to community involvement seems necessary as well.

The one key difference between the two target areas – the controversy over the program that existed in the Central Area and not in the southeast – seems to have had some effect on the program's implementation, though perhaps not in the manner expected. In general, the original controversy seems to have helped residents in both target areas take more control. In the east precinct, the controversy had a strong development-focus but the implementation has edged more towards a police-focus. In the southeast, where community organizations were able to be involved earlier on, the implementation is more balanced between police- and development-focused groups.

This suggests that concerns about opposition that are built into design and implementation from the outset may have more influence on the outcome of the program than the controversy itself. This is consistent with Joel Handler's claims that professionals must have a stake in cooperating with the community in order for those partnerships to work (Handler 1996). In the original target area, the program had already been designed; the changes to the program were an effort to quell that controversy. In the southeast, however, the program was proposed to the community as a community-driven program, thus its success was dependent upon the community feeling as though its input was central to the program.

Community, Policing and Governance

This book began with a framework for exploring the role of community involvement in crime prevention. I suggested that Weed and Seed promoted the opportunity reduction and order maintenance models and that those models might be seen as consistent with a governing through crime control strategy which is aimed at promoting and legitimating state authority by emphasizing state control in connection to crime. It is easier to demonstrate authority and results by tackling fear of crime or reducing opportunities for crime than it is by addressing crime itself. I return to those themes here, reflecting on how the dominance of opportunity reduction and order maintenance as illustrated by Weed and Seed promote governing through crime control. I suggest that this approach undermines the community-centered model and prospects for meaningful community involvement because it promotes police-centric policies and it does so most prominently in inner-city minority neighborhoods, precisely the communities most likely to be ambivalent about or downright hostile towards police presence.

Opportunity reduction strategies were least prominent in the Seattle Weed and Seed experience. While Weed and Seed initially advocated that police officers work with community groups on fortifying homes and businesses against crime, in Seattle this has clearly taken a back seat to other priorities. The Washington Insurance Council grant to Jackson Place, discussed in chapter four, involved extensive planning about the physical landscape, including lighting improvements, roundabouts and street changes to divert heavy traffic flow to other areas. In the whole scheme of the program, however, little has been implemented by way of opportunity reduction/target hardening strategies. Because the CAC and SECAC have had some control over the direction of both weeding and seeding activities, there has not been a focus on opportunity reduction strategies. The relative prevalence of these strategies elsewhere as well as the extent that they incorporate community needs and interests is a subject for future research but this analysis indicates that they are likely to be problematic because they center crime prevention around the police and, more importantly, deflect attention from broader concerns, such as economic development. This is precisely the reason that governing through crime control strategies proliferate: they do not involve broad social and economic development programs and they fund existing police programs that strengthen police authority and visibility.

   With respect to the second type of community involvement in crime prevention, order maintenance, these strategies are taking on increasing prominence in the public discourse and are a key component of the Seattle Police Department's move towards community policing. While they are sometimes the subject of criticism, such as in New York City where some believe Mayor Giuliani's zero tolerance policy has gone too far in addressing disorder, they also continue to be intimately linked with broad community policing strategies which are proliferating in urban centers across the country. While Seattle's Weed and Seed program did not explicitly set out to address disorder, the SPD's community policing program is firmly rooted in the tradition of 'broken windows' – the major foundation upon which order maintenance policing rests – and in problem-oriented policing, which seeks to reduce crime by addressing underlying problems and conflicts.

   This study challenges underlying assumptions of order maintenance proponents that a focus on law enforcement can effectively serve as the centerpiece of community revitalization. Furthermore, it suggests that order maintenance strategies are all too easily absorbed into a governance strategy that promotes crime control as a means of exerting state authority. The following discussion focuses on three key components of the order maintenance argument and illustrates that order maintenance provides legislators and criminal justice officials with ample opportunity to govern through crime control in three ways. First, it does not address fear of police harassment and abuse, independent of actual police harassment, thus further insulating police from scrutiny and legitimating their presence and activities. Crime prevention programs that do not take fear of police harassment as seriously as they take fear of crime, however, risk inefficacy in minority communities. Second, it promotes police discretion that could result in higher levels of incarceration for minorities, thus offering opportunities for state agents to use incarceration rates as evidence of effective state authority. Finally, and perhaps most importantly, it redirects attention away from basic community development concerns to achieve narrow law enforcement ends.

As noted in chapter two, James Q. Wilson and George Kelling argued that neighborhoods could decay into disorder and crime when seemingly small problems, such as broken windows on buildings, are left unrepaired. I will not repeat that argument here except to note that in its more recent version, Kelling and Coles advocate for order maintenance as the cornerstone of community-based crime prevention. They base this claim in part on the notion that fear of crime and disorder is best alleviated by police who can serve multiple aims, including reducing fear.

The findings of the research presented here indicate, to the contrary, that addressing fear of aggressive policing may be as important as addressing fear of crime in inner-city neighborhoods. As suggested in chapter two, order maintenance takes residents' fear of crime seriously and does not question its origins. It does not, however, give the same consideration to fear of police abuse or misconduct, thereby ignoring one of the primary concerns of residents of urban areas of high-crime, particularly black residents. Asking urban minorities to give police more discretion without also giving residents more of a voice in how their neighborhoods are policed and/or some control over police harassment, is asking for community residents who bear the brunt of aggressive police tactics to swallow a bitter pill.

Kelling and Coles argue that order maintenance policing must be responsive to community concerns and standards for order; but research on community policing has demonstrated that the police are often most responsive to the most dominant interests and voices in any given community which are unlikely to be the ones most frequently subject to policing activities (Lyons 1999; Greene and Mastrofski 1988). Indeed, chapters four and five presented several illustrations of how the police sought out those whose views were consistent with their own and even sought to discredit those who are overly critical.

In defending New York's zero tolerance policing strategy, Kelling observed that the fundamental issue to be dealt with in New York vis-à-vis crime is the fact that citizens endure tremendous fear as a result of disorder. "[T]he well-founded belief that in disorderly places, society has ceded control to those who are on the margin of or outside the law, and therefore that anything might happen in such places" (Kelling 1992, 25). But chapters four and five presented evidence that some members of crime-ridden communities may not see marginally criminal behavior as all that important. This calls into question the idea that disorder is the central problem. Historically, crime has not been the number one item on the list of concerns of residents of the Central Area, save perhaps the brief period in the late 1980s when crack cocaine appeared to be a serious problem. Even then, a close reading of the concerns of community councils reveals a deep and abiding belief that crime can best be dealt with by raising the economic and political power of the area. In Southeast Seattle, crime is ranked high as a concern but so are job opportunities and programs for youth. Research on the relationship between crime and disorder also calls into question the hypothesis that a narrow focus on disorder can effectively reduce crime (Sampson and Raudenbush 2001).

Kelling and Coles state that in order to achieve the goals of a safer community, police discretion must be enhanced.

> [We must] accept the legitimate use of police discretion while finding ways to limit its excesses. Police officers need the legal authority to respond to citizen demands for assistance in maintaining minimal levels of order…Finally, this discretion must be carefully shaped and controlled by law and policy to ensure that police authority is used equitably and that police order-maintenance activities strengthen lawful citizens control over neighborhoods while ensuring tolerance for diversity (Kelling and Coles 1996, 169).

There is little evidence, however, that police officers have a higher degree of tolerance for diversity than any other segment of society; indeed there might be evidence that there is a lower tolerance (see Smith, Graham, Adams 1991). Increased police discretion was at the heart of the Coalition to Oppose Weed and Seed's concerns about the program in the Central District and the SECAC's efforts to maintain control over weeding activities in the Rainier Valley.

Finally, Wilson and Kelling maintain that broken windows indicate that "no one cares" about the neighborhood. The interview data presented here indicate that the "no one cares" perspective is an *outsider* perception that can be reinforced by order maintenance advocates. No sentiment came through stronger in the interviews and participant observations than the feeling that these community leaders are people deeply committed to solving the problems in their neighborhoods. Indeed, some community leaders in the Central Area have felt that the police regarded their communities as filled with people who did not care when, in fact, their years of caring were often met with indifference by the police and their lack of resources went unacknowledged. Thus, the order maintenance view is rooted in an assumption about residents of high-crime neighborhoods that may not be particularly representative of the people who live in those neighborhoods. This is partly because order maintenance deflects attention away from the main components of the community-centered crime prevention strategy: a community-controlled role for the police and an emphasis on the issues that many feel are the root causes of crime, such as poor education and underemployment. Thus, the order maintenance model conflicts with citizen interests in addressing other potential criminogenic conditions and with concerns about police discretion and abuses of that discretion.   Furthermore, the 'no one cares' perspective legitimates the infiltration of state agents, such as federal, state and local law enforcement, into the area to do the 'clean up' work (weeding) that they perceive residents as unable or unwilling to do themselves.

Governing through crime sets up the choices for crime-ridden communities as an either/or proposition: either one supports the massive infiltration of criminal justice agents (not just in law enforcement guise but in social service connections to police programs as well), or one must be resigned to the 'do nothing' approach and abandon neighborhoods to blight, violence and deterioration.   This book has sought to demonstrate that this is a false dichotomy. Many critics of police do not wish to see the police completely hamstrung. Rather, they are implicitly (and sometimes explicitly) expressing deep concerns about having the police serve as the state's *central agents* of revitalization, renewal and restoration. This is precisely what the founder of Mothers for Police Accountability meant when she said, "We didn't need the police to save our community. We could do it ourselves."[1]   Given that this woman had a seat on Chief Stamper's African-American Advisory Council, actively works to improve police activity in the black community and travels around the country talking to community groups about police-community relations, she is clearly not interested in having the police "do nothing." Rather, she sees the police role as one player among many with the community and its needs serving as the central control over activities in the area. Similarly, Edith Norton, Wendy Overton and Sarah Malano, community activists who were critical of police department decisions about Weed and Seed in their areas, still worked closely with police and had strong interests in having police help communities address problems. But for each of these women, giving the police greater authority and greater discretion, particularly in the absence of a comparable increase in authority on the part of the community, risked subjecting residents of crime-ridden communities to the whims of officers who have already have a tremendous amount of power.

All of this is not to suggest that the order maintenance model serves no meaningful ends other than to enhance governance through crime control. Certainly the residents interviewed for this research are concerned about being able to walk freely and comfortably in their neighborhoods, about the potentially negative influence of disorderly activity on their community life, and about the ability of police officers to control gang and drug activity that threaten so many neighborhoods. But the research in this book suggests that community control of some policing activities may be needed to mitigate the punitive impulse and police department's narrow framing of urban problems. It also suggests that allowing community residents to have input into how to revitalize their communities might shift the focus away from police and onto other resources, thus making discretion problem less acute and reducing the tendency to govern primarily through crime control. In the end, it is not so much the goals of order maintenance but the tactics that are the problem. A police-centered strategy is almost bound to cause concern in inner-city neighborhoods.

Problem-oriented policing (Goldstein 1990) comes closer to the community-centered model of crime prevention than does the order-maintenance model because it recognizes the need to identify community concerns before being overly prescriptive. It also requires police to get feedback from as wide a range of community residents as possible, including those most likely to be affected by the adoption of a particular problem (Goldstein 1990, 143). Furthermore, problem-oriented policing attempts to reconcile concerns about policing with the positive role police can play in resolving urban ills. In particular, Goldstein notes that the communities most affected by any particular policy need to be consulted before that policy is enacted and that the police could do a better job of serving as advocates for community residents by enforcing laws that affect communities but are typically ignored, such as landlord-tenant laws, building inspections, and white collar crime.

Nonetheless, problem-oriented policing still sees the police as central to problem identification and problem-solving. Goldstein suggests that a key element of problem-oriented policing is for the police to identify and focus on the substantive problems of an area and to gain "an understanding of all the dimensions of a problem in the total community" (Goldstein 1990, 34). The "Proposed Weed and Seed Management Structure" put forth by the SPD and U.S. Attorney's office in Seattle suggests a similar strategy by putting law enforcement at the center of a variety of non-law enforcement activities, including employment and computer training, teen clinics and health programs.

But the interviews and participant observations in Seattle indicated that community leaders had little, if any interest in the police addressing non-crime-related problems and were more likely to see the non-crime problems as the cause of crime, rather than the other way around. Since many urban ills are interconnected – poverty, joblessness, drug addiction, poor schools, inadequate health care, drug dealing, car prowls, theft – what does it mean to say that the police should 'understand all the dimensions of a problem in the total community?' How much can the police really know about health care or employment programs? And are the police any better at knowing about those problems than other governmental agencies or community-based organizations? If not, then why place policing at the center of problem-solving? There does not appear to be much evidence that the police are any better at dealing with problems in their totality than anyone else. In fact, the police may make some problems worse by bringing the threat of arrest and incarceration into situations that can better be dealt with through other means. Goldstein's list of possible problems to be dealt with through problem-oriented policing include drug dealing and burglary – two areas in which law enforcement seems like an appropriate partner. But with other problems, like school truancy, the role of law enforcement is not so clear. In fact, in the controversy around Weed and Seed community leaders were downright nervous about police involvement with youth in areas like truancy.

There is also some question as to whether the police are in the best position to identify emerging problems and play an active role in placing the range of choices before the community.

> Police occupy a frontline position vis-à-vis social ills of community. They acquire large amounts of data and insights that can be used to clarify community problems, rather than wait until problems have reached significant magnitude to generate community concern and only then react to them (Goldstein 1990, 46).

The problem here is that community leaders in Seattle's Weed and Seed target areas frequently thought that the police misidentified problems and solutions. The CAC spent a great deal of energy advocating for reverse stings in the Central Area so that the community could demonstrate to the police what residents in the area had long suspected: that drug buyers were primarily coming from outside the area. Several police officers, including some administrators, told me outright that they did not believe this to be the case when the community first raised the possibility. Some community leaders even blamed the SPD for allowing gang violence to proliferate by ignoring concerns in the 1980s about the infiltration of gangs from California.[2]

Thus, the police can serve to limit the range of possible responses that exclude not only the unrealistic and illegal, but also the ones most amenable to community support. If community members want the police to engage in an activity that is not on the police agenda (because it is not cost-effective, because it does not strengthen police organization, because it limits discretion, underutilizes manpower, etc.), it may not get presented as an option. The findings of this research suggest that solving problems is far trickier than the academic and popular literature on crime prevention suggests. As policy scholars are all too aware, solutions depend on how problems are defined. What are the primary problems of urban blighted areas and how should they be addressed? That policy makers, local crime prevention professionals, and community leaders all answer these questions differently suggests that input from each level is required for crime prevention strategies to be effective.

The Continued Significance of Race in Crime Prevention Politics

News articles about police brutality and harassment reveal ongoing tensions between police and black Americans and growing anger at incidence of police use of force against minorities.[3] These tensions were renewed in the wake of the shooting death of Amadou Diallo, an unarmed West African immigrant who was killed by four white New York city police officers while standing outside of his apartment. The officers were later acquitted of any wrongdoing. The incident raised anew concerns by minorities around the country that the police treat all blacks as criminals and too often use force indiscriminately or, at least, inappropriately.

Another theme in the news has been the high degree of incarceration rates for blacks: approximately five blacks are in prison for every one that is at an institution of higher education and in 1999 nearly 1 million black Americans were incarcerated.[4] The way in which crime-ridden areas are policed can have an impact on the number of blacks that come into the criminal justice system in the first place. Black residents of the CD and southeast Seattle seem particularly concerned about young people in the area being caught up in the criminal justice system and landing in prison for longer periods of time.

Racial politics has played a role in the development of Weed and Seed in Seattle from the moment the program was first announced through recent efforts on the part of the SECAC to be responsive to diverse communities. As the flurry of activity on the topic after the New York shooting illustrates, the subject of law enforcement is a volatile and difficult one. The experience of Weed and Seed in Seattle demonstrates that serious consideration must be given to providing community members with some semblance of control over how their neighborhoods are policed, and that crime prevention programs need to be contextualized in concerns over broader economic, social and political development.

Generalizing from a single case study is always problematic. Nonetheless, given similar conflicts in other cities and the on-going tensions between urban minority communities and law enforcement, the Seattle case study provides an opportunity to draw some general observations about the salience of racial politics in crime control strategies. Furthermore, the relationship of Seattle's black community with the SPD has been somewhat less contentious than in urban areas with more concentrated areas of poverty and police departments with longer histories of racial bias. Thus, one might expect the Seattle experience to actually mute the racial issues and for those issues to be magnified in other urban areas.

There have been two dominant themes about race throughout this book: First, urban racial minorities, particularly blacks, living in high-crime areas tend to be wary of police. This is confirmed by a wide range of public opinion research on policing (Welch, et al. 1996; Reisig and Parks 2000, Weitzer 2000a; Weitzer 2000b). Hence, police-centered strategies, no matter how community-friendly, will, for the foreseeable future, be eyed with suspicion (see Kennedy 1997; West 1994; Tonry 1995). The reverse stings in the Central District helped generate some confidence and respect for the police among community leaders and deflected some of the law enforcement attention away from local minority youth and towards affluent whites. That this tactic was used only after intense pressure from the community, however, illustrates the difficulty neighborhood residents have in altering existing police strategies.

A second theme throughout this book has been the fact that community leaders in Seattle resisted the dominant explanations for criminality which see crime as the result of individual moral failing. They were much more likely to characterize the crime problem as a result of economic and social deprivation. While the tendency to keep policy agendas narrowly focused on law enforcement remains, possibilities exist for minorities to 'expand the scope of the conflict' (see Schattsneider 1960). "At the nexus of politics and policy development lies persistent conflict over where problems come from and, based on the answer to this question, what kinds of solutions should be attempted" (Rochefort and Cobb 1994, 3). This seems particularly true of crime because, as suggested earlier, if the crime problem is defined as a function of economic breakdown of cities, a solution might be revitalization. If it is defined as the moral breakdown of youths, solutions might be focused on punitiveness. To the extent that racial minorities are given a voice in how high-crime areas will be policed and how community revitalization will take place, the landscape of crime prevention and control could be significantly altered; the scope of conflict expands from addressing crime, victimization, fear and disorder to include fear of police misconduct and abuse and concern for broad economic and social development.

The overall prospects for changes such as these are not promising, however. Governing through crime control ensures that efforts to reconfigure the role of communities, question the centrality of police agencies, and address root causes of crime will be difficult at best. National policymaking continues to center urban revitalization around crime control and policies such as Three Strikes You're Out and mandatory minimums illustrate the salience of the punitive approach for policymakers. These programs may also be indicative of a more insidious trend which recalls the "dangerous classes" of the early part of the century when one's ethnic or racial group was seen as an indicator of criminality (see Gordon 1994). The rhetoric around gangs and drug activity seems particularly rife with racial prejudice, referring to youths as "predators," "monsters," and "animals."[5] Research on the role of race in sentencing recommendations by probation officers indicates that the criminal actions of racial minorities may be more likely to be seen as the result of bad character than bad circumstance (Bridges and Steen 1998). And research into the relationship between race, gender and age to outcomes in the criminal justice system has illustrated that young, black and Hispanic males pay a higher price for committing the same crimes as other groups (Spohn and Holleran 2000; Steffensmeier, et. al. 1998). The result is that black youths end up being recommended more often for incarceration and less often for alternative, diversionary programs than white youths who commit the same types of crimes.

To the extent that racial minorities continue to be associated with criminal behavior and the public discourse emphasizes law enforcement and punishment, community crime prevention and revitalization efforts are likely to remain focused on citizen assistance and support for aggressive police tactics.   Furthermore, as long as community crime prevention strategies empower police agencies as much or more than the communities being policed, they are likely to perpetuate imbalanced power relationships which allow the police to enact their own programs and have those programs rubber stamped as community-approved.

There is, however, another avenue for input that might bring the perspectives of racial minorities more to the forefront of community crime prevention. Crime control/prevention policies are rooted in dominant legal rules and norms that shape the manner in which the state can exercise control over its citizens and the responsibilities of the state to ensure equal protection.   While the Coalition to Stop Weed and Seed did not draw heavily upon the language of civil rights, the underlying themes of their opposition to the program parallel the language of equal opportunity and due process rights that have been the underpinning of legal contests over social and economic policy for the past 50 years. Minority groups (and women) have historically looked to the courts for assistance when confronting unresponsive state institutions about inequality. There have been numerous legal challenges to some of the more aggressive types of community policing and order maintenance strategies, such as gang curfews and loitering ordinances.   Those cases have produced legal decisions that parallel the community-centered views about police by noting that empowering police to move gang and drug activity out of a particular area might encourage police to stop youths based on more racial profiles than criminal behavior and that police have historically abused additional power for such purposes.

A 1999 Supreme Court case illustrates the legal logic at work. *Chicago v. Morales*[6] involved a Chicago ordinance that targeted gang activity in Chicago. The ordinance was invoked when "any person reasonably believed by a police officer to be a gang member is found loitering with any other person or persons in any public place. In such a circumstance, the ordinance requires the officer to order all the persons to disperse and remove themselves from the area." The officer is further required to arrest any person who does not "promptly" obey the order. The Illinois Supreme Court affirmed a lower court ruling that the ordinance was impermissibly vague and violated due process rights of the defendants. In 1999, the Supreme Court upheld the Illinois court decision.

The Supreme Court indicated that the ordinance "failed to give the ordinary citizen adequate notice of what is forbidden and what is permitted." The court also concluded that the ordinance "does not provide sufficiently specific limits on the enforcement discretion of the police." The Illinois Supreme Court also noted that: "Although persons of ordinary intelligence may maintain a common and accepted meaning of the word 'loiter,' such a term by itself is inadequate to inform a citizen of its criminal implication."[7]

These issues are similar to the ones raised by the Coalition to Stop Weed and Seed about the possibility of federal law enforcement agents coming into the target area and sweeping up young people based on their perception that youths were up to no good. Similarly, one of the concerns about the Chicago ordinance expressed by a black alderman in the city was that "people have to gather…and that the ordinance might inappropriately be applied to "young people on our block . . . going to school."[8] The ordinance, the court ruled, unconstitutionally criminalized status by criminalizing the mere presence of gang members in public.

Second, the court determined that the ordinance was also vague because it vested too much discretion in the police and was therefore open to arbitrary enforcement. The Illinois Supreme Court stated it this way:

> Moreover, when a law fails to provide standards regulating the exercise of its discretion, "the scheme permits and encourages an arbitrary and discriminatory enforcement of the law. [The law] furnishes a convenient tool for 'harsh and discriminatory enforcement by local prosecuting officials, *against particular groups deemed to merit their displeasure'"* Papachristou, 405 U.S… The city has declared gang members a public menace and determined that gang members are too adept at avoiding arrest for all the other crimes they commit. Accordingly, the city council crafted an exceptionally broad ordinance that could be used to sweep these intolerable and objectionable gang members from the city streets. As the Supreme Court has observed, ordinances such as the gang loitering ordinance are drafted in an intentionally

vague manner so that persons who are undesirable in the eyes of police and prosecutors can be convicted even though they are not chargeable with any other particular offense. Papachristou, 405 U.S. at 166, 31 L. Ed. 2d at 118, 92 S. Ct. at 845.[9]

This echoes the fears of community leaders in the Central Area that the Justice Department and Seattle Police had declared residents of their community "a menace" and had designed "weeding" as a means of ridding the area of young minorities who were perceived to be causing the crime problems.

While the Court did not specifically refer to race, it alluded to police differential treatment of racial minorities by referring to efforts to remove "intolerable and objectionable gang members" from the streets. Gary Stewart has argued that anti-gang ordinances are the contemporary equivalent of vagrancy laws which historically targeteded racial minorities and the poor (Stewart 1998). The capacity of the courts to slow the proliferation of inner-city crime prevention strategies that promote police discretion could serve as an important counter-balance to the governing through crime control strategy that promotes law enforcement policies with heavy police discretion. On the other hand, the Morales decision may itself be counter-productive because it hamstrings the ability of police and communities to work together to come up with alternative policing strategies (Meares and Kahan 1998). This is an interesting and important area for future research.

Conclusion

Stanley Cohen's formidable work on communities and social control strategies cautions against a myopic view of communities that focuses too heavily and narrowly on crime. Cohen argues that community development ought to occur for its own sake, not simply as a result of efforts to reduce crime. Indeed, communities that are not plagued with crime are able to address their needs – new traffic patterns to protect children, new and improved parks and schools, block parties and community fairs – for the sake of community development and solidarity. Inner-city neighborhoods, which tend to have high concentrations of lower-income people, particularly minorities, must justify their community development in terms of crime control. To the extent that they are restricted by police-centered approaches to crime, their community development will be further stunted by an inability to address concerns that might be related to criminal activity and that are most certainly related to community-building and solidarity. Cohen lays out the choices this way:

> The choice here is between two quite different political options. One would be the strategic use of social-control resources as an opportunity for welfare improvement. The alternative would be to divert scarce resources right away from the [social control] system and devote them to policies (family, educational, community, health, fiscal, etc.) which are not justified in control terms at all. To pursue my simple example: the first strategy would be to use the excuse of 'vandalism prevention' in order to build adventure playgrounds for kids living in high-rise apartments; the second would be to forget about vandalism and simply build the playgrounds as part of a neighborhood project. The advantage of the first strategy is (sadly) that it is politically more appealing and hence more likely to attract the scarce resources which have not been consumed by hard-end law-and-order budgets. Its corresponding disadvantage is that it is more vulnerable to pseudo-scientific attacks of the 'nothing works' type and will be readily abandoned if it cannot be politically justified in crude utilitarian terms. The advantage of the second strategy is its integrity, its direct appeal to values and its ability to be defended in its own terms - of which none of which [sic] elements, of course, has the slightest appeal to right-wing politicians controlling monetarist economies (Cohen 1985, 264).

Certainly in its embryonic form, Weed and Seed resembled the "vandalism prevention" of Cohen's example. It justified seeding programs almost exclusively in terms of crime prevention – making communities places to which criminals do not wish to return (or enter in the first place). Of course, one cannot expect a Justice Department program to ignore law enforcement. But this is precisely the point: programs to revitalize urban areas so often come with a law enforcement justification.

The data presented here also suggest that Cohen's second choice is the one which activists in and advocates for inner-city, minority communities would like to pursue. When Cohen says "forget about vandalism," he is clearly engaging in hyperbole. None of the people interviewed suggested that the police should not be involved in their communities or that they should not address certain types of crimes. At no time in the participant observations did anyone suggest that crime of any kind should not be addressed. On the contrary, as people most likely to be affected by crimes such as vandalism, the participants in Weed and Seed were deeply appreciative of the police presence at their meetings and the willingness of some officers to address their concerns.

At the same time, however, they were concerned about the effect of centering activity around policing. This is abundantly clear from the constant refrain of "too much weeding" that was heard from the moment Weed and Seed first arrived on the public agenda in Seattle to the present day development of the southeast's mission. There was the sense that crime prevention that promises community development cannot be centered on law enforcement, which has a volatile historic relationship with minority communities and which represents the government's legitimate use of force. In the long run, this is the unmistakable goal of residents of these areas. Crime appears to be a convenient way to organize residents and try to obtain resources. But, in their view, crime is the result of underlying problems that must also be addressed simultaneously.

As we have seen, the consequences of centering community development around law enforcement means and ends are serious problems for federal policy makers, local elected officials and police, and the communities which are the target of such policies.

The urban communities that face street crime on a daily basis may want more than just an attack on the criminals; the Seattle case illustrates that community leaders there wanted also the hope and promise that come from a more comprehensive development program than law enforcement can provide. Any community-oriented crime prevention program that does not acknowledge this will face deep opposition and risk reinforcing existing models that have already proven to be difficult implement and counter-productive.

Notes

[1]   Conversation with Mothers for Police Accountability founder during the Seattle Regional Weed and Seed conference, April 6, 1999.

[2]   Interview 17: November 11, 1998.

[3]   "A senseless Assault" *New York Times*, February 18, 1999. A27; "After shooting, an Eroding Trust in the Police," February 19, 1999; "Black Anger at British Police Abuse Boils Over," *New York Times* February 22, 1999; "British Report Finds Racism Pervades Police," *New York Times*, February 23, 1999; "Street Tactics by Police draw heavy criticism," *New York Times* March 18, 1999; "In Police shooting, Civil Disobedience on Tight Schedule," *New York Times*

3/19/99. "A Well-blazed Trail for the Police," *New York Times*, March 18, 1999; "Boston's Police Solution," *New York Times,* March 3, 1999.

4 "War on Crack Retreats, Still Taking Prisoners," *New York Times,* February 28, 1999, "Number of blacks in prison nears 1 million," *Seattle Times.* March 2, 1999.

5 "Broken windows, mended kids," *Tampa Tribune*, October 19, 1997; "About New York: Youths' voices aren't silent, just ignored," *New York Times*, September 5, 1998; "Churches united against drug violence," *Courier Journal* (Louisville, KY), September 18, 1997.

6 527 U.S. 41; 119 S. Ct. 1849.

7 117 Ill. 2d 440, 68 N.E. 2d 53, October 17, 1997.

8 Respondent's Brief to the Supreme Court.

9 117 Ill. 2d 440, 68 N.E. 2d 53, October 17, 1997.

Bibliography

Banfield, Edward. 1965. *Big City Politics*. New York: Random House.

Baumgartner, Frank and Bryan D. Jones. 1993. *Agendas and Instability in American Politics*. Chicago: University of Chicago Press.

Bayer, Ronald. 1981. Crime, Punishment and the Decline of Liberal Optimism. *Crime and Delinquency 27*: 169-190.

Bayley, David. 1988. Community Policing: A report from the devil's advocate. in Jack R. Greene and Stephen D. Mastrofski. *Community Policing: Rhetoric or Reality*. NY : Praeger.

Beckett, Katherine. 1997. *Making Crime Pay: Law and Order in Contemporary American Politics*. New York: Oxford University Press.

Beckett, Katherine and Theodore Sasson. 2000. *The Politics of Injustice: Crime and Punishment in America*. Thousand Oaks, CA: Pine Forge Press.

Blumberg, 1978. The Practice of Law as a Confidence Game in Austin Sarat and Sheldon Goldman, ed. *American Court Systems: Readings in Judicial Process and Behavior*. San Francisco: W.H. Freeman.

Bridges, George and Sara Steen. 1998. Racial disparities in official assessments of juvenile offenders: attributional stereotypes as mediating mechanism. *American Sociology Review 63*: 554-570.

Butterfield, Fox. 1995. *All God's children: the Boskett family and the American tradition of violence*. New York: A. Knopf.

Cirel, Paul, Patricia Evans, Daniel McGillis, Debra Whitcomb, *Community Crime Prevention Program: Seattle, WA 1977*. National Advisory Commission on Criminal Justice Standards and Goals.

Cobb, Roger W. and Charles D. Elder. 1983. *The Political Uses of Symbols*. New York: Longman.

Cohen, Stanley. 1985. *Visions of Social Control*. Cambridge: Polity Press.

Cover, Robert. 1992. Violence and the Word. In Austin Sarat and Thomas R. Kearns. 1992. *Law's Violence*. Ann Arbor: University of Michigan Press.

Cullen, Frances T. and L. Q. Cao, J. Frank, R.H. Langworthy, S.L. Browning, R. Kopache and T.J. Stevenson. 1996. 'Stop or I'll shoot":   Racial differences in support for police use of deadly force. *American Behavioral Scientist 39*: 449-460.

Dahrendorf, Ralph.   1985.   *Law and Order.*   London: Stevens and Co.

Derthick, Martha.   1972.   *New Towns In-Town.*   Washington: Urban Institute.

Dubow, Fred and David Emmons.   1981.   The Community Hypothesis.   In Dan A. Lewis, Ed. *Reactions to Crime.*   Beverly Hills, CA: Sage Publications.

Dubow, Fred, Edward McCabe, Gail Kaplan.   1979.   *Reactions to Crime: A Critical Review of the Literature.*   Law Enforcement Assistance Administration.   National Institute of Law Enforcement and Criminal Justice.   National Institute of Justice, Department of Justice.

Durkheim, Emile.   1958.   *The Rules of Sociological Method.*   Glenco, IL: Free Press.

Edelman, Murray.   1964.   *The Symbolic Uses of Politics.*   Urbana: University of Illinois Press.

Edelman, Murray.   1971.   *Politics as Symbolic Action.*   Chicago: Markham.

Edelman, Murray.   1988.   *Constructing the Political Spectacle.*   Chicago: University of Chicago Press.

Feeley, Malcolm M. and Austin D. Sarat.   1980.   *The Policy Dilemma: Federal crime policy and the Law Enforcement Assistance Administration.*   Minneapolis: University of Minnesota Press.

Feeley, Malcolm M. and Jonathan Simon.   1992.   "The New Penology: notes on the emerging strategy of corrections and its implications." *Criminology 30*: 449-474.

Feeley, Malcolm M. and Jonathan Simon.   1994. Actuarial Justice: the Emerging New Criminal Law.   In *The Futures of Criminology*, ed. David Nelken.   New York: Sage Publishing Co.

Fleissner, Dan.   1997.   *Community Policing: A Stage Assessment Model.*   Seattle Police Department, Grant and Contract Services.

Fleissner, Dan, Nicholas Fedan, Ezra Stotland, David Klinger.   1991.   *Community Policing in Seattle: A Descriptive Study of the South Seattle Crime Reduction Project.*   Seattle Police Department.

Fleissner, Dan W.   1997.   *Community Policing Stage Assessment Model for Implementation Planning and Organizational Measurement.*   National Institute of Justice Research Project Final Report.   Office of Justice Programs, U.S. Department of Justice.

Fowler, Floyd Jr., Mary Ellen McCallen, Thomas W. Mangione. *Reducing Residential Crime and Fear: The Hartford Neighborhood Crime Prevention Program.* Law Enforcement Assistance Administration, United States Department of Justice. December 1979.

Friedman, Lawrence. 1993. *Crime and Punishment in America.* New York: Basic Books.

Garland, David. 1996. The Limits of the Sovereign State. *The British Journal of Criminology* 36: 445-470.

Goldstein, Herman. 1990. *Problem-oriented Policing.* New York: McGraw Hill.

Gordon, Diana. 1994. *The Return of the Dangerous Classes.* New York: W.W. Norton.

Gordon, Andrew, Hubert Locke, Cy Ulberg. 1998. Ethnic Diversity in Southeast Seattle, in *Cityscape: A Journal of Policy Development and Research 4 (2):* 197-219.

Gordon, Margaret T., Hubert G. Locke, Laurie McCutcheon and William B. Stafford. 1991. Seattle: Grassroots Politics Shaping the Environment. In *Big City Politics in Transition.* Newbury Park, CA: Sage Publications.

Gossett, Larry and Mike Williams. *Seattle's Central District: A community study.* Central District Community Council. May 19, 1977.

Greenberg, Stephanie W., William M. Rohe and Jay R. Williams. 1985. *Informal Citizen Action and Crime Prevention at the Neighborhood Level: Synthesis and assessment of the research.* National Institute of Justice.

Greene, Jack R. and Stephen D. Mastrofski. 1988. *Community Policing: Rhetoric or Reality.* New York: Praeger.

Gurin, Patricia, Shirley Hatchett, James S. Jackson. 1989. *Hope and independence: Blacks' response to electoral and party politics.* New York: Russell Sage Foundation.

Hall, Stuart. 1978. *Policing the Crisis: Mugging, the State and Law and Order.* New York: Holmes and Meier.

Handler, Joel F. 1996. *Down from Bureaucracy : the Ambiguity of Privatization and Empowerment.* Princeton, N.J.: Princeton University Press.

Hunt, Alan. 1993. *Explorations in Law and Society: Towards a Constituitive Theory of Law.* New York: Routledge.

Katznelson, Ira. 1981. *City Trenches: Urban Politics and the Patterning of Class in the United States.* New York: Pantheon Books.

Kelling, George. 1988. *Police and Communities - The Quiet Revolution.* Washington, D.C.; National Institute of Justice.

Kelling, George. 1992. Measuring What Matters. *The City Journal,* Spring.

Kelling, George L. and Catherine M. Coles. 1996. *Fixing Broken Windows.* New York: The Free Press.

Kennedy, Daniel B. 1990. Facility Site Selection and Analysis through Environmental Criminology. *Journal of Criminal Justice 18:* 239-252.

Kennedy, Randall. 1997. *Race, Crime and the Law.* New York: Vintage Books.

King, Gary; Robert O. Keohane, Sidney Verba. 1994. *Designing Social Inquiry: Scientific Inference in Qualitative Research.* Princeton: Princeton University Press.

Krislov, Daniel. 1997. Ideology and American Crime Policy, 1966-1996: An Exploratory Esssay. In Friedman, Lawrence M. and George Fisher eds. *The Crime Conundrum: Essays in Criminal Justice.* Boulder, CO: Westview Press.

Krislov, Samuel and Susan O. White 1977. *Understanding crime: an evaluation of the National Institute of Law Enforcement and Criminal Justice.* Committee on Research on Law Enforcement and Criminal Justice, Assembly of Behavioral and Social Sciences, National Research Council.

Lavrakas, Paul J. Community-Based Crime Prevention: Citizens, Community Organizations, and the Police. In Lawrence, Joseph B. *Crime, Communities and Public Policy.* Center for Urban Research and Policy Studies. 1995.

Lewis, Dan A. and Greta Salem. 1981. Community Crime Prevention: An Analysis of a Developing Strategy. *Crime and Delinquency* 27: 405-421.

Ligurio, Arthur J. and Dennis P. Rosenbaum. 1986. Evaluating Research in Community Crime Prevention: A critical look at the field. In Rosenbaum, Dennis P. *Community Crime Prevention: Does it Work?* Beverly Hills, CA: Sage Publications.

Lindsay, Betty and Daniel McGillis. 1986. Citywide Community Crime Prevention. In Rosenbaum, Dennis P. *Community Crime Prevention: Does it Work?* Sage Publications.

Livingston, Debra. 1997. Police discretion and the quality of life in public places: courts, communities, and the new policing. *Columbia Law Review* 97: 551-672.

Lyons, William T. 1999. *The Politics of Community Policing: Rearranging the Power to Punish.* Ann Arbor, University of Michigan Press.

Manning, Peter. 1977. *Police work: the social organization of policing.* Cambridge, Mass: MIT Press.

Marion, Nancy E. 1994. *A History of Federal Crime Control Initiatives, 1960-1993.* Westport, Conn.: Praeger.

Massey, Douglas S. and Nancy A. Denton. 1996. American Apartheid: The Perpetuation of the Underclass. In John Arthur and Amy Shapiro eds., *Color, Class, Identity.* Boulder, CO: Westview Press.

Mastrofski, Stephen. 1988. Community Policing as Reform: A cautionary tale. In Jack R. Greene and Stephen D. Mastrofski. *Community Policing: Rhetoric or Reality.* New York: Praeger.

McCann, Michael W. 1994. *Rights At Work: Pay Equity Reform and the Politics of Legal Mobilization.* Chicago: University of Chicago Press.

McPherson and Silloway. 1981. Planning to Prevention Crime. In Dan A. Lewis, ed. *Reactions to Crime.* Beverly Hills, CA: Sage Publications.

Meares, Tracy L. and Dan M. Kahan. 1998. Law and (Norms of) Order in the Inner-City. *Law and Society Review* 32: 805-838.

Merry, Sally Engle. 1990. *Getting Justice and Getting Even : Legal Consciousness Among Working-class Americans.* Chicago: University of Chicago Press.

Migdal, Joel S. 1994. *State Power and Social Forces: Domination and Transformation in Third World.* New York: Cambridge University.

Miller, Lisa. L. 1994. *Competing Visions of Crime Control: The case of Seattle's Drug Traffic Loitering Ordinance.* Masters' Thesis, University of Washington.

Nagel, Stuart, ed. 1983. *Encyclopedia of Policy Studies.* Urbana, IL: University of Illinois.

Piven, Frances Fox and Richard A. Piven. 1979. *Poor People's Movements: Why They Succeed, How They Fail.* New York: Vintage Books.

Podolfeskey, Aaron M. 1985. *Rejecting Crime Prevention Programs.*

Pressman, Jeffrey L. and Aaron Wildavsky. 1973. *Implementation.* Berkeley: University of California Press.

Quinney, Richard. 1975. *Criminology: Analysis and Critique of Crime in America.* Boston: Little Brown.

Reiman, Jeffrey H. 1979. *The Rich Get Richer and the Poor Get Prison: ideology, class and criminal justice.* New York: Wiley.

Roberts, Julian V. 1997. *Public Opinion, Crime and Criminal Justice.* Boulder, CO: Westview Press.

Rochefort, David A. and Roger W. Cobb. 1994. *The Politics of Problem Definition: Shaping the Policy Agenda.* Lawrence, Kan.: University of Kansas.

Roehl, Janice A. and Robert Huitt, Mary Ann Wycoff, Antony Pate, Donald Rebovich and Ken Coyle. *National Process Evaluation of Weed and Seed.* Department of Justice, Office of Justice Programs, National Institute of Justice Research in Brief. October 1996.

Rosenbaum, Dennis P., ed. 1986. *Community Crime Prevention: Does it Work?* Beverly Hills, CA: Sage Publications.

Sampson, Robert J. and Stephen W. Raudenbush. 2001. Disorder in Urban Neighborhoods: Does It Lead to Crime? *National Institute of Justice, Research in Brief.*

Sampson, Robert J. and Dawn Jeglum Bartusch. 1998. Legal Cynicism and (Subcultural?) Tolerance of Deviance: The Neighborhood Context of Racial Differences. *Law and Society Review 32.*

Sarat, Austin. 1978. Alternative Dispute Resolution, in Austin Sarat and Sheldon Goldman, ed. *American Court Systems: Readings in Judicial Process and Behavior.* San Francisco: W.H. Freeman.

Sasson, Theodore. 1995. *Crime Talk: How Citizens Construct a Social Problem.* Hawthorne, N.Y.: Aldine de Gruyter.

Savitch, H.V., John Clayton Thomas. Ed. 1991. *Big City Politics in Transition.* Newbury Park, CA: Sage Publications.

Schattsneider, E.E. 1960. *The Semisovereign people: A realist's view of democracy in America.* New York: Hold, Rinehart and Winston.

Scheingold, Stuart. 1984. *The Politics of Law and Order.* New York: Longman.

Scheingold, Stuart. 1991. *The Politics of Street Crime.* Philadelphia: Temple University Press.

Scheingold, Stuart. 1998. Constructing the New Political Criminology: Power, Authority and the Post-liberal State. *Law and Social Inquiry 23.*

Seattle-Everett Real Estate Research Committee. 1981-1998. *Seattle-Everett Real Estate Research Report*. Seattle, Washington.

Skogan, Wesley G. 1988 Community Organizations and Crime, in Michael Tonry and Norval Morris, *Crime and Justice* Chicago: University of Chicago Press.

Skolnick, Jerome H. and James J. Fyfe. 1993. *Above the Law: Police and the excessive use of force*. New York: The Free Press.

Simon, Jonathon. 1993. *Poor Discipline: parole and the social control of the underclass*. Chicago: University of Chicago.

Simon, Jonathon. 1997. Governing Through Crime, in Friedman, Lawrence M. and George Fisher eds. *The Crime Conundrum: Essays in Criminal Justice*. Boulder, CO: Westview Press.

Smith, Douglas A., Nanette Graham, Bonney Adams. 1991. Minorities and the Police: Attitudinal and Behavioral Questions, in Michael J. Lynch and E. Britt Patterson, *Race and the Criminal Justice System*. New York: Harrow and Heston.

Spohn, Cassia and David Holleran. 2000. The Imprisonment Penalty Paid by Young, Unemployed Black and Hispanic Offenders, *Criminology* 38: 281-306.

Stahl, Anne L., Melissa Sickmund, Terrence A. Finnegoan, Howard N. Snyder, Rowen S. Poole, and Nancy Tierney. 1999. *Juvenile Court Statistics 1997*. Washington, D.C.: Office of Juvenile Justice and Delinquency Prevention.

Steffensmeier, Darryl, Jeffrey Ulmer and John Kramer. 1998. The Interaction of Race, Gender and Age in Criminal Sentencing: The Punishment Cost of Being Young, Black and Male. *Criminology* 36: 763-797.

Stewart, Gary. 1998. Black Codes and Broken Windows: The Legacy of Racial Hegemony in Anti-Gang Civil Injunctions. *Yale Law Journal* 107, 2249.

Taylor, Michael. 1982. *Community, Anarchy, and Liberty*. New York: Cambridge University Press.

Taylor, Quintard. 1994. *The Forging of a Black Community: Seattle's Central District through the Civil Rights Era*. Seattle, WA: University of Washington Press.

Taylor, Ralph B. 1998. Crime and Small-Scale Places. Crime and Place: Plenary Papers of the 1997 Conference on Criminal Justice Research and Evaluation. National Institute of Justice – Office of Justice Programs, Bureau of Justice Assistance. July 1998.

Thompson, E.P. 1975. *Whigs and Hunters*. London: Allen Lane.

Tonry, Michael. 1995. *Malign Neglect*. New York: Oxford University Press.

Tyler, Tom R. and Robert J. Boeckmann. 1997. Three strikes and you are out, but why? The psychology of public support for punishing rule breakers. *Law and Society Review* 31: 237-265.

University of Washington Urban Design/Economic Development Studio. "Master Plan for the Central Area. December 16, 1992.

Vega, David. 1997. Can Political Incorporation Help African Americans? A case study of Seattle, Doctoral dissertation, University of Washington.

Walker, Samuel. 1994. *Sense and Nonsense about Crime and Drugs*. Belmont, CA: Wadsworth Publishing Co.

Weitzer, Ronald. 2000a. Racialized Policing:Residents' Perceptions in Three Neighborhoods. *Law and Society Review* 34: 129-155.

Weitzer, Ronald. 2000b. White, Black or Blue Cops? Race and Citizen Assessments of Police Officers. *Journal of Criminal Justice* 28: 313-324.

Welch, Susan, Michael W. Combs, Lee Sigelman and Timothy Bledsoe. 1996 Justice for All: Still an American Dilemma, in Obie Clayton Jr, ed. *An American Dilemma Revisited: Race Relations in a Changing World.* New York: Russell Sage Foundation.

West, Cornel. 1994. *Race Matters*. New York: Vintage Books.

Wilson, James Q. 1992. The Contradictions of an Advanced Capitalist State. *Forbes* 150: 110-116.

Wilson, James Q. 1975. *Thinking about Crime*. New York: Basic Books.

Wilson, James Q. 1989. *Bureaucracy: What Government Agencies Do and Why They Do It*. New York: Basic Books.

Wilson, James Q. and Richard J. Hernstein. 1985. *Crime and Human Nature*. New York: Simon and Schuster.

Wilson, James Q. and George L. Kelling. 1982. The Police and Neighborhood Safety. *The Atlantic*. 25: 29-38

Zimring, Franklin E. and Gordon Hawkins. 1992. *The Search for Rational Drug Control*. New York: Cambridge University Press.

Index